W9-DCZ-171

Allen, Devere, 1891-1955.
　　The fight for peace.　With a new introd.
for the Garland ed. by Charles Chatfield.
New York, Garland Pub., 1971 [i. e. 1972,
c1930]
　　2 v. (740 p.)　illus.　(The Garland library
of war and peace)

　　1. Peace.　I. Title.

The
Garland Library
of
War and Peace

The
Garland Library
of
War and Peace

The
Fight for Peace

by
Devere Allen

In two volumes

Vol. I

with a new introduction
for the Garland Edition by
Charles Chatfield

Garland Publishing, Inc., New York & London
1971

Library of Congress Cataloging in Publication Data

Allen, Devere, 1891-1955.
  The fight for peace.

  (The Garland library of war and peace)
  1. Peace. I. Title. II. Series.
JX1952.A65 1972   327'.172   74-147439
ISBN 0-8240-0228-8

Introduction

Always the peace movement has sought for unity within its ranks. Seldom has the movement found it. . . . unity is only, after all, one phase of the fight for peace. Of infinitely more importance is the question, which is the sound approach to a warless world? The unfriendly critic of the peace movement may nevertheless be excused for his insistence that what we cannot work out in the clash of honest differences of opinion can scarcely be worked out among the diversified and 'opinionated' nations on the quarrelsome earth.

— *Devere Allen*[1]

There is nothing abstract about these words for anyone acquainted with the organizational history of the peace movement in the nineteen-sixties. They characterize the divisions within SANE early in the decade, the rise and quick demise of a broadly-based coalition envisioned in the Turn Toward Peace, the competing claims for resources and attention of the civil rights and peace movements in the middle years, the shifting alliances and internal quarrels behind the thrilling mass coalitions in public evidence at Washington and elsewhere. Never more vigorous than in the Vietnam crisis, the movement has never been united on more than specific projects. It is hard to

---

[1] The Fight for Peace *(New York: Macmillan Company, 1930),* p. 522.

5

believe that Devere Allen was writing in 1930.

He was in England when the first copy of The Fight for Peace *reached him from the Macmillan* Company. *Journalist and pacifist that he was, Allen was sensitive to public opinion and political stereotypes; and he was appalled when he saw the book jacket: "Think of the state of mentality that would select yaller [sic] as the color for a jacket on this book!" he wrote.² Besides, he felt that the portrait on the jacket made him look youthful and effeminate, while the biographical details on the inside flap would convince many potential readers that he was "the sort of radical with a chip on [his] shoulder, looking for a fight." Years later his wife recalled that he had disposed of the jackets on almost all the copies in his possession.*

Sans *jacket, the book deserves to endure as a radical and analytical critique of the peace movement in America until almost 1930. It yielded also the first comprehensive history of the movement; and Merle Curti, whose ground-breaking* American Peace Crusade, 1815-1860 *had been published scarcely a year before, characterized Allen's work as having "admirable factual accuracy."³ However faithful to the past,* The Fight for Peace *was not essentially a narrative history. It was an historical analysis aimed at*

²*Allen to Albert MacLeod, November 25, 1930, Devere Allen papers, Swarthmore College Peace Collection.*

³*"Warriors for Peace,"* The Nation, CXXXII *(January 21, 1931), p. 76.*

*establishing perspective from which the peace
movement in general and Devere Allen in particular
could crusade effectively. It was intended to
document both the futility of what Allen called the
old line peace orthodoxy and the danger of
exclusiveness in war resistance — both the search for
ways to obviate warfare without really questioning
the legitimacy of the war system and the temptation
for radicals to insist upon total abolition of war
without regard for the strength of the peace coalition.*

*Its author had shown a keen interest in history and
social issues as a student at Oberlin College. There
during World War I he and some friends published an
antiwar paper,* The Rational Patriot. *In this way he
came to the attention of pacifists in the East, and
soon he became executive secretary of* The Young
Democracy, *the forerunner of numerous youth
organizations. After the war Allen edited* The Young
Democracy, *trying to bring Americans in touch with
politically-oriented youth groups in Europe. When
the journal was taken over by* The World Tomorrow
*in 1921, Allen joined the staff where he was a
principal editor for a decade, helping to make the
magazine the most vigorous exponent of the social
gospel after World War I. Increasingly he and his
colleagues — John Nevin Sayre, Anna Rochester,
Kirby Page, Reinhold Niebuhr, and Norman Thomas,
among others — tried to apply that gospel to politics.
Allen became an officer in the pacifist Fellowship of
Reconciliation and the League for Industrial Democ-*

7

INTRODUCTION

racy, *and he was chairman of the executive
committee of the League for Independent Political
Action.*

*Already he was a popular speaker, had written on
social issues and radical causes for a variety of
magazines, and had edited one book,* Pacifism in the
Modern World.[4] *At the same time, he cultivated a
private interest in genealogy, folklore, and history.
Thus, Devere Allen established qualifications then
unique among writers on the peace movement: a
serious student of history, he was also an
organization-wise activist. He was an indefatigable
worker. He produced* The Fight for Peace *over a
period of two years by working into the early
morning hours, sometimes until daylight, after a full
day's work.*

*Some of the material in this book is drawn from
Allen's previous writing — notably the chapter on
women in the peace movement, the parody on peace
plans on pages 243-44, and the case for war
resistance. Most of the book was fresh, though, and
included material drawn from books and tracts for
which Allen had scoured bookstores and libraries in
this country and abroad.*

*He took an historian's pleasure in correcting
established misconceptions and inaccuracies. He
managed an impressive mass of material. His style*

[4]*(Garden City, N.Y.: Doubleday, Doran, 1929), reprinted in the
Garland Library of War and Peace, New York, 1971.*

8

was, as John Haynes Holmes correctly observed, "simple, clear, forceful, touched with humor, and on occasion hard-bitten with wise and penetrating irony."[5] *Still, the book is heavy reading. Why?*

It is heavily larded with direct quotations, as Holmes complained, but this material makes forgotten people and events vivid and authentic. More critically, the book is organized topically although its substance is largely historical. Consequently, both the story and the analysis are thrown back upon themselves repeatedly. Although the book is convincingly developed, therefore, it is not arresting unless one already understands the problems to which it is addressed.

The first ten chapters constitute a discussion of alternative strategies of the historic peace movement considered in chronological order. Allen is at his critical best in dissecting the flaws in various strategies. All of them are deemed important and worthy; none is sufficient; and each suffers the same defect of obscuring the essential problem of war itself by concentrating on some specific cause or cure of war. The many single-issue crusades had resulted in a tendency toward exclusiveness, faction, division within the movement.

Allen argued in chapters eleven and twelve that the forces of militarism have become, by contrast, inclusive and concentrated. They encompass industry,

[5] *Review of* The Fight for Peace *in the New York* Herald Tribune, Books *(February 15, 1931), p. 15.*

9

science, and government. They exert concentrated influence on educational facilities, media and news, and public celebrations; they operate on all facets of the public mind to legitimatize warfare. In short, they constitute "a vested interest determined to use its power in order to create an overwhelming demand for more of the same vast power." [6]

At this point in the book Allen introduced five chapters on the narrative history of the organized peace movement in America in order to suggest why it has become relatively ineffective against the "military juggernaut." He drew from his organizational survey the same lesson he had drawn from his comparison of peace strategies: effectiveness requires a coordinated peace movement with a core of radical pacifists fixing its attention on war itself as the essential problem, on justice as a necessary concomitant to order, and on a willingness to confront warfare directly and personally. Allen made, as Merle Curti observed, "the most persuasive case for the efficacy of war resistance, or the consistent refusal to compromise under any circumstance whatever with the war system." [7] *He argued, too, that pacifists must relate the cause of peace to labor and social reform. But he insisted as well that radical pacifists must not make either radical politics or war resistance into an exclusive strategy. The peace movement must become as inclusive and concen-*

[6] The Fight for Peace, p. 356.

[7] *"Warriors for Peace,"* The Nation, p. 76.

10

INTRODUCTION

trated as the forces of war. No wonder, then, that Devere Allen was piqued by the suggestion of either effeminacy or aggressive exclusiveness on the cover of his book.

Upon his return to the United States Allen worked toward the kind of movement his analysis implied. He tried to bring Americans into closer touch with European peace and radical forces through special news sections in The Nation *and* The World Tomorrow. *He helped to create a Pacifist Action Committee, a coordinated core of radical pacifist groups. He promoted pacifism among Socialists and campaigned as a Socialist candidate for the Senate from Connecticut.*

In 1933 he launched a venture new to the peace movement, the No-Frontier News Service (later Worldover Press). He supplied regular news and analysis to newspapers and the church press in order to focus attention on the relationship of developing international affairs and peace initiatives. By the time of his death of 1955 he was delivering material to nearly 700 newspapers and magazines in 62 countries. It was his way of working for a more inclusive and concentrated movement. In 1936-37 Allen was in charge of publicity for the half-million dollar Emergency Peace Campaign which mobilized popular support for neutrality; but the operation of his news service and the unfolding drama in Europe absorbed more and more of his time, so that gradually he

11

INTRODUCTION

moved away from the core of peace activism.

Meanwhile, a coterie of pacifists played almost the role Allen had envisioned for them. They formed a radical pacifist core within a broadly-based coalition of peace forces. In the twenties they had learned techniques of mobilizing segments of public opinion for political pressure. With their experience and resources, and with fairly well-defined foreign policy goals, they held the initiative in the movement until about 1937. After that the traditional internationalists, conservative in the face of change and wedded to concepts of international organization for peace and order, shifted increasingly toward collective security. At the same time they adopted the public opinion-forming techniques of the pacifists.

These, in turn, cast about for new allies in their effort to retain national neutrality. By 1938 they had formally aligned with Socialists under Norman Thomas, and in 1940-41 they even flirted with America First until its Fortress America foreign policy and its conservative domestic policies proved to be too much for them. As political effort looked ever more like a cul-de-sac, the radical pacifists reaffirmed the religious basis which Devere Allen had discerned, finding in it strength to endure the relative isolation from political forces which he had feared. The movement became fractured and somewhat exclusive in wartime. It remained so until the drive to reinstate conscription, the hazards of nuclear testing, and then the crisis over Vietnamese policy created

12

pressures for a newly concentrated and comprehensive political effort.

In close retrospect that coalition appears to have been largely ad hoc. Allen's analysis and prescription remain as salient as ever for those who take the fight for peace seriously. Cautious internationalists may still ponder the historical futility of seeking peace and order without confronting war itself and injustice; they may be wary of dealing with mechanisms for resolving conflicts without wrestling with fundamental pressures and policies. And what of the responsibilities of modern radicals? There are sound ethical and political reasons to avoid illiberal dogmatism whether religious or secular, in theory or in action: ethically it leads toward self-righteousness; politically it breeds obscurantism. "It matters incalculably. . . whether war is abolished and left behind with a host of other discarded institutions," Allen reminded the radicals of his time. "If he can hold out no hope of furthering that great achievement," the radical "may still deserve and win respect; but he will always seem the spokesman of a cult, a denizen of an ivory tower, a voice crying in a sterile wilderness." [8]

Charles Chatfield
Department of History
Wittenberg University

[8] The Fight for Peace, *p. 540.*

THE FIGHT FOR PEACE

THE MACMILLAN COMPANY
NEW YORK · BOSTON · CHICAGO · DALLAS
ATLANTA · SAN FRANCISCO

MACMILLAN & CO., LIMITED
LONDON · BOMBAY · CALCUTTA
MELBOURNE

THE MACMILLAN COMPANY
OF CANADA, LIMITED
TORONTO

THE
FIGHT FOR PEACE

By

DEVERE ALLEN

EDITOR, THE WORLD TOMORROW

NEW YORK

THE MACMILLAN COMPANY

1930

To Marie

WHO GAVE THE SPARK
AND FOSTERED THE FLAME

FOREWORD

THE American movement for world peace has behind it a century of pioneering. Neglected until recently by historians, ignored by the savants who compile encyclopedias, there has been no public comprehension of the force this developing enterprise has exerted on our national life and character.

Nowhere yet is there an adequate record of the organized war against war which first took form in the United States and to which the early American peace societies so gallantly contributed throughout the world.

The rôle of the movement, it is true, has largely been defensive. The story is chiefly one of hard defeats and illusory successes. There have been victories, none the less, and noble, agonizing struggles, quickened into colorful drama by some of the world's most gifted personalities.

These men and women, their aims and deeds, their splendid loyalties and their betrayals, their cautious compromises and their daring ventures, should be indelible. Yet they have perished from all common knowledge. More vital and more vivid than many who are better known, under the corrosion of incredible disregard they have disappeared from the living pages of the past.

Small wonder that our discussions of war and peace teem with untrue generalities; that so much peace planning is unpoised by real perspective; that so many literary and oratorical flights above the battle reveal the absence of an earth-inductor compass.

The farmer, the chemist, the teacher, for example—and by now increasingly the social scientist—have access to a body of experience. Not so the engineer of peace. Every new effort he makes is still a pioneering venture. His process is almost entirely trial and error. Availing himself of no lessons from the past, he labors under the impulsion of ideas which are oftentimes remote from present-day reality.

This book is not, however, a history of the peace movement. In favor of a more popular treatment, and through a desire to apply the obvious lessons of experience to a time which needs them sorely, I have departed from the method of the chronicler—though not, I trust, from sound historic fact.

For definite reasons I have liberally resorted to direct citation. First, to remove any doubt regarding the authenticity of the material. Further, to eliminate the boredom of abundant footnotes—which, for the reader who wishes to investigate for himself, are grouped at the end of the book. And further still, to convey not only the meaning of ideas and persons, but more interestingly the emotional and intellectual flavor of which they were compounded.

Unorthodox views must invariably run a severe critical gauntlet. It ought to be so. One test in particular should be ruthlessly applied to such a work as this. Has the writer, in order to establish a preconceived thesis, either deliberately or unwittingly selected untypical facts and quotations in order, willy-nilly, to prove a case? Few of those who have inquired even superficially into the literature of the peace movement of previous days will be free from this suspicion; and it cannot be denied that each organization has emphasized its own historic mission and has presented its own efforts and leaders without any attempt at a critical evaluation. Important facts, when unfavorable, have often been entombed in diplomatic silence. The answer in the present instance lies entirely in the sources, to which I will assist all skeptics.

Again, thoughtful readers will regard one hundred and fifteen years—the life span of the organized peace movement— as a brief time in the life of nations. They may feel moved to defend the peace groups from certain of the book's critical observations on the ground that in so short a period no substantial success in the abolition of war could reasonably be expected. They may charge the writer with unwise impatience. To this argument I reply that to-day, at least, the nature of modern warfare is such that the times cry out for more, not less, impatience. Humanity is not faced with a problem in abstract mathematics but with a knife-blade at its jugular vein.

With reiteration, I have borne down on the need of a more drastic opposition to war, the war system, and its perpetuators. For this I offer no apology. The supporters of war are the ones who must be ever on the moral defensive—they and the advocates of conventional work for peace: the former because of their destructive record in the past, the latter because of their too general ineffectiveness and their almost perpetual confusion.

The evidence of experience, to be sure, is only a partially useful guide for present and future policy. No one appreciates more than I what Randolph Bourne once called the wisdom of inexperience. There is stirring among the younger spirits of the world a new determination, a new realism, a new and striking grimness which bodes no good to Martian idols. The relatively rapid growth of this new attitude dates almost entirely from the World War and its aftermath, and is mainly independent of the earlier work for peace.

There is, though, ample reason why the past should be brought nearer. For the story of the peace movement reënforces, often by sheer contrast, the vigor and validity of more thoroughgoing methods. The social value of these methods is implied throughout the book and they are set forth explicitly in the final chapters.

DEVERE ALLEN.

CONTENTS

CHAPTER I
THE PIONEERS

Some mysterious unconscious impulse appears to be a concomitant of natural order. This impulse has always been unsettling the existing conditions and pushing forward, groping after something more elaborate and intricate than what already existed. This vital impulse, élan vital as Bergson calls it, represents the inherent radicalism of nature herself. This power that makes for salutary readjustment, or righteousness in the broadest sense of the term, is no longer a conception confined to poets and dreamers, but must be reckoned with by the most exacting historian and the hardest-headed man of science.—JAMES HARVEY ROBINSON, in The Journal of Philosophy, Psychology, and Scientific Methods.

CHAPTER I

THE PIONEERS

BETWEEN the events of the early nineteenth century and those of the corresponding period in the twentieth, there is a striking parallel. In each instance a series of economic factors, coupled with nationalistic rivalries, irresponsible statesmanship, and dependence on balances of power for security, had culminated in colossal warfare. Each time the settlement which followed was arranged by the great powers with scant concession to the sensibilities of smaller countries seeking to influence the decisions of the peace conference. Each settlement contained the germs of future wars, and the various war zealots came from each conflict little chastened.

In the last century, as in this, there ensued a revulsion of sentiment against such wholesale slaughter. Renewed interest in world peace was evoked in many conscience-stricken people, and occasioned a great increase in anti-war activity.

Of one hundred and twenty-seven years terminating in 1815, England had spent sixty-five in war and sixty-two in "peace." The young United States on its own part had gone through the senseless War of 1812, which never had whole-hearted popular support and which gained not a single thing originally stated as our war aims. This experience, plus the affront to decency in the shambles of Europe, was responsible, if not for the first clear outcry against the curse of war, for the rapid emergence, here and there, of more and more peace partisans.

Gathering strength from feeble beginnings, this new passion for the abolition of war was speedily crystallized into the world's first peace societies. In 1813, at the crest of Napoleon's prestige, Dr. David Bogue, a London preacher of considerable

fame, delivered a sermon on "Universal Peace," in the course
of which he made the following significant suggestion: "As we
live in an age of societies to combine individual efforts for
public benefit, why should not one be formed for promoting
peace among the nations of the earth?"

Years afterwards, in describing these early days and their
eventuation in organized peace efforts, one of our American
peace journals piously but shrewdly observed: "No individual
deserves the sole honor of originating this movement; it was
the result of providential causes operating powerfully on the
mass of minds throughout Christendom." [1]

On the night of June 7, 1814, William Allen, an English
Quaker—linguist, educator, preacher, man of science, and pub-
lisher of *The Philanthropist*—thumbed the pages of his diary
and made the following laconic entry: "A meeting to consider
of a new Society to spread tracts, etc., against war." [2] But
the meeting in William Allen's house did not result, until
June 14, 1816, in the actual establishment of the Society for
Permanent and Universal Peace, with its declaration that
"War is inconsistent with the spirit of Christianity and the
true interest of mankind," and with ten original members,
comprising Churchmen, Non-conformists, and Friends. This
occurrence, and Allen's interest in peace societies, is not even
mentioned in the forty-six-page sketch of his life in the five-
volume set of *Quaker Biographies* published during 1916 by
Friends in the United States! Not the least of the world's
injustices is the regrettable inability of long-dead men to write
their own life stories in perspective.

By virtue of the delay in England the honors, arguing by
the calendar, came to this country. For, entirely unknown
to each other at the time, three peace societies were formed
here during 1815. One, under the presidency of David Low
Dodge, a devout Presbyterian, in New York City on the sixteenth of August; another on the second of December, at
Vienna, Ohio, chiefly composed of Friends; while the evening
of December twenty-eighth witnessed a gathering in the home
of the Reverend William Ellery Channing, composed mainly
of Christian ministers of liberal denominations under the

leadership of the Reverend Noah Worcester, who there organized our most vigorous early anti-war group, the Massachusetts
Peace Society.

Behind this culmination were years of idealism manifested
in the teachings and the lives of Quakers, Shakers, and other
religious bodies whose principles embraced pacifistic tenets,
Find work for international peace at any stage of the movement's development, and you will not seek far before discovering the quiet, persevering handiwork of Friends. Long had
they labored to spread their principles of peace.

One of their farthest-flung voices, using the language of the
printed page, was that of Anthony Benezet, early foe of
slavery, apostle of practical good will in everyday living, and
pamphleteer of pacifism. Of meager stature and stalwart modesty, he refused to have his portrait done, exclaiming, "Oh,
no, no! My ugly face shall not go down to posterity!"

Posterity can spare his face, for it has some knowledge of
his force of character. It was he who, upon the outbreak of the
Revolution, possessed the temerity to scatter where he could,
to many in high places in this country and abroad, a pamphlet
expressing his *Thoughts on the Nature of War*. In 1780
came another from his pen, *The Spirit of Prayer, with Some
Thoughts on War*. The kind of thoughts he broadcast rang
with passionate outspokenness:

What thievery bears any proportion to that which, with the
boldness of drum and trumpet, plunders the innocent of all they
have? . . . What honor has war gotten, from its thousands and
tens of thousands of men slaughtered on heaps, with as little
regret or concern as at loads of rubbish thrown into a pit? Who
but the fiery dragon, would put a wreath of laurel on such heroes'
heads? Who but he, could say unto them, Well done, good and
faithful servants? Youths in "nameless numbers" have been
either violently forced or tempted in the fire of youth and full
strength of sinful lusts, to forget God, eternity, and their own
souls, and rush in to kill or be killed, with as much furious haste
and goodness of spirit as a tyger kills tyger for the sake of his
prey.

Twenty-one years later, in 1801, appeared a pamphlet by
the Reverend Job Scott—New Englander, Quaker by choice,

globe-trotter of good will, prolific author, a man so conscientious that he suffered privation during the Revolution rather than accept paper currency issued to finance the war—entitled *War Inconsistent with the Doctrine and Example of Jesus Christ, in a Letter to a Friend.* Over the next third of a century at least five editions in this country and England were put out, and circulated widely. Forthright in speech, this Scott:

> I have not merely to oppose men who oppose all the order of society, by committing depredation and offence universally; but those who interlard the system of blood-shed with the profession of christianity. . . . I therefore avow the following proposition as a sentiment closely connected, and one with the nature of true christianity, and as a sentiment which will finally prevail:
> *That war, in every shape, is incompatible with the nature of christianity; and that no persons professing that religion and under the full and proper influence of the temper and mind of Christ, can adopt, pursue, or plead for it.*

First of all publications directed against war, exclusive of those by Friends, was in all probability *The Battle Axe,* by Timothy Watrous. Watrous was an outstanding member of the Rogerenes, a rebellious sect of eastern Connecticut. While the Rogerenes because of their disavowal of warfare were locally referred to as "Quakers" on some occasions, they were distinct in origin and different in doctrine. Watrous could not get his pamphlet printed, so fiery was it, and so jubilant over the success of the Revolution which had just ended were the people. His son, also named Timothy, revised the manuscript, while another son, Zachariah, inventor of the coffee mill, devised a printing press for the sole purpose of putting out this scathing attack on war.

Even had there been no others prior to 1809—and the chances are there were—several students who deserve our eternal thanks for making a record of the pioneers [3] are thus technically in error when they follow without qualification the lead of the early American Peace Society, which said in 1828, in its first general circular letter, that "the first tract, composed professedly and exclusively for the cause of peace, which—

so far as is known to this board—ever appeared in this country, was written by a merchant of the city of New York in the year 1809, and was entitled, *The Mediator's Kingdom Not of This World.*" One author, forgetting the teachings of Laotse, Confucius, Buddha, and Jesus; overlooking the writings of Sully and the Abbé St. Pierre, William Penn, and many others, goes so far as to call this publication "the earliest peace literature in the world!" ⁴ This merchant-author was David Low Dodge.

The error regarding the American pamphleteers indeed is merely technical, and noted here simply for the sake of the record; not only because David Low Dodge accompanied his pamphleteering with organization, but because, riding in on the wave of nausea over the horrors of the Napoleonic insanity in Europe, his influence was the greatest thus far of the early peace crusaders. Dodge really "started something." "If war," he declared, "is an inhuman and cruel employment, it must be wrong for Christians to engage in it."

Such an insinuation was too much for the good Christian soldiers in the congregations of Manhattan. They sprang to arms, and in the name of the Nazarene poured execrations on the aristocratically poised and dark-haired head of the thirty-five-year-old dry goods merchant. And when, five years later, Dodge came out with a still more pointed onslaught against war, *War Inconsistent with the Religion of Jesus Christ,* the clamor was louder than before. What? Take war away from Jesus? Where then would be his ministers, zealously assuring their flocks that the cross and the cutlass were Holy Twins when used against Great Britain—in that instance—for the defense of Right? A committee of three literary men, one a clergyman, had issued an attack on Dodge's earlier pamphlet, calling their defense of war, *The Duty of a Christian in a Trying Situation.* Dodge followed with a rebuttal which won him some adherents. But the second pamphlet of that first war year as it slowly spread about, uncorked so many vials of wrath that one can understand why the organ of the Massachusetts Peace Society should have said of Dodge's organization:

In August, 1815, a small number of worthy characters formed a Peace Society in the City of New York; but for some prudential reasons, they deferred for several months a public avowal of the existence of such a Society.[5]

Measured in relative terms, the influence of Dodge's writings was tremendous; they were republished in other cities, and their author's influence on the peace movement, though his radicalism alarmed a great many, remained considerable for years. "Some," he once confessed, "who were favorable to the doctrines of peace judged that, with a bold hand, I had carried the subject too far; and doubtless, as it was new and had not been much discussed, I wrote too unguardedly, not sufficiently defining my terms." [6] That, of course, is a matter of judgment on which there may be difference of opinion even now. In any case, he spoke with truth when in later years he modestly asserted on behalf of his pamphlets, "These publications gave the first impulse in America, if we except the uniform influence of the Friends, to inquiry into the lawfulness of war by Christians."

After Dodge, the deluge! Came a pamphlet—author unknown—called *Thoughts on the Practical Advantage of Those Who Hold the Doctrines of Peace Over Those Who Vindicate War, Addressed to Those Who Follow Peace with All Men.* In Norwich, Connecticut, David Low Dodge's father-in-law, the Reverend Aaron Cleveland, a renowned anti-slavery preacher who had been converted by his son-in-law—to whose opinions he had been at first inhospitable—preached a pair of sermons on "The Life of Man Inviolable by the Laws of Christ"; and stable citizens of ye olde Connecticut gossiped wonderingly about these radical ideas.

In Boston the Reverend Daniel Chessman, a young Baptist only a year out of Brown University, poured his burning peace views into a fifty-two-page manuscript which he called *An Essay on Self-Defence, Designed to Show that War is Inconsistent with Scripture and Reason.* It rivals in force and cogency the modern arguments on the authority of the Gospels, with a deal of secular polemic power added.

New York peace campaigners seized upon the works of Erasmus and in 1813 brought out a booklet of selections from his *Antipolemus, or the Plea of Reason, Religion and Humanity Against War,* beginning:

If there is in the affairs of mortal man any one thing which it is proper uniformly to explode; which it is incumbent on every man, by every lawful means, to avoid, to deprecate, to oppose, that one thing is doubtless war.

while Adna Heaton, in his twenty-thousand-word pamphlet published in New York, on *War and Christianity Contrasted,* was discomfitingly inquiring of professing followers of Jesus:

Can the christian appeal to his conscience, that he has in him the same mind that was in Jesus his Lord, when he prays for vengeance on his enemies, or indulges emotions of hatred or revenge toward them? Can he say, that he walks as his Master walked, when under the direction of his lust, his feet run swiftly to shed blood?

And the Reverend Samuel Whelpley, under the pen-name of "Philadelphus," was publishing broadcast a series of *Letters Addressed to Caleb Strong, Esq., Late Governor of Massachusetts, Showing* (provided anyone ever got beyond the title) *That Retaliation, Capital Punishments, and War, are Prohibited by the Gospel; Justified by no Good Principle; Not Necessary to the Safety of Individuals or Nations; But Incompatible with Their Welfare; and Contrary to the Laws of Christ.*

But there are pamphleteers and pamphleteers. King of them all so far as brilliant style and argument are counted, was Noah Worcester, prime mover and corresponding secretary of the Massachusetts Peace Society. He is second in the chronological order of great leaders in the movement. Worcester had served in the Revolution. He was already fifty-six years old when, on Christmas Day of 1814, he let loose upon the world the most effective pamphlet on the question ever written: *A Solemn Review of the Custom of War; Showing that War Is the Effect of Popular Delusion and Proposing a Remedy.* Worcester was never a radical, like Dodge, who, he thought, had gone too far. But just as his mild pseudonym of "Philo Pacificus" concealed a pen of mighty power, so his rotund, benevolent countenance, fringed with whitening hair, hardly revealed the keen, clear mind that worked so trenchantly behind it.

So strong was even Worcester's pamphlet, that one shudders to think what a dressing-down this Revolutionary War veteran would receive from the super-patriotic spirits of the D. A. R. and other effervescent loyalists in the present time, should they ever fall upon his writings. Happily for the public accord, original copies of his tract are as scarce as saints, and the edition brought out in 1904 by the American Peace Society is minus most of his frank strictures on war-making governments.

One shudders more, however, to realize that this historic tract narrowly escaped the fate of Daniel Chessman's manuscript—to remain unpublished through the lack of funds. Once published, it received an amazing circulation for those days; two members of the Society of Friends made financially possible the free distribution of several thousand copies; it was translated into other languages and was still being read in Europe many years after its issuance. Its immediate acclaim is pleasurably described by Worcester in these words:

It is now about three years since he [Worcester is writing in the third person] offered that work to publishers. But the subject was so new and the prospect so gloomy, that, while they were friendly to the sentiments, they declined publishing even a small edition at their own risk; and he, having need to be cautious, agreed with his generous printer to share with him in the *profit* or the *loss* which should occur on the sale of the edition. Now, in this country and Great Britain, that tract has passed through as many as *ten* or *twelve* editions—two of which amounted to 22,000 copies.*

This from *The Friend of Peace,* edited in Boston by Noah Worcester for nearly fifteen years, and described with charming incorrectness in a peace magazine of October, 1927, as follows:

The first periodical devoted exclusively to the cause of international peace was titled the Friend of Peace. It was the product of Noah Webster, the first number being published in Philadelphia in 1816.*

The 1816, anyway, is right! And with respect to its fertility of ideas, its zest, its readability, and its solid informational content—considered, of course, in relation to its handicaps—the term of "first" has something more than a chronological justification.

In France, the "Society of Christian Morals," having for its object the application of the precepts of Christianity to the social relations of life, but largely interested in work for international peace, was set under way on the fifteenth of August, 1821—chiefly through the influence of an English ironmaster, Joseph Tregelles Price, who gave to William Allen the idea of establishing the first peace society in England.

A peace society was organized at Geneva, Switzerland, in 1830, by the Count de Sellon. By 1825, there were about twenty-five separate peace societies functioning in the British Isles.

In the United States, meantime, they had been steadily on the increase. In Maine, Rhode Island, Connecticut, Pennsylvania, New Hampshire, Massachusetts, Vermont, North Carolina, and other states, peace societies of local influence were springing up, one after another, until by 1828 there were about three dozen of them altogether.

On the tenth of February of that year, it was voted by the Peace Society of Maine, "that it is expedient to adopt measures for the formation of a national peace society." Similar votes were taken in most of the other societies; until, on May 8, 1828, an amalgamation of these friendly groups was effected under the federative title of The American Peace Society, and our first national peace organization was an actuality.

Around these dry bones of fact were wrapped the dreams and energetic devotion of the next great leader in the movement's history. William Ladd, never a literary light, but a genius at organization and a persuasive speaker, was a comparative newcomer in the cause; and here as in many another period, a newcomer proved to be its salvation. Ladd owed his abhorrence of war and his zeal for peace partly to the personal inspiration of his friend, the late President Appleton of Bowdoin College, and perhaps more to the famous pamphlet of Noah Worcester. At first a conservative, he became a radical by conviction though never by temper; able to see the sincerity in those of other views despite his stoutly maintained personal convictions, he overleaped with his reconciling spirit the vast distances still unshortened by telegraph, telephone, or railroad, and kept alive an incredible fellowship and unity; a oneness sustained more than eighteen years.

More of this man's work and thought will be brought out in later chapters. It is enough to note here that the labor of Dodge, the great awakener, and that of Worcester, the convincing preacher by the printed word, had now passed to the leadership of Ladd, the gifted organizer. All three were indispensable; and all three belong in the roster of our great immortals.

CHAPTER II

THE RELIGIOUS URGE TO PEACE

He never failed to say and keep up his paternosters every morning, whether he remained in the house, or mounted his horse and went out in the field to join the army. It was a common saying among the soldiers that one must "beware the paternosters of the Constable." For as disorders were frequent, he would say, while muttering and mumbling his paternosters all the time, "Go and fetch that fellow and hang me him up to this tree"; "Out with a file of harquebusiers here before me this instant, for the execution of this man"; "Burn me this village instantly"; "Cut me to pieces at once all these village peasants who have dared to hold this church against the king!" All this without ever ceasing from his paternosters till he finished them—thinking that he would have done very wrong to put them off to another time; so conscientious was he!—"M. le Constable de Montmorency," from *Lives of Distinguished Men and Great Captains*, by the ABBÉ DE BRANTOME, 1527-1614.

CHAPTER II

THE RELIGIOUS URGE TO PEACE

THESE pages are not written just for Christians. But they are written out of facts.

To-day, the organized forces struggling directly for peace embrace all creeds, all faiths, and those with no religious affiliations at all. Not only the churches, but an immense variety of sectarian bodies are lined up against war, and among them are labor groups, some of the radical political parties, and individuals, naturally of the utmost imaginable diversity. Nevertheless it remains true that in organized Christianity the peace movement had its origin; and so for a time, until we reach the developments of later years, we shall confine our attention largely to the relation between peace work and Christianity.

The first peace organizations were directly associated with the Christian religion. Most of their officers were ministers. David Low Dodge was a conservative churchman, though not an ordained preacher. Noah Worcester was a Congregational divine. William Ladd, though a retired sea captain, joined the Second Congregational Church at Minot, Maine, and later took his ordination vows.

At the end of its first year, the Massachusetts Peace Society announced a total of one hundred and seventy-three "respectable members"—without mention of any other category—and its respectability was enhanced, no doubt, by the inclusion of "more than 50 ministers of religion." Though the ratio dropped the next year—eighty clergymen out of three hundred and four members altogether—"the greater part of the new members are persons of respectable standing and influence," which meant, at that time, certainly, that they were in good status with the churches. Many of the societies held their annual meetings on Christmas night.

Uniformly the anti-war impulses of those early days were rooted in the pious devotion of conscientious Christians. You might paraphrase the famous remark of Horace Greeley that "all Democrats are not horse thieves, but all horse thieves are Democrats," and declare with truth that while all Christians were not peacemakers, all peacemakers were Christians. All, that is, in the peace societies.

No Christian pacifist of to-day need flatter himself that he has contributed any substantial originality to the religious case for peace. The special responsibility of Christians for the abolition of war, because of Jesus' teaching, was recognized by all pioneer spokesmen of the cause. Noah Worcester, in his *Solemn Review,* expressed the typical attitude among the anti-war minority when he declared:

If the Christian religion is to put an end to war, it must be by the efforts of those who are under its influence. So long, therefore, as Christians acquiesce in the custom, the desirable event will be delayed.

Acquiesced they have, and delayed it is; for from that day to this, the professing Christians of every country have had two different attitudes in time of peace and one less attitude in time of war.

Would it not be possible to match, almost word for word, in our Christian anti-war literature of to-day (except that now it would be put more mildly, possibly) the following passionate protest of Noah Worcester in 1815?

It may be doubted whether a complete history of all the conduct of infernal spirits, would contain anything more inconsistent, more abominable, or more to be deplored, than has appeared in the history of *warring Christians.* To behold two contending armies, from Christian nations, so deluded as mutually to offer prayers to the same benevolent God, for success in their attempts to butcher each other, is enough to fill the mind of any considerate person with amazement and horror.

The precise meaning of Jesus' teachings in respect to war

was fully as much a matter of concern to these early peace workers as to any modern Christian pacifist. "Is it not a circumstance worthy of some notice," dryly remarked a writer in *The Friend of Peace* in 1816, "that Jesus omitted to say, 'Blessed are the war makers; for they shall be called true patriots'?"

Nor did they fail to challenge the orthodox war exegesis of their clerical opponents. When confronted with Jesus' reference to his coming to bring, not peace, but a sword, or his driving the money changers out of the temple—the stock in trade of every similar anti-pacifist critic of to-day—they retorted usually with almost the same general facts and reasoning as those employed, say, by the distinguished Biblical scholar, C. J. Cadoux, author of *The Early Christian Attitude to War* (1919). Thomas Clarkson in England—whom William Lloyd Garrison called in a sonnet "the good man eloquent"—had published his *Essays on the Doctrines and Practice of the Early Christians, as They Relate to War.* Joseph John Gurney, the English Quaker, wrote on the subject also. And Jonathan Dymond, another English Friend, whose premature death at the age of thirty-two deprived the peace movement of a mind it ill could spare, bequeathed to posterity his keenly analytical *Inquiry into the Accordancy of War with the Principles of Christianity, etc.*

The work of Clarkson, Gurney, and Dymond was speedily available to the peace movement in this country and served as the basis of such widely circulated dissertations as that, for example, issued in 1836 by Professor Thomas C. Upham of Bowdoin.[1]

The scholarship of these pioneer peace writers is most interesting. They quote Tertullian; they use Origen's work against Celsus; they tell the dramatic story of the youthful pacifist martyr Maximilian; they demonstrate so admirably that one rather questions why many later comments should be needed, the reasons why a typical early follower of Jesus drove down a spiritual stake with the firm declaration, "I am a Christian; therefore I cannot fight." The example of the faithful, how-

ever, has had almost as little practical influence on the majority
of later Christians as Jesus has himself.

The Battle over Army Chaplains

No less than Christian pacifists since the World War, were
the spokesmen of the early peace societies exercised by the rôle
of military chaplains. Says one of the early tracts of the
American Peace Society:

> Statesmen of our own, though at the hazard of being branded
> as infidels, have objected to the employment of chaplains among
> our soldiers, on the ground that the religion they teach is incom-
> patible with the duties of war. . . . If war is wrong, its chap-
> lain, employed for its support, *must* countenance what the gospel
> condemns; and hence his very office is unchristian. . . . We judge
> not the *men;* we merely condemn their *business* as unchristian.
> So the gospel itself does; so common sense is fast coming to do;
> and posterity will yet look back, and wonder how any ambassador
> or disciple of the Prince of Peace could ever have lent himself to
> such a libel of blood on his peaceful religion. Would you have war
> cease? It never can so long as Christians support it by their
> prayers.[2]

Especially interesting is this early attitude of the American
Peace Society in view of the fact that as recently as December,
1921, the same Society's journal boasted how the organization
"has stood by the United States Government in all of its wars
of over a century." This apostasy was a trifle exaggerated,
happily, for as we shall later see, the record really stands at
nearer half and half.

There have always been found some to hold with firmness.
George Fox, founder of the Society of Friends, was offered
in 1650 a captaincy in the army of the Commonwealth, but
promptly declined.

> I told them I knew from whence all wars did rise, even from
> the lust, according to James' doctrine, and that I lived in the
> virtue of that life and power, that took away the occasion of all
> wars.[3]

The March 19, 1835, issue of *The Christian Mirror* contains
a striking letter from the Reverend Stephen Thurston, of

Maine, stating why he refused an offer to serve as chaplain in the militia.

If it is right for me to act as chaplain to the militia at home, it would be right for me to join the army in that capacity in time of war. . . . If I were to join the army in this capacity, I should be expected to impart, on all suitable occasions, moral and religious instructions to the soldiers. Suppose that on the eve of some important battle I should preach from the well-known words of our Saviour, "Put up thy sword into its place; for all they that take the sword shall perish by the sword"; or the words, "Love your enemies"; and suppose that I should speak according to the spirit and the meaning of these texts; should I be considered as acting the part of a good chaplain? Would it be a suitable preparation for a work of slaughter upon which they were soon to enter? But would not such preaching be in perfect accordance with my duty as a minister of the gospel of peace? And is it not evident that my duty as chaplain to an army would be quite inconsistent with my duty as a minister of Christ?

And in complete agreement with such a view, Professor Upham declared:

We assert it with entire confidence, that, were it not for the countenance which they receive from professed Christians in the ranks of the army and particularly from the chaplain, the soldiers themselves, hardened as they are by the tendency of their occupation, would experience more misgivings, more doubt, more compunction of heart in their work of destruction and blood, than they are now generally found to do. They conclude, and very naturally too, if a preacher of the Gospel, a commissioned minister of the Most High, with all his capabilities for forming a moral and religious judgment of things, approves their employment and prays for its success, it would be an excess of scrupulosity in them to entertain a doubt.

From then until now, the attack on the idea of military clergy has been constantly recurrent. One of the most recent critics is Bishop Francis J. McConnell, of the Methodist Episcopal Church:

I am sure, however, that the chaplaincy, as at present conceived of in the armies of all nations alike, aims at spiritual ministry only in a secondary fashion. Governments establish chaplaincies for

the increase of the effectiveness of the fighting forces. Let not the
Church befool itself on this point. The interest of war parties in
religion for their own side is the same sort of interest they have in
poison gas for the enemy—just the desire to make their own side
win more quickly.⁴

And yet the alliance between the church and the military is
just as strong officially as ever; the bond between the two is
not relaxed. And should another conflict come, ministers of
the religion of Jesus will doubtless be found in abundance to
bolster up the fighting men's morale, that they may better wield
the bayonets and hand grenades and liquid fire and lethal gases.

Not the whole long century of protest in the name of Jesus;
not the many citations from the early Christian martyrs; not
the intermittent drumfire on the backs of chaplains, have
availed to turn the Christian world as a whole from its first
allegiance to the gods of battle.

War and the Missionary Enterprise

While the late great Christian War was on, church leaders
confessed lugubriously in private, and occasionally in the open,
to a certain worry over its effect on missions. Then and ever
since, missionaries have brought back experiences revealing the
distrust of Christianity by "the heathen"; though non-Chris-
tians, like Gandhi in India, have almost uniformly found no
quarrel with Jesus himself. And just as the peace societies
have lost few opportunities to publish these outside criticisms
of gunboat Christianity, their early prototypes were steadfast
in the same unwelcomed service. Said *The Friend of Peace*
in 1816:

The warring character of Christian nations has for ages been
one of the greatest obstacles in the way of extending the light of
the gospel. Indeed it has occasioned a dreadful eclipse of this
light, and hid it under a bushel. The Peace Societies wish to
remove the cause of this eclipse, and the great obstacle to the
conversion of the pagans.

They were still wishing, when a couple of decades later the
Reverend Mr. Simpson, an earnest missionary to one of the

South Sea Islands, wrote back home and complained because the natives were learning that Christian countries, so-called, slaughtered each other's populations in war. The native leaders became eagerly imitative, but suffered defeat in a military expedition against some neighbors. Whereupon, says Mr. Simpson, "a great falling off in our adult and children's school followed, and has continued to a great extent up to the present time." And William Ladd, commenting on this episode, succinctly noted "progress": "The spears have disappeared from Rurutu, and the nations now fight, like Christians, with muskets."

About this time Dr. Joseph Wolff, the missionary and traveler, was telling his audiences of the Jewish listener in London who had startled him one day by saying: "You go to war, and you call the Lord Jesus Christ the Prince of Peace, and you pray to him, as the Prince of Peace, to aid your warriors to vanquish your enemies." [5] Thus Professor Upham was reminding his Christian readers that the emperor of China, in refusing admittance of the Christian religion, gave as his reason that "wherever the Christians go, they whiten the soil with human bones." [6] And a little later, Joshua P. Blanchard, one of the most undiscourageable fighters for peace, was saying in *The Christian Citizen:*

Missionaries of the Cross do not hesitate to encounter the storms of ocean, the dangers of pestilential climates and untried privations, that they may administer this panacea for universal evil, vainly imagining that the message of divine life they carry will be able to withstand the counteracting martial aggressions which accompany it, or that a truth will have power to produce the peace and joy and righteousness in a foreign land it has hitherto failed to effect in their own.

Said the Reverend Rufus W. Clark of Portsmouth before the American Peace Society in 1851, of the natives who had shown persistent hostility to our missionaries:

Their hatred arose from the dread of Christian armies, and their horror of the refined cruelties and awful barbarities of Christian battles.

At a huge peace meeting in Mystic, Connecticut, in 1884, the Reverend R. McMurdy, leader in the movement for arbitration, drove home the bitter words of the melancholy King Theodore of Abyssinia:

First came the missionaries, then the consuls, and after them, the armies.

—thus anticipating the same doubt of the churchly ambassadors' usefulness expressed by a pacifist during the World War in verses drenched with lye:

> If you can flood the world with Holy Bibles
> And follow them abroad with Holy Bombs.[7] . . .

No wonder that a missionary, Dr. James M. Yard, exclaimed in 1927:

So many missionaries have faced bitter criticism of Chinese and Indians since 1918. The Orientals say, "You preach love, peace, brotherhood—what do you mean? There never was fought such a cruel, fiendish war as you Christians have just engaged in. What good is Christianity anyway?" [8]

Well, what good is it? Good for a great deal and not all failure! But for how many centuries longer the missionary can labor under such a handicap with the non-Christian world; and how long he will continue to tolerate the position of rank hypocrisy in which he is perpetually kept, is not a purely academic query.

Significant was the petition sent to the United States Legation at Peiping (then Pekin) by twenty-five American missionaries in 1924, urging that "no form of military pressure, especially no military force," be used to protect them or their property, and that in the event of their capture or death at the hands of lawless persons no money be paid for release and no indemnity be demanded. "We take this stand," they said, "believing that the way to establish righteousness and peace is through bringing the spirit of personal good will to bear on all persons under all circumstances, even through suffering wrong without retaliation."

Significant also was the declaration of the great international missionary conference at Jerusalem in 1928 that "the protection of missionaries should only be by such methods as will promote good will in personal and official relations," and that mission societies "should make no claim on their governments for the armed defense of their missionaries and their property." Here is a portent of great promise. How thoroughly it may be embodied, how uniformly it may be tried in actual practice under critical tests, only time can reveal.

The ability of the Christian religion to confront the world with the war viper coiled contentedly in its bosom has seemed endless. There have been heartening signs of awakening conscience in the last few years. Yet even now, no adequately deep or pervasive repentance has been manifested. And this despite the outcries over the betrayal of the church's founder, despite the witness of the early Christians, despite the anomaly of fighting parsons, and despite the obvious embarrassment about the ever-contradictory Christian missions.

CHAPTER III
A GREATER "GREAT ILLUSION"?

The loud little handful—as usual—will shout for the war. The pulpit will—warily and cautiously—object—at first; the great, big, dull bulk of the nation will rub its sleepy eyes and try to make out why there should be a war, and will say, earnestly and indignantly, "It's unjust and dishonorable, and there is no necessity for it." Then the handful will shout louder. A few fair men on the other side will argue and reason against the war with speech and pen, and at first will have a hearing and be applauded; but it will not last long; those others will outshout them, and presently the anti-war audiences will thin out and lose popularity. Before long you will see this curious thing; the speakers stoned from the platform, and free speech strangled by hordes of furious men who in their secret hearts are still at one with those stoned speakers—as earlier—but do not dare say so. And now the whole nation— pulpit and all—will take up the war-cry, and shout itself hoarse, and mob any honest man who ventures to open his mouth; and presently such mouths will cease to open. Next, the statesmen will invent cheap lies, putting the blame on the nation that is attacked, and every man will be glad of those conscience-soothing falsities, and will diligently study them, and refuse to examine any refutations of them; and thus he will by and by convince himself that the war is just, and will thank God for the better sleep he enjoys after this process of grotesque self-deception.—MARK TWAIN in *The Mysterious Stranger,* written in 1898, published posthumously in 1916. (Used by permission of Harper and Brothers.)

CHAPTER III

A GREATER "GREAT ILLUSION"?[1]

HOPE springs eternal, and undaunted by recurrent disillusionment, the peace societies never ceased to dream of different days within the institution of the Christian Church. They envisaged always a little church around the corner, wherein might yet occur the marriage of the Church and Jesus, sending forth disciples of international peace until the whole of Christianity should be won to its own professed ideals and program for the human family.

Said William Ladd in 1824:

> Perhaps at no time since the apostolic age has pure and undefiled religion so generally prevailed, as at the present; nor has peace among Christian nations been so general. There is scarce a "speck of war" in the horizon. There has been a very evident change in public opinion respecting war. And we have great reason to hope that the time is not far distant, when men "shall beat their swords into plowshares and their spears into pruning hooks, and nation shall not lift up sword against nation, neither shall they learn war any more." [1]

Noah Worcester, a decade earlier, had begun to glow with hope because of the certainty with which, he felt, the clergy would rally to the cause. In the peace societies, he ventured to believe,

> we may hope to engage every true minister of the Prince of Peace and every Christian who possesses the temper of his Master. . . . The Bible Societies, already formed in various parts of the world, must naturally, and even necessarily, aid the object now proposed. Indeed, the two objects are so congenial, that whatever promotes the one, will aid the other. Nor is it easy to see how any Bible Society could refrain from voluntarily affording all possible encouragement to peace societies. The same may be said of all missionary societies, and societies for propagating the gospel.

Still more imbued with fervor, he exclaimed in another place:

> Where is the godly minister of any sect, or where is the man renowned for talents and virtue, who has attended to the subject, that feels any disposition to oppose the efforts for the abolition of war? Truly we have not heard of so many as *three* respectable opponents, among all who have read what has been written on the subject. Was there ever a subject brought forward in our country, so novel and half so interesting, which met with so little opposition? May we then not humbly hope in God that in less than fifty years from this time, our country will be as free from war advocates, as it is now from advocates for the African commerce in slaves?[2]

This was assuredly a robust expectation; for far in advance of abolitionist sentiment, public opinion was unitedly opposed, throughout the North, at least, to a further continuance of the slave trade.

"Fifty years from this time!" The Northern armies were then being disbanded while the South looked on in sullen helplessness: and the United States lay exhausted from one of the bloodiest conflicts in history, at which other nations where slavery had been abolished without bloodshed and with a modicum of bitterness, could only stare aghast.

And yet, Noah Worcester's prophecy was modest in comparison to another he printed incidentally at about the same time:

> If we may calculate on a progressive increase for years to come, proportionate to that of last year, we may pretty confidently expect, that at the commencement of the year 1820, there will not be found in New England a single advocate for the custom of war, among all the ministers of religion in every denomination.[3]

In one sense, neither the long-term nor the short-term prophecy was wrong. For by 1820, the evidence seems to indicate, there was not left one clergyman in New England—or elsewhere—who believed in war. And at the end of the Mexican and Civil wars, were there any ministers who did not ardently believe war wrong and peace the way of right? You are doubtless asking, What is wrong with this picture?

Since the pioneer peace work began to spread its influence, it has won practically all ministers and most "respectable" laymen to its cause. Peace societies have grown through the passing years, and they have welcomed the interest of the clergy and churchmen who, after every war, have once more devoted themselves to the ideal of brotherhood.

After every war—there is the answer to the paradox. A ministry flocking to the banner of peace in 1820, and calling persistently for peace throughout the hundred years since then; yet during times of testing, when wars came on—once, twice, thrice, four times—blessing all these wars (and the innumerable lesser hostilities in between) when it was popular to do so, giving armed violence its full and free support, and finding each time reasons plausible enough to justify its action. Like the clergy in each instance, on the other side. Like the clergy in all nations, on all sides of every conflict.

Yes, the pulpits and the pews of Christian churches have been for peace, through all the last loud century. Yet wars have come, the altars have been our best recruiting stations, and in this whole long time the church has never so much as attempted an opposition to war that actually amounted to a snowball in the muzzle of a "seventy-five."

But there had been substantial precedent. From the capture of the church by Constantine about 312 A.D.—regarded first as the capture of Constantine—the Christian religion has served as Mars' faithful handmaid.

One of the Crusaders wrote home to his highly pious family that "our men returning in victory, bearing many heads fixed on pikes and spears, presented a glorious spectacle for the people of God." [4]

As kind old Saint Bernard put it, so thought the Church: "The Christian who slays the unbeliever in the Holy War is sure of his reward, the more sure if he himself be slain. The Christian glories in the death of the infidel, because Christ is glorified."

The mediæval Spaniards, seeking to carry their religion into everyday life, as it were, used to call their warships by devout

nomenclature: "The Blessed Virgin," "The Holy Ghost," "The
Most Holy Trinity," "The Conception," "St. John the Baptist." Philip II sent out his Great Armada only after many
hours on his knees in prayer for victory; and the English after
defeating Philip's fleet, struck off a medal bearing the inscription in Latin, "God blew at them and they were dispersed."
The old British falcon of the sea, Sir John Hawkins, named his
buccaneering slaveship the "Jesus." Our own battleship
"Princeton" boasted a mammoth gun called "The Peacemaker"
which in 1844 ironically blew up and killed the American
Secretary of State and almost did away with President
Tyler.

The New England Pilgrims, so central were firearms in
their way of life, measured distance by a musket shot; they
came to a pond, for example, "about a musket shot broad and
twice as long." [5] The Massachusetts colonists put a bounty of
a hundred dollars on Indian scalps; and unlike William Penn,
relied upon their aim for safety. [6]

The Puritans' old training days on Boston Common were
gala celebrations; prayers and psalm-singing were followed by
a banquet, and after this came target practice, with guns and
cannon, at a stuffed human figure, for prize awards offered to
the best marksmen. [7]

The men from the Hartford settlement who participated in
the bloodthirsty massacre of the Pequots at Mystic, Connecticut, under Captain Mason, were cheered on their way by a
minister:

Your cause is the cause of heaven, the enemy have blasphemed
your God and slain his servants. [8]

As Indian children and defenseless women and youths
roasted to death in the flames wantonly spread through the
fort by Mason's men, prayers were wafted toward the sky
from the lips of a so-called man of God, who, after victory,
blessed the bestowal of young, attractive captives into slavery
among the settlers' families. Mason's fellow-leader Underhill,
in answer to later criticisms of the ferocious butchery (which

sickened even the Englishmen's allies, the Narragansett Indians) explained it in this way:

> It may be demanded, Why should you be so furious? Should not Christians have more mercy and compassion? But I would refer you to David's war. . . . Sometimes the Scripture declareth women and children must perish with their parents. . . . We had sufficient light from the word of God for our proceedings.

So thought Richard, first of the New England Mathers, who from his pulpit publicly raised a pæan of praise because "on this day we have sent six hundred heathen souls to hell."

The same spirit that prompted President Oakes of Harvard University in 1675 to brand liberty of conscience as "the firstborn of all abominations" [9] served in matters military to howl down those who would not fight. Long before the Revolution, during the French and Indian Wars, President Samuel Davies of the College of New Jersey (later Princeton University) took keen delight in serving the Lord with pro-war sermons. In one he got out of his system a quotation often employed by others in succeeding years:

> . . . methinks the cowardly soul must tremble lest the imprecation of the prophet fall upon him, *Cursed be the man that keepeth back his sword from blood.* [10]

Spirit of Seventy-six

And then the Revolution. The military services of the preachers are glowingly set forth by J. T. Headley in his *Chaplains and Clergy of the Revolution*—a book brought out in 1861 as a stimulus to the ministry of that tense time. "Oh, how deep down," says Headley, "in the consciences of men had the principles of that struggle sunk, when they made those Puritans forget the solemn duties of the sanctuary for the higher duties of the battlefield."

Now there are principles and principles; and no matter how high the principles adduced at every crisis by the clergy who went berserk, the simple fact is that, collectively, they have backed any and every war that came along, with only a handful of overridden dissenters. Somehow that bleaches out the sanctity of pro-war principles.

But nothing ever fazed the war-mad pulpiteers. Dr. Robert Davidson of Maryland addressed at different places the troops of the Continental Army, assuring them that the war was of God. Dr. Samuel West of Dartmouth turned his homiletic artillery on the loyalists and non-warring sects alike, and thundered: "God has manifested his anger against those who have refused to assist their country against its cruel oppressors"; and flung upon all and sundry non-military minds the curse of Meroz:

Curse ye Meroz (said the angel of the Lord), curse ye bitterly the inhabitants thereof, because they came not up to the help of the Lord against the mighty.

Dr. Langdon of Harvard, three weeks before the Battle of Bunker Hill, declared to the Colonial Congress at Cambridge after recounting the joyous destruction of British lives at Chelsea:

If God be for us, who can be against us? . . . He can command the stars in their courses to fight his battles, and all the elements to wage war with his enemies. He can destroy them with innumerable plagues, and send faintness into their hearts, so that the men of might shall not find their hands.

Illusion

Hopes; and hopes betrayed. Of such a mixture were the coming years composed.

In Providence, Rhode Island, on the twenty-sixth of February, 1816, the Reverend Thomas Williams counseled, on a literalistic basis, patience and good cheer, for God would end war when he wanted to—and perhaps might want to soon.[11]

In a circular letter of the Massachusetts Peace Society in 1816—its bow to the universe—"the time we hope, is near," so it was stated, "when not only ministers, but all classes of Christians, will be 'of one heart and soul' in ascribing praise to the

'God of Peace' that they lived to see that day in which Peace Societies were formed in our land."

Judge Thomas Dawes, at the second anniversary of the Massachusetts Peace Society, bespoke himself with frankness:

What a solecism, that two adverse armies of Christians should be drawn out in battle array, each by its chaplains invoking the Lord of Hosts, and calling for the destruction of the other . . . whilst hungry vultures on the neighboring rocks are watching with impatience to enjoy the carnage.[11]

But while the peace societies spread, their influence on the masses and on governments was little more than nil; and how about the Christian community Worcester visualized as flocking to the standard? Said *The Friend of Peace* for January, 1821, in somewhat sobered tone,

Considerable additions have recently been made to the Massachusetts Peace Society and to the branch societies in Jaffray and Hollis, N. H.; it is however much to be regretted that Christians in general are so little disposed to promote an object of such infinite importance to themselves, to their posterity, and to the world.

Northward in Portland, Maine, on Christmas, 1827, another preacher, the Reverend Charles Jenkins, said a thing or two:

As yet a large portion of the class of nominal Christians who perceive, that the Bible reveals a system of religion adequate to bring the human family universally to cease from individual and national hostilities, have appeared to wait in indolent expectancy, until the Most High shall be pleased to make the gospel more fully reveal its power, in every where and entirely meeting the moral exigencies of the world.[12]

William Ladd, a little later, gave the picture as he saw it in these words:

Religion is still made subservient to war in *every* Christian nation. Christian ministers discover no inconsistency with their sacred duties, in praying for the success of the bloody struggle and for the destruction of their enemies.[14]

Leonard Bacon, the well-known New Haven pastor, spoke for the cause with boldness. Said he, at Hartford, 1832:

The impropriety of a Christian minister's bearing arms; the necessary exemption of the professed minister of Christ from all the bloody laws and rituals of military honor, has always been more or less distinctly recognized by the common sentiment of Christendom, from the days of the apostles to this hour. Why? Simply because it was always felt, even in the darkest age of chivalry, that the spirit of the gospel is irreconcilably at variance with the spirit of wartime enterprise.[15]

But the cause of peace, said Thomas S. Grimké, of South Carolina—sturdy anti-war campaigner if there ever was one —before the legislature of Connecticut and the citizens of New Haven, also in 1832,

can never triumph until the Christian clergy, individually and as a body, shall condemn, universally and unconditionally, war and the warrior in every form as they have condemned private violence and the duellist.[16]

Apparently, however, despite some striking gains that will be noted, the churches as a rule weren't doing it. The fourth annual report of the Hartford County Peace Society, dated 1832, declared:

We appeal to the affecting fact of many of the disciples of the Prince of Peace being yet found among the advocates of war, and some even on the battlefield, as proof that the subject demands particular and distinct attention.

Said Ladd, toward the end of 1834, writing as "Pacificator":

The "appeal to heaven" by duel has long since been condemned by all true Christians, but the "appeal to heaven" by war, a much greater barbarism, still remains sanctioned by the church, and is preceded by fasting and prayer. Ah, when will Christians be enlightened on this subject also?[17]

There are many now who would like to know the answer. Some in that time were openly coming out for peace, and others were under too much pressure yet to do so. Through *The Calumet* in 1835—organ of the American Peace Society at that time—it was announced that two hundred and ninety-one ministers, whose names were printed, had promised to preach once a year on peace. But said the editor:

> There are yet other names with some of our agents which have not yet been reported to us, and a great number of ministers preach in favor of the cause of Peace, who have not thought proper to give in their names.

War scares had flamed up toward France, toward England; and the government was busy putting the fear of God into the hearts of the various Indian tribes. In December, 1840, *The Advocate of Peace,* the present American Peace Society periodical, asked—and in the same breath answered— a rather pointed question:

> Is the church as a body now reclaimed from her war-degeneracy of ages? Alas! essentially the same sentiments pervade the great mass of both nominal and real Christians throughout the world. Here and there you may find a little Goshen in this vast moral Egypt; but I gather from evangelical writers even in our own country the most ample proof that the Church of Christ is even now gangrened with the war-spirit, and lending her sanction to principles and practices which would render this custom perpetual.

In 1845 the sober Judge William Jay expressed the opinion to the American Peace Society in its annual meeting that "the folly and sinfulness of war and the inconsistency of military ambition with the spirit of Christianity, are themes rarely discussed in our pulpits." About the same time Roswell Rice, Jr., of White Creek, New York, who admitted that he was a professional orator and yet who, as far as I can discover, was never incarcerated for it, opined with hammer-like emphasis that he caught sight of things he would rather not hear told in Gath and Askalon, to say nothing of his native village:

> In this luminous day, when the gospel of light beams with such lustre, I behold certain objects strange in appearance. They are those Ministers of the sacred desk, who pretend to preach the gospel of the Son of God, yet are Mahometans at heart—believe in shedding blood—teach their people the same precept; and instead of preaching the doctrine of the Saviour, they are recom-

mending the greatest sin for virtue, that was ever perpetrated by man.[18]

On to Mexico

The time had arrived for the proponents of slavery and expansion to ride across the Rio Grande, abstract a highly desirable slice of territory, and thus contribute to the liberation of the Mexican people and their general improvement. In Boston the parents of the boys sent southward as missionaries of the bullet were given faith in the eternal justice of heaven by their pastor, who thanked God that

not only have no serious disasters attended the American Arms in Mexico, but that the national feeling of the people had been gratified by victory.[19]

The war passed by. Over in England, the sojourner who was perhaps this country's greatest man of peace, Elihu Burritt, and about whom more is coming in these pages, wrote in his little paper, as if whistling to keep his backbone strictly vertical:

If every one of the hundreds of thousands of Christian congregations, scattered over the face of the globe, would have a finger, like John the Baptist's, pointing the rebuke of the gospel, with unsparing honesty and unwavering precision, against all the systems of violence and oppression which fill the world with misery, lamentation and woe, the Peace Society, and all the other Societies that have recently celebrated their birthdays in this metropolis, might disband tomorrow; and all the populations of the earth might sing, with a hope that has its hand upon the reality of its aspiration,
"There's a good time coming,
Wait a little longer." [20]

But there wasn't. What was coming had been predicted by Noah Worcester in his later years with uncanny accuracy. It was foreseen—though the intervention of the War with Mexico detracted from the absolute correctness of the prophecy—by William Ladd, who wrote in *The Calumet* for May-June, 1833:

There is no reason to doubt, that the next war in which this country shall be engaged, will be a civil war—a war of brother against brother, of the son against his father,—and the very materials of war which we have been heaping together will be expended in the work of mutual destruction, and the military spirit which we have so carefully nurtured will be found, at last, to have been employed in whetting our swords for the throats of our brethren.

North and South

It came, and all was chaos. The effect of that war on the peace movement will be brought out in a later chapter. The clergy, both in the North and South, ran true to form.

There was the usual little handful who refused to bless the conflict. The Reverend Benjamin Franklin, an early Middle Western preacher of some fame among the Disciples' denomination, and who had opposed the Mexican War on Christian grounds, held out against the new war also, suffering a heavy loss in the circulation of his paper, *The Christian Review,* being driven to the expedient of discussing war in general with no specific reference to current happenings, and ultimately of stopping even that. There were one or two other ministers, such as the Reverend J. W. McGarvey, who did not hesitate to say boldly in print that whatever happened, their love for people on the opposite side of the fighting lines would not abate.

But these, as the record overwhelmingly shows, were far from typical. For example the Reverend R. L. Stanton, D.D., Professor in the Theological Seminary of the Presbyterian Church at Danville, New York, assured the people—oh, familiar phrases!—that "God is in the war"; and, so far as "our" soldiers are concerned, "His strong arm will give them the victory." Toward England, not without some reason, leaving Christly counsels out of the reckoning, he hurled fiery warnings of a vengeance yet to come. "There are duties to be discharged," he said to the approval of no small section in the churches,

which can be met only by an exhibition of the national power of the United States towards those who have forever blackened their honor in endeavoring to work our ruin. . . . But this is "venge-

ance," cry the timid and the meek. It is *justice,* we reply; and a
justice which will meet the approval of heaven.[21]

A delegation of clergymen actually waited upon President
Lincoln and demanded that he wage the war more vigorously.

And this is the conflict whose outbreak followed in less
than three months a letter in *The Advocate of Peace* by a too-
hopeful optimist who had thus sized up the peace-war status:

> Peace principles make slower progress than we desire, and yet
> they *do* make progress. Wars grow briefer, and less ferocious,
> and God seems to be overruling the conflicts of nations so as to
> further the great end in man, viz., to fill the earth with peace and
> joy.[22]

The years between then and the War with Spain were once
more filled with mingled hope and disillusion. The American
Peace Society, which had raged at the pacifists during the
Civil War, gave ground somewhat in public influence to the
Universal Peace Union, a much more radical body. But in
the churches boys' brigades were springing up and on the
part of the military and naval professionals there was a
grim determination to wring more preparedness out of public
apathy.

And yet, so many and so genuine had been the accomplishments of the anti-war campaigners in this period, it
seemed, that who could find fault when, in 1895, the feminist
and humanitarian, Belva A. Lockwood, before the Triennial
Women's Council at Washington, in her turn saw through
rosy spectacles? After pointing out the heavy odds faced by
the peace societies, she exclaimed:

> But we hold on with unwavering hope in the belief that the day
> is not distant when the Christian world will be relieved from the
> curse of war, for even now the Christian ministry are combining
> with us against this unholy warfare, this slaughter of the inno-
> cent and the death of the many for the emolument of the few.[23]

Spain—and the Filipinos

Three short years, and the country was plunged into an
unnecessary, execrable, yet popular war, to be followed by

the campaign against the recalcitrant Filipinos, and the emergence of this country as a full-fledged member of the imperialist powers of the world. Once more the ministry did
its "duty." Said Ernest Howard Crosby shortly after:

If you address a miscellaneous audience at the Cooper Institute
in New York—an audience of some fifteen hundred, composed
neither of blackguards nor gentlemen—and tell them as I have
that war is a relic of barbarism which has no business to show
itself at the beginning of the twentieth century, they will cheer
you to the echo, and scarcely a man will be found to make a protest. I have also spoken to audiences of well educated Christians
and I have found them cold. Only once were my hearers unanimous against me without exception, and that was when I was
invited to address a meeting of Protestant ministers.[24]

But the optimists, bless them, will not down. In 1901 the
Honorable Andrew J. Palm of the Pennsylvania State Legislature was telling the audience at the thirty-eighth anniversary of the Universal Peace Union that "ministers will soon
be scarce who apologize for war." [25] And at Richmond, In-
diana, eight years later, the Honorable John Watson Foster,
Secretary of State under President Benjamin Harrison, expressed the conviction that "the spirit of Christianity is
becoming more and more inspired by the teachings of its
founder, the Prince of Peace, and in the future the pulpit
and the pew will be found largely arrayed against the warlike
propensities of the masses." [26]

This newer Christian spirit, unfortunately, lacked time to
get up steam. It always does. Just as progress in loving
enemies was under way, an enemy appeared. And that was
quite enough for most of the churches. Loud in their praiseworthy protests against the war in Europe, their revulsion
of feeling once the government called them, was all the
greater for the prosecution of the struggle.

Over Here

In his recent book, *A Brass Hat in No-Man's Land* (Cape
and Smith) Brigadier General F. P. Crozier of England says

with brutal bluntness that "the Christian churches are the finest blood-lust creators which we have, and of them we made free use."

In Connecticut, Governor Holcomb used the churches to take a census of the state's war materials in terms of men, because, as he put it, "I recognize that the churches in Connecticut count among their members and attendants the people whose influence as a whole, can, perhaps, do more than that of any other body of citizens."

"In flag draped pulpits," as the papers had it, "the pastors of New York, men of peace, sounded the call to arms."

"To hell with Germany," shouted the Reverend Dr. Bustard in Cleveland, to the cheers of his flock; while in New York Dr. Charles A. Eaton fervently declared, "I want to stand before God and tell Him I have walloped the Germans in the face. If you find a man lurking around that looks like a spy take him out and put a bomb under him and blow him straight to the Kaiser—blow him straight to hell."

The Reverend James A. Francis (Baptist) of Los Angeles was moved to say, "I look upon the enlistment of an American soldier or sailor as I do on the departure of a missionary for Burma." Bishop Richard J. Cooke (Methodist) of Helena, Montana, waxed regretful because von Bernstorff was not hanged, and called for conflict until there was an "unconditional surrender." The Reverend Dr. John Roach Straton (Baptist) felt certain that "the very angels of God have been fighting with our soldiers." Rabbi Joseph Silverman was able to see mankind brought nearer to brotherhood by the War than by centuries of religious teaching. The Reverend William Mole Case (Presbyterian) of Eugene, Oregon, discovered that "Christ is at the heart of this war. It is the holiest war the world has ever known." In Waukegan, Illinois the Reverend Howard Ganster (Episcopalian) constructively suggested "the organization of a society for the committing of murder of persons who do not stand up or who leave the building when 'The Star Spangled Banner' is played." The Reverend Billy Sunday (evangelist) separated the just from the unjust: "You are either a patriot or a black-guard traitor. . . . Stop your damn knocking. I tell you that I am getting sick of it." The Reverend Dr. Albert C. Dief-fenbach (Unitarian) explained that "we are in this war be-cause we believe it is a judgment of God that only by force of arms can we save the world. As Christians, of course, we say Christ approves. But would he fight and kill? . . . There is not an opportunity to deal death to the enemy that he would shrink from or delay in seizing!" The Reverend Dr. Newell Dwight Hillis, anxious to be fair-minded about it, stated his willingness to forgive the Germans "just as soon as they are all shot." [27] The writer of this book, though he did not support the War, wrote bitter (and amateurish) verses declaring that never again could the world's children use German toys because they would be covered by bloody finger-prints. It was a time of hysteria, and no one can pretend to have utterly escaped.

Missionary societies accepted special donations from war propagandists and circulated among the clergy thousands of free copies of such books as *The Man Foch,* by Clara E. Laughlin and *The Cross at the Front,* by Thomas Tiplady.

Here and there lone voices were raised in protest. In a Methodist conference one minister even ventured to stand and assert, "If I have to choose between my country and God, I have made up my mind to choose God. I am an American, but a Christian first." But stentorian voices crying "Shame!" and "Traitor!" soon howled him down. Everywhere the imprudent Christians received practically the selfsame treat-ment.

The War-Time Message of the Federal Council of Churches, adopted in special session assembled at Washing-ton, May 8-9, 1917, included among its genuinely idealistic aims, and quickened no doubt by a wholly laudable love of the boys embarking for the camps, inevitable consideration of morale, and avowed its purpose "to hearten those who go to the front."

The American Branch of the World Alliance for Inter-

national Friendship Through the Churches prefaced a series
of hopes for after-war days with the resounding call:

The Church of Christ in America should prove itself the loyal
and efficient servant of the nation at this time of testing.

The Church Peace Union, the League to Enforce Peace—
that supreme anomaly of all time—with the coöperation of
the World Alliance and the Federal Council's Commission on
International Justice and Good Will—established the National Committee on the Churches and the Moral Aims of
the War, the first aim being—you are allowed one guess—
"to win the war against autocracy." [28]

In the figures of the American Bible Society, 6,678,301
Testaments were distributed among the belligerent forces of
all nations; but in that host of active combatants apparently
few noticed Jesus' teachings. In fact it seemed, as General
Foch well stated, "The Bible is certainly the best preparation
that you can give an American soldier about to go into battle
to sustain his magnificent ideal and his faith." [29]

And ditto in the battlements back home. As the Inter-
church World Movement put it, in a post-war advertisement,
"Every officer of the Government with a war message appealed to the churches first of all."

And the churches certainly responded. In Oberlin College,
where world peace had been preached heartily for many years,
the congregation of the oldest church arose and sang:

> When Tyrant feet are tramping
> Upon the commonweal,
> Thou dost not bid us bend and writhe
> Beneath the iron heel;
> In Thy name we assert our Right,
> By sword or tongue or pen;
> And e'en the headsman's axe may flash
> Thy message unto men. [30]

How fortunate for militarism has been the fact—as witness the songs of the Christian churches through the ages—

that "sword" rhymes with "Lord," whereas "Peace" lacks a deistic or celestial consonant!

What was labeled once by Ernest Howard Crosby as *Militaritis clericalis* had the country in its sway. Little children in the Sunday schools poured out their dimes to build a battleship; and a popular song in the erstwhile quiet basements of spired edifices was the stirring martial ditty, sung with lively rhythm by gay young voices:

> Soldier boy, soldier boy, where are you going,
> Waving so proudly the Red, White, and Blue?
> I go to my country where duty is calling;
> If you'll be a soldier, you may come too.

"What you do, do quickly," admonished a Liberty Loan poster in the first days of the War. And the churches did it; did it all too quickly, it happened, to realize that this was exactly the advice vouchsafed by Jesus, in John 13:26-27, to Judas.

The black and sickening record of those years will not bear close retelling. If it could be obliterated, what a blessing that would be!

But now it can't be wiped out, for one all-impelling reason: the far too meager symptoms of repentance. Few qualms indeed are outwardly displayed by the millions in the churches' memberships. Conjure up a daydream—one of those daydreams it is said that pacifists are fond of—and picture a mad stampede of people to change their ways toward war to coincide more closely with the Man of Love.

And what you really have will be the opposite.

I would not be a prophet of despair. Mine is no voice of chronic pessimism. But a realistic evaluation of the gains— with which I shall deal in more detail in a later chapter—must check them not in terms of war-renouncing individuals, fine as so many of these are, nor yet in terms of pro-peace declarations from on top by churchly bodies. We have to ask ourselves, Are the great bulk of the people in the churches moved by so passionate a mood, so basic a conviction, that they will hold out long if once again the trumpet blows in Washington? Is there sufficient warrant for the familiar-sounding statement, made lately by a sturdy Christian pacifist, that "there is now a widespread awakening"? Or are we merely at the same old stage within the cycle?

I do not say. I do not know. If another pen may trace, a hundred years ahead as mine has now, the course of Christian policy on war, what words will flow out on the mute and waiting paper?

CHAPTER IV
REPENTANCE, LTD.

AFTERMATH

Have you forgotten yet?
For the world's events have rumbled on since those gagged days,
Like traffic checked awhile at the crossing of city ways:
And the haunted gap in your mind has filled with thoughts that
flow
Like clouds in the lit heavens of life; and you're a man reprieved
to go,
Taking your peaceful share of Time, with joy to spare.
But the past is just the same—and War's a bloody game . . .
Have you forgotten yet?
Look down, and swear by the slain of the War that you'll never
forget.

Do you remember the dark months you held the sector at
Mametz—
The nights you watched and wired and dug and piled sandbags
on parapets?
Do you remember the rats; and the stench
Of corpses rotting in front of the front-line trench—
And dawn coming, dirty-white, and chill with a hopeless rain?
Do you ever stop and ask, "Is it all going to happen again?"

Do you remember that hour of din before the attack—
And the anger, the blind compassion that seized and shook you
then
As you peered at the doomed and haggard faces of your men?
With dying eyes and lolling heads—those ashen grey
Masks of the lads who were once keen and kind and gay?

Have you forgotten yet? . . .
Look up, and swear by the green of the spring that you'll never
forget.

(Taken from Siegfried Sassoon's *Picture Show*,
by permission of the publishers, E. P. Dutton and Co.)

CHAPTER IV

REPENTANCE, LTD.

Sir Philip Gibbs has voiced a perennial inquiry:

There is one world-wide organization of people, already pledged in the most solemn way to the principles of peace, charity, and human brotherhood, without distinction of class or race. They are under the most sacred obligations to forgive their enemies; they are under a law which forbids them to kill their fellow-men. They are the people of the Christian churches. Is it asking too much that these people should get busy and fulfill their vows and prove the sincerity of their faith?

But since the War they have been getting busy. Some of them, though comparatively small in point of numbers, have turned in frank repentance from the war machine and method, throwing their lives with the utmost abandon into the ranks of radical peace societies. But as far as the overwhelming majority are concerned, they are desperately engaged in following for the most part the identical ways of work for peace that have engrossed the energy of conservative peace workers for a century—the net result of which, in actually abolishing war, need not be told to anybody.

Yet there have been fine services. One of these is the share taken by the religious forces of the country in arousing public opinion for the Washington Conference on the Limitation of Armament; some practical good resulted, even though most of the "limitation" was on near-obsolete naval weapons. Conspicuous and deserving of great praise, is the effective attack on Mobilization Day, later more euphemistically labeled as Defense Day; an attack which buried it, perhaps forever. To the Federal Council of Churches, as well as to the peace societies, should go the credit for this fine maneuver of defense.

Through this same body and the organizations affiliated in the National Council for the Prevention of War, a dangerously lethargic opinion was aroused in 1927 against a threatened war on Mexico, and further serious meddling, already dangerous enough, in China; though in respect to Nicaragua, we did not fare so well. And in regard to military training, the churches have been on the whole responsive. The Methodist General Conference of 1928 not only made an appropriation for peace education; but by a vote of over eight to one registered itself as strongly opposed to compulsory military training in colleges and all military training in high schools. Singularly effective, also, was the prompt protest in the early part of 1928 against the Administration's naval expansion measure, flattening out a program of seventy-four ships to sixteen.

From 1921 to 1924 the chastened post-War mood burned strongly. The Reverend Samuel McCrea Cavert, General Secretary of the Federal Council of Churches, in a report to the Administration Committee of that body, had unequivocally stated:

There is only one way out. The churches of every nation must teach their people that war is a crime, the utter denial of everything for which the churches stand. They must declare that murder is murder, even when ordered by the state, and that the moral law is as binding on nations as on individuals, that in the relations of nations as of individuals reason and justice, determined by an impartial tribunal, must supplant the resort to naked force, that to the development of agencies of international cooperation must be given the energy that nations have hitherto given to preparation for war.

And the World Alliance asserted in annual convention, 1923:

The churches of the world should solemnly declare that war as a method of settling disputes is anti-Christian, and therefore every effort to outlaw war and provide judicial substitution will receive their hearty support.

In the National Study Conference on the Church and World Peace, composed of representatives from twenty-eight com-

munions, came a message in December, 1925, which reached
the high-water mark of all coöperative Christian peace expression since the War. "We are determined to outlaw the whole
war system," said the conferees. Soon a *Syllabus of Topics,
Problems, and Suggestions for Study Groups* was prepared by
the conference's continuation committee, and for the first time
in recent years, so far as I can find, Christians in the churches
were given an opportunity to consider fairly two basic alternative attitudes to war: the first alternative, Participation; the
second, Non-Participation. Real work had been put in on this
study; and the suggestive bibliography, along with a mixture
of pacifist and anti-pacifist literature, even included the 1905
reprint of our old friend, David Low Dodge.

But times and seasons change, not always for the better.
By the following Armistice Day, something had happened.
The Federal Council's message for 1926 threw overboard
all such categories as participation or non-participation in warfare. Instead the churches were counseled at the very beginning against "the ineffectual way"—including "merely negative
attitudes and policies in opposition to war preparations and to
war." The core of the "effectual" way, when reached
through a lot of resounding but decidedly ethereal phrases, was
none other than that boon companion of the legalistic meta-
physicians in the old-line peace societies—the outlawry of "aggressive" war. Shot through with terminology of political caution, asking merely for unilateral and partial disarmament, the
difference between this message and the one described before
constituted the greatest let-down in the shortest time that has
been witnessed since the Armistice.

With this question of "aggressive" war, I propose to deal in
a later place. I pause here only long enough to express the
sober conviction that, as compared with the principles of Jesus,
the elimination of "aggressive" war is on a par with the abolition of "aggressive" gangrene. This plausible will-o-the-wisp
still lures the peace societies; but time will show if vision does
not, that the laborer for peace who goes romping after this
illusion is but one

Who stems a stream with sand,
And fetters flame with flaxen band.

The 1927 statement of the Federal Council, however, was chiefly an appeal for support of the Briand-Kellogg treaties for the renunciation of war "as an instrument of national policy." It was accompanied by a memorial presenting five points of belief: the first, "that war should never again be resorted to by civilized nations as the means for settling disputes or enforcing claims," and the second (the inevitable nullification?) "that war, save for self-defense against actual attack, should be outlawed and declared by the nations to be an international crime."

It is a satisfaction to state that in a message to the churches dated January, 1928, the Council once more definitely, if thereby confusingly, declared that "war, in its spirit and modern practice, is the negation of everything to which the gospel of Jesus bears witness," and further contended that "the Church can be satisfied with nothing less than the complete abolition of (no qualifying adjective!) war." Yet even here, all mention of a possible policy of non-participation in an actual war is conspicuously absent.

Surpassing the first Study Conference on the Churches and World Peace, the second, meeting at Columbus, Ohio, March 6-8, 1929 with one hundred and twenty-four delegates from thirty-five bodies boldly declared:

We therefore hold that the churches should condemn resort to the war-system as sin and should henceforth refuse, as institutions, to sanction it or to be used as agencies in its support.

And more! For it stated:

We hold that the churches should support and sustain with moral approval individuals who, in the exercise of their right of conscience, refuse to take part in war or in military training.

A brave, adventurous stand was reiterated against war and military training and armed intervention in Latin America by the 1930 Study Conference. The World Peace Commission of the Methodist Episcopal Church has shown a genuine vision in its work. The Quakers have shown an awakened interest in peace education, and in all denominations a ferment is stirring.

Increasingly the churches are emphasizing the Pact of Paris as a basis for the final outlawry of all war. This emphasis is natural and right. Their danger is that they may withhold support from the further aspects of the war-outlawry and war-abolition program, deluded by a short view and an ungrounded optimism into mistaking partial for complete accomplishment.

Moved and Seconded
At thirty man suspects himself a fool;
Knows it at forty and reforms his plan;
At fifty chides his infamous delay,
Pushes his prudent purpose to resolve,
In all the magnanimity of thought
Resolves and re-resolves; then dies the same.[1]

So, says the cynic in one, with the churches; though cynicism cannot hold out long. Judged, however, by the paving of the road alone, it is hard to tell the approach to the Infernal Regions from that to the City of God. In no sense is that road a one-way street. Turn to this side or the other, the paving is the same: high purposes.

Thus George Odell, in *The Christian Science Monitor,* in 1924:

A survey of the declarations on peace that are being issued by religious bodies shows conclusively that there is a growing conviction among churchmen that war is immoral.

They have come thick and fast, assuredly. They are a mixture, as should be expected. But a rather high percentage of them ring with more than pious platitudes, and one or two are striking for the lengths to which they go.

Most of the resolutions passed soon after the War were only sound and sweetness, signifying nothing. But in 1923 occurred the sensational proceedings of the Student Volunteer Convention at Indianapolis, with its hundreds of young and radical pacifists brought to light, and the reverberations that followed on many a campus. The clutch of the war neurosis was loosening. A little band of dynamic and highly competent religious pacifists, with unanswerable logic, winged down upon pulpits and upon the platforms of conventions. At church conferences everywhere, peace preëmpted the center of discussions. The cause of peace—and pacifism—was distinctly on the move. Freed from wartime delusions, learning that the skies did not fall even though congregations sometimes got a little nervous when bold words were said in the name of the bold young Nazarene, one religious group after another voiced its war abhorrence in resounding tones.

Make no mistake. There may be serious doubt whether the rank and file behind their representatives would ever go as far in practice or even in theory. And such drastic resolutions as have been adopted had to make their way against strong opposition. No one can rightly say that such and such a church thinks so and so on war.

The standing committee of the General Conference of the Methodist Episcopal Church had agreed on a most forthright resolution. It read:

While recognizing the freedom of the individual member to follow his own conscience, but remembering that the church is the visible expression of Christ in the world, we as an organization, separate ourselves from war and take no part in its promotion.

But, after the memorable fashion of large bodies, the conference as a whole on May 14, 1924, killed off the resolution.

Earlier the Unitarian Ministerial Association, by a postal ballot, had adopted a resolution possibly more challenging. The vote stood ninety-one for and eighty-seven against, with thirty-six not voting upon this declaration:

Whereas we see that war is the most colossal and ruinous social sin that afflicts mankind today; that it is not only futile but suicidal, and that recognition of this fact is necessary to the continuance of civilization; that it is inherently the defiance of common sense and the denial of common humanity,—we therefore, as ministers of religion and public teachers of morality declare now in time of peace our deliberate determination never to sanction or to participate in a war; we affirm our conviction that churches as such ought to refuse cooperation with governments in waging war; and we memorialize the American Unitarian Association at its coming session in May to repudiate the entire war system— economic exploitation, imperialism, and militarism—to the end that our fellowship may take an honorable, if not a leading, part among religious bodies in the abolition of war.

What happened to this invitation I scarcely need to say. But the energy behind it did not expire with the recommendation; and the same courageous and spirited minority, in varying proportions, grows in practically all denominations.

Early in 1928 the Central Pennsylvania Conference of the Methodist Episcopal Church passed a drastic peace resolution and referred it to the General Conference of that denomination, where it was not received as enthusiastically. It asked its "entire church"

to withdraw completely its sanction of and its participation in the war system, and that it shall determine to throw its entire spiritual and moral energy behind the creation of a system of peace. . . .

Introduced into the North East Ohio Conference of the same denomination by the Reverend Charles B. Ketcham, and adopted on the twenty-eighth of September, 1925, by a large majority, the following is in all probability the most drastic resolution of any thus far passed in this country:

Whereas, by the united judgment of Christian leaders everywhere, war today is recognized as our most colossal and far-reaching social sin; and

Whereas, our own Methodist Episcopal Church has declared through its General Conference that "war is the supreme enemy of mankind";

Therefore, be it resolved by the North East Ohio Conference of the Methodist Episcopal Church that the day has come when our Methodist Episcopal Church as a part of the Church Universal, the Body of Christ in the World, should in its corporate capacity refuse to sanction or support any future war.

And, be it further resolved that recognizing the great Protestant principle of individual judgment in matters of personal conduct, we do not presume to pass judgment upon the right of any individual in the event of war, to follow his own enlightened conscience, whether it takes him into the forces of armed defense or into the ranks of conscientious objectors.

Another notable pronouncement on war is that of the National Council of Congregational Churches, which adopted as part of its *Statement of Social Ideals* in 1925, a section on International Relations, one paragraph of which would make a tremendous difference, if at all adhered to, in another war:

The church of Christ as an institution should not be used as an instrument or an agency in the support of war.

The Quadrennial Meeting of the Federal Council of Churches at Rochester, New York, in 1928, drew up a suggested article to be added by the constituent bodies to the statement of the Social Ideals of the Churches. It said, "That the Churches stand for: The renunciation of war and the refusal of the Church of Christ as an institution to be used as an instrument or an agency in the support of war." The General Assembly of the United Presbyterian Church has definitely called this article to the attention of its congregations, and as a matter of record it has been ratified by the Presbyterian Church in the United States (South). At its 1929 convention the last-named body declared that

The historic position of our Church is that the function of the Church is purely spiritual. We believe that this principle should apply in time of war as well as in time of peace, and that therefore the Church should never again bless a war or be used as an instrument in the promotion of war.

While they mark a great step forward—for even resolutions have an educative value—such statements are not typical. There have been literally dozens of vague, evasive declarations and a great many in between, which, nevertheless, affirm the incompatibility of war with the religion of Jesus.

Meantime, there is not only a pacifist but a militarist wing in the churches, which loses no opportunity to berate the peace crusaders. The churches as a rule still bless the colors on gala military occasions; many non-student sections of the Y.M.C.A. do little to weaken the affection (now the war is over!) of the military; army and navy chaplains are still officially recognized by church bodies as legitimate clerical representatives; and the one thing spoken as an "open sesame" and a reassurance by the men of Christ whenever they plead for peace is "though I am no pacifist . . .;" or, it may be, "I am a Christian, *but.* . . ."

How strongly, then, dare honest thinkers lean hope on the best of resolutions?

There is light on this point also, in the history of the early peace societies. Concentrating their efforts on the churches, between 1815 and 1840 in particular, they won their way to a certain status and prestige. Churches in greater numbers gave over their platforms to such men as Worcester and Ladd and others who were scarcely more ahead of their time, alas, than they are of ours. A harvest of pacific resolutions soon resulted. Look at a few and see if they do not seem familiar!

One winter's morning late in 1818 Noah Worcester opened a letter with a blurred return address. The man of peace found that it came from the old town of Springfield, New York. Its message, however, was quite clear. From the "Conference of the Methodist Reformed Church," it declared that

War and bloodshed have had their rise and support too much among professors of religion [i.e. adherents]. But we trust and believe that the day is near—if it has not already come—when the children of the same family will no more join in the diabolical practice of murdering one another, because required so to do by unsanctified national rulers. . . . Therefore, we will from henceforth consider ourselves a Peace Society.[2]

"Every church ought itself to be a peace society," said the Reverend Peter Ainslee, a modern pacifist, not long ago.[3]

At a meeting of Vermont Congregational and Presbyterian ministers in 1820 it was voted that Christians had too long been under the power of the war appeal, and ought to give support to peace societies.[4]

And now see how they stiffen up! Thomas S. Grimké's address at New Haven in 1832—which, incidentally, made William Ladd a thorough pacifist—had had a widespread influence; and too, the early members of the peace societies had been given time for deeper thinking.

A conference of Baptist ministers at Boston, 1832, pronounced *"all war* utterly inconsistent with the spirit of the Gospel." [5]

By the Lincoln County Conference in Edgecomb, Maine, in 1833, it was declared that "we consider the practice of war as inconsistent with the spirit of the principles, and the millennial triumphs, of the Gospel."

But in the same year, by the New England Conference of the Methodist Episcopal Church, it was

Resolved, that as a body of Christian ministers, they feel themselves called upon to record their solemn judgment, that the waging of all offensive war is in direct opposition to the benign spirit of the religion of Christ.

Let no conservative peace campaigner fail to note that safety valve, *"offensive* war."

At the same time a smaller body, the York (Maine) Conference, was joining in with those who counted war contradictory to the religion of Jesus; as also was the case with the newly formed peace society in Cincinnati, and another in the Bowdoin Street Church of Boston.

The resolutions of a hundred years or so ago were not much less radical than those of now. They were not useless, certainly. In the task of building up a public opinion that helped prevent a threatened war with France and another with Britain at about this time, they probably had a share.

And yet, one may close his eyes and in imagination see the cavalry of Scott crashing through the Mexican cactus in 1847; the Blue and the Gray battering each other's ranks to pieces on the fields of Gettysburg; the weak ships of Cervera's squadron going down in Santiago Harbor and the natives of Luzon writhing under the "water cure"; the mud-encrusted doughboys slaughtering and being butchered by the Germans at Château Thierry, in the Argonne Forest, and at St. Mihiel— men against whom they had no personal enmity and with whom they shared the experience of being victimized with lies of wartime poison pens; and at most times in between our major conflicts, around the Everglades, along the Mississippi and on the Western Plains, blue-coated men in deadly war with copper-hued Americans, a series of campaigns which William Penn's warm vision had proved to be unnecessary.

At the anniversary meeting of the Windham County (Connecticut) Peace Society in 1832 a new song was sung, which had been composed (doubtless in a hurry!) by one of the members. Two lines of it posed a question:

> Christians! can you idly slumber
> While this work of hell goes on? [6]

There rests the riddle of the future. It was a former chief of staff in the Army, General Tasker H. Bliss, who, after the World War, hammered home this stern admonishment:

The responsibility is entirely upon the professing Christians of the United States. If another war like the last should come, they will be responsible for every drop of bloodshed. [7]

How widely—and how deeply—do the Christian churches see it in that light? It is always possible that we may find out much sooner than we think. In the test of a crisis the future reaction from the stained-glass followers of love's great teacher, is like that outraged lad who lies at Arlington: "*Known But to God.*"

CHAPTER V

TWIN WARS: "AGGRESSIVE" AND "DEFENSIVE"

The right way to resist tyranny is not to kill the tyrant, but to refuse to coöperate in his tyranny.—A. FENNER BROCKWAY, M.P.

CHAPTER V

TWIN WARS: "AGGRESSIVE" AND "DEFENSIVE"

At no time in the history of the peace movement has it been undivided over the question of defensive war. To-day the cleavage is as sharp as ever.

"Personally," says the Reverend S. Parkes Cadman, "I make a differentiation between wars of defense and wars of aggression." [1]

"If you get rid of aggression," declared Lord Robert Cecil during his visit to the United States, "you get rid of war." [2]

The influence of the conservative peace societies has been thrown behind the "outlawry of aggressive war." Though the term "aggressive war" does not appear in the Covenant, the League of Nations has not yet explicitly disavowed the sanctions of armed force implicit in its articles, to be hurled overwhelmingly at a nation guilty of "aggression." The Locarno treaties are built along substantially the selfsame lines. Even the original Levinson-Borah plan for the Outlawry of War, while relying only on the sanction of public opinion against a nation breaking the law by going to war, in effect allowed "defensive" war. The Pact of Paris is practically on the selfsame status. The great bulk of the peace movement accepts the differentiation between wars of "defense" and wars of "aggression."

There is nothing new in this theoretical distinction.

Early in 1814, the Reverend John Lathrop of the New Brick Church of Boston so pleased his congregation by a sermon that they arranged to have it printed. It was a *Discourse on the Law of Retaliation.* It went pretty far—for a war year; but Dr. Lathrop still had one foot in the war system. Said he:

The true subjects of the Prince of Peace will be the last men on earth to blow the trumpet of war. They will never take the sword but in defense of rights highly important, and such as are essential to their safety and happiness.

In thirty-three years "they" were, as all men know, waging a bitter war of conquest to the southward. "They"—for all of these battling invaders from the United States were still (if the clergy's word be taken for it) "true subjects of the Prince of Peace."

In the same year of 1814, however, David Low Dodge was hammering away with stern realism and appealing to the teachings of his religion:

The fact is, however, that no man can, on gospel principles, draw a line of distinction between offensive and defensive war so as to make the former a crime and the latter a duty. . . .[*]

How little did Dodge appreciate the inventiveness of legalistic minds! Let him go on:

But suppose this principle adopted by governments. Could they prosecute war while they left every individual in the free exercise of his conscience to judge whether such war was offensive or defensive and to regulate his conduct accordingly? Would it be possible for governments to carry on war if they depended for support on the uncertain opinion of every individual? No; such a procedure would extinguish the vital strength of the war and lay the sword in the dust. The fact is well known, and monarchs declare war and force their subjects to support it. The majority in republican governments demand and enforce obedience from the minority. , . .

Hence we see that the acknowledged principles of defensive war are the vital springs of most of the wars that agitate and desolate our world. The pretended distinction between offensive and defensive war is but a name. All parties engaged in war proclaim to the world that they are fighting in defense of their rights, and that their enemies are the aggressors; while it may be impossible for man to decide which are most in the wrong.

But the peace movement as a whole could not agree with Dodge. "The truth," declared the Lady in Shaw's *Man of Destiny*, "is the one thing nobody will believe."

In Boston, Noah Worcester's quill scratched across the manuscript of his *Solemn Review* the plausible sentence:

As soon as offensive wars shall cease, defensive wars will, of course, be unknown.

And the peace movement, turning its back on Dodge and his followers, started its hundred years' campaign against *aggressive* war.

"So long as defensive war is admitted," urged the Reverend Samuel Whelpley in 1818, "all wars can easily be proved to be defensive, by a system of martial logic." A good phrase— "martial logic." Through its entire history, the peace movement has used that logic; no better compliment has ever been paid to the power of tradition over human thought.

Also in 1818, Andrew Ritchie Esq. delivered a conservative address to the Massachusetts Peace Society. It was the Society's third anniversary. Said Ritchie, to the approval of many listeners:

When we see the world filled with nations which are restrained from aggression because it will be opposed by force, we ought to consider, whether we promote peace by denying the use of force. Should we not increase the temptation to hostilities, by removing the principal ground of apprehension from the mind of the aggressor?

There's martial logic for you! And yet that address of Ritchie's, spoken one hundred and ten years ago, could be used by some of our most active peace workers to-day without the change of anything but the obsolete punctuation. The elimination of "aggressive" or "offensive" war has always been the preoccupation of the peace movement's "best minds." Channing himself, along with President Kirkland of Harvard and three others, prepared an address on war, on behalf of a convention of Congregational ministers. You can guess what they said in the course of a really passionate denunciation of war; but here it is, exactly:

Unquestionably there is a wide difference between offensive and defensive war. But every war is offensive, at least on one part;

and if offensive war can be prevented, defensive war will of course
be superseded.

Sounds reasonable, does it not? Nearly everybody thought
so. A few years later, one of the tracts of the American Peace
Society presented a series of forceful quotations against war,
selected from the words of ancient and modern seers, comprising "eminent pagans," "warriors," "statesmen," "philosophers,"
"men of letters," and "theologians." In summing up, the compiler asked his readers to

mark how far the extracts above go against war. They do not
directly touch the vexed question concerning wars purely defensive; but they are strong against the whole war system.*

The whole war system? Achilles had his heel; and the peace
movement has had this pet distinction without a difference.

In 1838 a resolution favoring a Congress of Nations was
introduced in the Massachusetts State Legislature. One of its
clauses read as follows:

Resolved, That offensive war is incompatible with the true
spirit of Christianity.

The peace forces have never obtained a real Congress of Nations. But they have to-day a League of Nations based on the
same conception, essentially, as manifested in the early resolution.

And in spite of the fact that the American Peace Society's
plan for a Congress of Nations did not contemplate the use of
punitive force against an aggressor, and relied on public opinion
—as does modern outlawry—William Ladd, as General Agent,
and George C. Beckwith, as Secretary, in their introduction to
the volume *Prize Essays on the Congress of Nations,* issued
in 1840, took almost the identical position developed by modern
outlawrists: the position that in this matter the question of
defense is neither germane nor of very great importance. Said
Ladd and Beckwith:

With the question of the lawfulness of defensive war, or its
consistency with the spirit of the gospel, these Essays have nothing to do. It is entirely irrelevant to the subject.

All this, if truth were told, was something of a diplomatic gesture. For Ladd had gone through a change, prior to this, from a halfway to a radical pacifism. In 1834 he had frankly pointed out that change:

> I am well aware that the American Peace Society does not decide on the lawfulness of defensive wars; but the longer I have studied the subject, the more I am convinced that all war is unlawful for a Christian, though I must confess that I was long unwilling to come to that conclusion.[5]

When President Allen of Bowdoin College wrote for *The Calumet* a series of articles justifying defensive war, and repeating the old, old "martial logic"—"if offensive wars were abolished, there would be no need to agitate the question of defensive war"—Ladd replied, with sympathy but with no budging from the view arrived at through long thought:

> It is the most forcible defence of the right of defensive war I have ever seen. In short, it reasons in the same manner as I myself reasoned, though much more forcibly, for many years after I was an advocate of peace; and it is the same manner in which many of the friends of the peace society now reason.[6]

How strong the radical minority in the peace movement finally became, will be related in another chapter. But it is significant to note here that one year later, 1835, Ladd said in the columns of *The Calumet:*

> The majority of those who conduct the affairs of the American Peace Society are decidedly opposed to all war, offensive and defensive.[7]

It was in 1836 that Professor Upham made his moving appeal to the peace movement to abjure the old distinction. With page on page of the best argument ever written up to that time, he called definitely on the peace societies for a shift of basis to the more radical position:

> So long as we admit that defensive wars are allowable, on Christian principles, so long we grant, for all practical purposes, everything which the advocates of war wish.[8]

To many came the new conviction; but not to all or even a majority of the rank and file. In my own copy of Upham's book is written this comment, brown with age but none the less emphatic as it reels across the margin:

If all the world would adopt the principle, *never* to be aggressive in war, war would never come. This would as effectually secure peace, as to adopt the principle that defensive war is never justifiable. Never *declare* war.

But even the conservative Judge William Jay, President of the American Peace Society, son of the illustrious diplomat, John Jay, in 1842 expressed the opinion that

The last plea that can be urged in behalf of war, is that it is indispensable in self-defence. To this we reply that every war is professedly defensive, while scarcely any is so in fact.°

And in 1843, before the American Peace Society, Andrew Preston Peabody—then thirty-two and as yet unmoderated by a Harvard professorship and the mass pressure of the Civil War—asserted succinctly:

I know that we have been accustomed to speak and hear of defensive wars; but there are no such wars.

In 1847 Joshua P. Blanchard was writing to *The Christian Citizen,* Elihu Burritt's paper, to say:

Vain is the deluding pretence that war is ever made for the defence of right or the enforcement of justice.

Then came the war against Mexico and soon the internecine war of 1861 to 1865. On the verge of the bitter sectional conflict the Reverend Samuel J. May, an abolitionist and (then) pacifist as well, published an address before the American Peace Society as delivered May 28, 1860, in which he said:

You would remind me perhaps, that the moralists of no Christian nation sanction offensive, aggressive wars—that it is only for the sake of self protection that they would have their several nations keep themselves armed; and only *defensive* wars that any of them would justify. Ah! this is one of the chief delusions

which have cheated the so-called Christian world of the truth as it
is in Jesus, on this paramount subject.

May, of course, found bitter opposition. He sent this address, as others, to Edward Everett Hale, who was later (long
after the Civil War) to be called "the grand old man of the
peace movement," and wrote in pencil across the front of it,
significantly, "And is this also 'All Bosh'?"

Scarcely had the country caught its breath after the slaughter
when the Franco-Prussian War broke out across the water;
and those who had led public opinion here on behalf of the
Civil War burst forth in violent denunciation of the European
conflict. Henry Ward Beecher, conspicuous among them,
qualified his condemnation of war by telling his people on Sunday morning, July 30, 1870:

All the sentimentality about not using force, where force is the
only thing that can be used, is surplusage and waste. I do not
believe in using force if you can help it, but I do believe in using
it when you cannot help it.

Clarifying his position a couple of years later, he returned to
chant the well-known theme:

Now, I do not take the ground that all defensive wars are
wrong. I do not think they are. I do not believe that the use of
physical force to maintain the great moral ends of justice, liberty,
and national life can yet be dispensed with. The time is coming
when it can be dispensed with, but that time has not come yet.[16]

Nor will it ever come, so long as war is confused or glossed
over by the non-analogous term "physical force." In that very
same year, the Peace Association of Friends in America was
circulating in this country a reprint of a London tract. It said:

Is it not . . . a strong presumption against the soundness of a
principle such as that on which you take your stand, who are the
advocates of only defensive war, that it cannot in any case be
acted upon without leading by a necessary sequence, as inevitable
as fate, to all the iniquities and atrocities of the entire system?

In 1893 the penitent powder maker, Alfred Nobel, scarcely
realizing how trite his idea was, wrote that if all states in true

solidarity would agree to turn against the first aggressor, war would become impossible. The odor of guncotton, obviously, still clung about his nostrils.

So raged the argument from side to side, in far too frequent controversy for recording here. Suffice it further to say that when the World War cut its red gash in humanity's side, and the great majority of leaders in the peace movement were busily engaged in leading this country into the War, there was the Reverend John Haynes Holmes to raise the query that simply will not down:

Go through all the history of the world—study all the persecutions, outrages, slaughter, martydoms, wars—search out the motives that determined these tragedies of blood and iron. And I venture to prophesy that, in every case, it will be found that the injury was wrought because some man, or institution, or country, felt it necessary to defend something which was assailed and in danger, therefore, of destruction. What indeed is defense after all, but aggression from the other point of view? [11]

Yet even the World War, supreme example of a conflict the one aggressor in which a multitude of experts have not yet been able to determine, did little to deter the peace movement from its pursuit of this plausible will-o'-the-wisp. The clergy, the international legal lights, and the statesmen of Europe, unite with many of our best-known workers for peace to vociferate the old refrain: "Get rid of aggressive war and you get rid of all war." To-day they stand in agreement on this point with Colonel P. S. Bond, advocate of heavy preparedness programs, believer in leaving the work of peace-making entirely up to the Creator, who declared his conviction in a militaristic pamphlet issued in 1925, that

We shall have peace when the aggressor among nations is as certain to encounter overwhelming force as would be an aggressor among the states of the American Union. [12]

A certain element of humor is not lacking in this alliance! I do not know where in the record of the peace movement it can be excelled, with one exception. The Massachusetts Peace

Society, as we have seen, affirmed the necessity of differentiating between offensive and defensive wars, giving the latter, even if reluctantly, its blessing. Yet when its committee of inquiry, in 1820, investigated as painstakingly as possible the causes of all the major wars from that time back to the days of Constantine—two hundred and eighty-six wars in all—and classified "assailants" and "defendants," they could report not one true defensive conflict! It is as easy for statesmen to determine the exact responsibility for an aggression as for moralists to fix the precise dimensions of a sin. More naïve than most, but expressive of the common point of view, was the Honorable James Williams, author of a mid-century book, *The South Vindicated:*

As for a war of aggression, we will never wage it, except in self-defense.

The attempt to suppress "aggressive" wars merits comparison with the proverbial search of "a blind man in a dark room looking for a black cat that isn't there."

International Blind-Man's Buff

The word "war" may mean either a state of hostility or actual combat. In current usage no clear distinction is made; even among writers on international law the two meanings are seldom completely differentiated.

Says John Bassett Moore:

Much confusion may be avoided by bearing in mind that by the term war is not meant the mere employment of force, but the existence of a legal condition of things in which rights are or may be prosecuted by force. Thus, if two nations declare war one against the other, war exists though no force whatever may as yet have been employed. On the other hand, force may be employed by one nation against another, as in the case of reprisals, and yet no state of war may arise. In such a case there may be said to be an act of war, but no state of war.[18]

By taking a clear term such as "act of war," and distinguishing a mere legal war status from such actual violence of combat, it is possible to draw a sharp distinction of great importance to this present discussion.

There may be theoretically a defensive war, but practically there can be no defensive warfare. There may be a status of defense, but there can be no defensive acts of war.

The distinction is valid. And because it is valid, the peace movement is unrealistic when it confines its labors to the abolition of "aggressive war."

I

No uniformly reliable definition of an aggressor nation is possible. Until recently, efforts to supply a definition stigmatized as the aggressor an invading nation. On this basis so distinguished a jurist as Professor Moore has conceded the impracticability of determining the aggressor.[14] Invasions, or declarations of war, do not necessarily warrant the allocation of all the guilt to the invader or the nation taking the initiative. Wars are not isolated phenomena; they originate in policies, usually a culmination of cumulative reprisals, the true origins of which are often impossible to ascertain.

Let any man seek fairly to determine any country which has a reasonable, complete claim to Alsace-Lorraine, or for that matter, almost any piece of irredentist territory. Many of these have changed hands so often, with changes of language and cultures, that no truly just settlement can be made. As a matter of sad fact, there is in justice no criterion for possession. Possession is all ten points of the law. Even forced signatures to war settlements can never be questioned on grounds of injustice, as between individuals in private affairs.

It is *policy* that warrants condemnation often as much as an open state of war. By policy, sometimes without actual conflict, as much injustice, as much cruelty, may be inflicted as in warfare. The blockade of Russia following the Bolshevik revolution was an act fully as cruel and destructive as many a minor war, yet it does not fit the terms of this inadequate definition. Hallam, in his *Constitutional History of England* was aware of just such influences of policy when he pointed out that

The aggressor in war is not the first that uses force, but the first who renders force necessary.

Again, the nations of the world to-day whatever be their faults do not reside behind impassable walls. Frontiers are traversible; given a border difficulty, even at best it is hard to tell whence came the first marauders. And given a border with mobilized forces drawn up on either side, it is often impossible to fix responsibility for any invasion followed by conflict. As a matter of fact, it is not only impossible at the time, but frequently impossible forever. Where is the man or the men who can state with certainty the place along the French frontier where either the French or the Germans crossed in 1914, and which did the first crossing? And even so, of what importance was the crossing in comparison to the infinitely greater significance of the policies which had been breeding war on both sides of that border for more than a generation?

The violation of demilitarized zones, the commission of a so-called overt act, the violation of treaties—these are often put forward as bases for the determination of an aggressor. They are sufficiently reliable tests to fit certain cases, to apply with clarity to some conceivable wars; but they fit too seldom to constitute any safe basis for the selection of a guilty nation against which other nations ought to turn their scorn if not their joint forces. The weakness of these tests becomes apparent when their practical operation is frankly faced.

The demilitarization of land areas may accomplish much to ease the tension between suspicious possessors of contiguous territory. Article Nine of the rejected Geneva Protocol provided that a violation of the rules governing a demilitarized zone should be deemed tantamount to a resort to war. When the existing demilitarized areas are examined, however, it will be seen that usually they consist of territories having international economic importance, yet for which none of the involved nations would desire to risk a war; but which, if a war for some other purpose were undertaken, they would scarcely then hesitate to use for military or naval considerations.[16] The aid given to a peaceful mood by these unfortified areas, such as Luxembourg, the shores of the Dardenelles and Bosphorus, our far Pacific Islands, et cetera, should not be minimized. Yet it is sheer folly to believe that if a war policy is decided on, any nation involved in the non-militarization of such zones would feel obligated to respect them.

And who by objective criteria can define an overt act? Nations sometimes go to war about an act which they label as overt, and sometimes fail to go to war. An overt act, if defined practically on the basis of experience, is simply a hostile act which will not be tolerated without war. Sometimes it is cleverly provoked. Where the line is drawn depends, actually, only on circumstances, public opinion, or other unrevealed governmental desiderata. As a test by which to determine an aggressor the overt act criterion is all but worthless.

Numberless treaties have been broken without the consequence of war. The treaty of 1778 between the United States and France, by which this country was to be an ally in any defensive war, was violated when England and France joined battle: our refusal to give France even non-military aid was based on the ground that although England had started the ball rolling by expelling the French ambassador, France had really provoked the war.

Is it sensible or prudent to stigmatize every breach of a treaty as an act of aggression? Bear in mind what treaties often are:

> So long, however, as fraud and violence are permissible factors in the conclusion of treaties; so long as mere superior power and the threat of its use are legitimate instrumentalities in exacting submission to the harshest terms, it is absurd to speak of "the faith of treaties"; many of them, in fact, deserve no more to be fulfilled than a promise extorted from an innocent pedestrian by a nocturnal highwayman.[16]

It all depends. And because it all depends—depends on the particular case in point, and depends on whether hostilities result—the uniform identification of treaty-breaking with utter international depravity would not be feasible. It would often be unjust, unrealistic, and productive of reprisals and up-heavals out of all proportion to the nature of the offense. Not always, to be sure; but often enough to make this test inadequate in fastening the onus of aggression.

Even here, the relation is close between non-fortification and policy, between overt acts and policy, between treaty-observance and policy.

And policies, in the last analysis, are based on economic interest. Lord Ponsonby has failed to find a single substantial war in the last hundred years that was fought over the violation of a treaty. Nor are territorial considerations so simple as they seem to those who assign all war guilt by the moral arbitrament of acreage. As a matter of fact, nations seldom fight to protect their soil as such from invasion; most of the wars that tear the human race apart are never fought "in defense of hearth and home." As Norman Angell once pointed out, England, for a supreme example, has fought defensive wars during the last nine hundred years in all quarters of the globe but one—England.[17]

Said an editorial in *The World's Work* for April, 1927:

> With our trade spread throughout the world and the world's gold in our pockets, it is more essential than ever that we should have our military establishment prepared not only for the protection of our interests in case of war between two other powers, but also for protection against aggression by other powers or groups of powers.

We do not fight alone to defend our land, our homes, our loved ones, if indeed we ever do. We fight to defend our national interest; and our national interest knows no bounds save those of interplanetary space.

The Aggressor As a Non-Arbitrating Nation

In recent years an attempt has been made to define an aggressor differently. As put by Father John A. Ryan of the National Catholic Welfare Council, an earnest voice for peace, it runs like this:

I think that aggressive war should be defined and also, legitimate self-defense. The only workable definition of the former is war made by a state which refuses to submit its case to arbitration.[18]

That is to say, a state which goes to war without arbitration *after having agreed to do so.*

Early in 1928 sixty persons of prominence in public affairs published a definition of aggression:

The aggressor nation in war is the nation that, having failed to settle its dispute by conference, conciliation, arbitration, appeal to judicial procedure or other peaceful means, initiates an attempt to settle it by war. (If preferred, the words, "in violation of its treaty obligations" may be inserted before the word "initiates.")

These proposals in essence go back to our old friend the League to Enforce Peace from which Woodrow Wilson derived many of the ideas in favor of military sanctions written into the League of Nations' Covenant in Articles X and XVI. The Executive Committee after adopting its program in the spring of 1915 issued an interpretation of Point 3 in that program. It read as follows:

The signatory powers shall jointly employ diplomatic and economic pressure against any one of their number that threatens war against a fellow signatory without first having submitted its dispute for international inquiry, conciliation, arbitration or judicial hearing, and awaited a conclusion, or without having in good faith offered so to submit it. They shall follow this forthwith by the joint use of their military forces against the nation if it actually goes to war, or commits acts of hostility against another of the signatories before any question arising shall be dealt with as provided in the foregoing.[19]

As earlier pointed out, the threat of such joint armed force in the background is the original basis of the League of Nations' program for security, though the League has not defined what constitutes aggression. It is the underlying basis of the Locarno treaties which define aggression essentially as the failure to arbitrate. The Pact of Paris leaves to each signatory the decision as to what action shall be taken against a violator of the Treaty; force is neither mandatory nor barred. In short, the world's existing peace machinery in varying degree depends on using the possibility of armed action against an aggressor.

But the attempt thus to define the aggressor is substantially as futile as the definition based on invasion. It breaks down in theory and will most certainly break down in practice unless nations change in the next few decades more than may reasonably be expected.

Nations are still bound by balance-of-power alliances and commitments, maintained despite the League and Pact. All Europe is chained by a network of treaties and defensive agreements, some known and some unknown, most of them executed by the members of the League in direct violation of its spirit and some in contradiction to the letter. Such, to cite one example only, is the political-military treaty consummated in secret among France, Poland and Roumania against Hungary, Russia, Germany and Bulgaria and revealed by accident in 1926. *The Manchester Guardian* stated, coincidently with the treaty's publication, "Of all the four possible enemies named, three are fellow-members of the League of Nations, one a fellow-member of the Council, and statesmen of Warsaw and Bucharest calmly envisage the likelihood of a sudden attack being made by any or all of them."

In any future war, of Europe certainly, it will be even harder than before to limit the conflict to a war between two countries. And there will not be one aggressor but a group of aggressors, acting with full common knowledge. Try to settle if you can who will be the aggressor on the theory of two involved powers! Especially when the body to decide in most cases must be the Supreme Council of the League.

How will the Council perform this task? Section 7 of Article XV of the Covenant reads as follows:

> If the Council fails to reach a report which is unanimously agreed to by the members thereof, other than the Representatives of one or more of the parties to the dispute, the Members of the League reserve to themselves the right to take such action as they shall consider necessary for the maintenance of right and justice.

Such action need not be military, and the Council can only recommend. But what it will be unless real disarmament proceeds with great rapidity, unless the policy of regional defensive-offensive alliances is speedily foregone, unless there is soon apparent a more unselfish economic spirit than manifest hitherto, does not require a great flight of imagination.

Boycotting the Aggressor

Of a piece with this effort to define aggression is the plan, sponsored in England by Mr. Henry Wickham Steed and in the United States by Professor James T. Shotwell, to have the United States ban the shipment of arms and goods in another war to a nation branded as an aggressor. This project has been endorsed at some of our peace conferences, notably the International Good-Will Congress held at St. Louis in November, 1927, and the Third Conference on the Cause and Cure of War in Washington, in January, 1928.

Infinitely more salutary and potent as a war deterrent would be the serving of a ban on all participants in another war. But our refusal of the more conservative project at Washington— for informally it was immediately snubbed—was on no such high ground. Primarily it was turned down because a great many influential members of the Senate shared the view of President Coolidge, whom the papers quoted, guardedly as usual:

. . . he was said to take the position that the United States has certain commercial and other rights that might not be best served under such an agreement.[20]

To the credit of the House Committee on Foreign Relations be it said that when Mr. Theodore E. Burton introduced a resolution to ban the shipment of war materials (unless permitted by Congress—there's the joker!) to a nation held by the President to be an aggressor, the Committee finally changed the resolution, and it was reintroduced by Mr. Burton on January 18, 1928 (with the joker still retained but otherwise significantly modified) "to prohibit the exportation of arms, munitions or implements of war to any nation which is engaged in war with another." A similar resolution was introduced by Representative Hamilton Fish, Jr.

Thus far, however, neither branch of Congress has seen fit to deal seriously with so realistic and important a resolution.

Tied up in many people's minds with the idea of directing an overwhelming force against an aggressor, is the conception of armies as police. Few fallacies so palpably without foundation gain currency and continue so long to confuse popular thought. An international police force, acting under the direction of a coördinated central delegated authority, might have some justification and use when employed against uncivilized tribes; though it is not the uncivilized but the civilized countries that menace world peace. While the nations are wedded to this aggressor ideology, any use of force will be in actuality not the exercise of police power, but open, unrestrained and ruthless war, no more to be checked at will, once started, than a prairie fire.

The first step taken within any country to insure the functioning of the police is the total disarmament of its citizens. When the nations cease to carry pistols and daggers on their hips and up their sleeves, the conception of an international police force will perhaps cease to be purely academic.[11]

An Ethereal Distinction

Underlying the reasons adduced thus far against the definition of an aggressor is the fact that aggression depends less on whom than on what. Variously, all of the plans for the definition of the aggressor nation rely upon such phrases as "a country *going to war* without submitting its case to arbitration"; or "a country commencing *hostilities*," or "a country *making an attack*." None of these schemes, however, define adequately what truly constitutes an attack, or hostilities, or going to war.

Does mobilization fall under these heads? If it does, it is entirely outside the strict limits of the definition. If it does not, what person who knows anything whatever of modern wars and the circumstances of their beginning will venture to say precisely where mobilization ends and war commences? Let the reader for himself lay hold of the material now available on the origins of the World War, and chart the precise points at which each of the nations actually "began hostilities," "went to war," or "started to attack"! He will have at least as many different points charted as there were participating nations, from the assassination of the Archduke by Serbian nationalists to the secret agreement between Italy and the Allies.

If these definitions cannot stand up as theory, may they not perhaps work better when it comes to practice? Few who live in this world and study the ways of governments, even though of robust faith in human institutions, could find any substantial evidence to warrant such a hope.

The distinction between aggression and defense in terms of war is as ethereal as it is arbitrary; and the attempts to write it down in the law of nations is a delusive over-simplification.

II

There can be no defensive warfare or "war for law" without aggression. The military experts know this well. What advocate of the abolition of "aggressive" war ever drew fire from the militaristic wing of our population? What military leader ever acknowledged playing the part of an aggressor?

Napoleon, before his death, asserted that he had never waged any other than strictly defensive wars. Earlier than that by far, measured in terms of bloodshed, the French National Assembly in the constitution of September 3, 1791, avowed an abandonment of wars of conquest.

As far back as 1833, a writer in the American Peace Society's journal was reminding his readers, "It is a favorite military maxim that the most effectual means of defending a country is to carry hostilities into that of the enemy."

In a drive for Congressional appropriations in 1861—just before the Civil War broke out—Colonel R. Delafield, acting as the War Department's "official spokesman," published a

huge volume on *The Art of War in Europe.* After pleading
for the fortification of our coasts, he says,

> . . . then with our resources we may feel secure and with other
> means at command, fit out armaments to meet our enemy on their
> own coasts, the most advantageous means of annoying them and
> adding to our own protection.

The late Rear Admiral Mahan exercised a tremendous influence on world public opinion relative to the importance of
sea power, and fathered a number of significant naval policies.
Among his contributions to United States naval progress, according to a Navy booklet issued in 1927, was "the abandonment of a strictly defensive naval policy."

Rear Admiral Bradley A. Fiske, another zealous advocate
of gigantic preparedness, makes it tactically plain in his book,
The Art of Fighting (1922) that

> . . . unless the defendant does at some time act offensively, he
> will surely be vanquished.

Consider the War Department's Training Regulations on the
subject, dated September 3, 1921:

> The object to be attained by training is to enable the Army
> to wage offensive warfare. While training must cover certain
> phases of defensive doctrine and police doctrine, the Army must
> definitely understand that these are only means to the definite end
> —offensive warfare—and every individual in the military service
> must be imbued with the spirit of the offensive.

Ex-Senator James W. Wadsworth, always a keen student of
military matters and a dependable booster for preparedness, led
the fight against the treaty banning poison gases, in December,
1926, which forced that treaty back into committee. He
stated quite frankly, as one of his reasons for favoring the use
of poison gas, that it constituted a valuable offensive weapon
and that it is necessary, for real defense, to take the offensive.

Major-General Charles P. Summerall, Chief of Staff, in
discussing the war of the future at the opening exercises of
the War College, in 1927, warned the specialists in destruction,

Whether the enemy strikes on our mainland or overseas, we must pour into the theatre of operations and into the battle line.[22]

What did the general mean by "overseas?" He might have meant, with prophetic insight, almost anywhere. Three days later, at Providence, Rhode Island, he elaborated his thesis:

We are prone to overlook the number of campaigns waged by American armed forces on foreign soil—the war with Tripoli, the expedition into Canada in the War of 1812, the War with Mexico, the Spanish War, the Philippine Insurrection, the Boxer Rebellion, expeditions to Haiti, Santo Domingo, and Nicaragua, the Vera Cruz expedition of 1914, the Punitive Expedition into Mexico in 1916, and the World War, during which the American flag was seen in France, Belgium, Italy, Northern Russia, Siberia, and finally in Luxemburg and on the Rhine with the Army of Occupation. . . . We seldom realize that, as a nation, we have since our birth 150 years ago been forced into armed conflict against more foreign nations than have either France or Germany during the same period.[23]

It hardly seems necessary to point out that in all these campaigns, and the ones on our own home territory also, we have fought after the sound tactics of defense. That is to say, by aggression.

The weapons were no less lethal, the lying no less prevalent, the hatred no less drummed up for its deadly purpose. *The Calumet* in 1834 asked a pertinent question,

Can a war of any kind be carried on without warlike weapons, swords, muskets, and cannon? But these are all *offensive* and *defensive* weapons. The shield and the helmet are weapons of defence; yet where is the defensive soldier who would think himself sufficiently panoplied with no other implements than these? [24]

Said the circular letter of the American Peace Society in 1828,

When we shall hear of a nation's waging defensive war without committing aggression, we may perhaps, withhold our censure; and when we shall see a defensive war *carried on on Christian principles,* we shall certainly approve of it.

There have been wars waged by great powers against weak

peoples, who have sometimes fought back. For many years to come, under the spread of imperialism to the less developed portions of the earth, we shall witness such disgraceful high-handedness. Even in these cases, however, from the first moment when the oppressed people resort to the war method in defense, defense exists no more except as a euphemism. It is aggression from then forward, on both sides of the conflict, but with one side capable of employing it to immensely better advantage than the other—by whom, as a matter of fact, the use of war is proving of less and less practical value irrespective of its awful cost in devastation and in life.

No matter how the battle goes, war is always the winner.

III

Defensive war, so-called, does not defend. The militarists are right: the only sound war-way to defend a homeland—apart from the interests for which wars are usually fought—is by offensive action, by carrying the war into the enemy's preserves. Once an aggressive expedition of this character has failed and the enemy strikes our shores, we may turn against him every device of destructive science, every artifice of propaganda, and yet from the time war begins, we have failed in our defense. The price of war is always high. It only remains to be seen whether, technically the losers, we are forced to pay a price that prostrates us for many years—as the South was prostrated by the Civil War—or, technically the winners, the conflict exacts a price that we can pay with a more or less decent chance of economic and cultural recovery. With the increasing economic interdependence of the nations, thinner, thinner grows the line between vanquished and victors. Hence, even in the case of a true war-status of defense, there is no escape from disaster.

But shall we not come to the defense of the weak when they are threatened? What about Belgium, for example? The answer is clear, and will be dealt with in a later chapter. Assuming that Belgium was neutral in 1914—it is not excusing Germany to show that she was not—how "defensive" of the weak was the war method in Belgium as compared, for example, to the non-military protest of Luxembourg? Or with the passive resistance of the Germans in the Ruhr (imperfectly sustained though it was) after the technical ending of the War? Used for a shambles when Napoleon's army was finally driven from her soil, Belgium was forced in just a century to bow once more before a cruel invader, one of her former friends; and since the war, we have seen her, rescued from this latest devastation, signing away her "neutrality" by a military compact with France. How long shall these grim jokes go on?

One serious query remains, however, not to be dismissed lightly. If the aggressor cannot rightly be defined, how then apply non-violent sanctions such as ostracism or the pressure of public opinion? Surely, even for a moral victory, there must be some method of focusing condemnation where it is deserved.

There is. First we have to admit that almost never, excepting for the cases of imperial piracy against small nations, is guilt all on one side; in practically every war-threatening controversy between great powers, the culpability has to be divided, in varying proportions. And next we have to recognize that the best test of an "aggressor"—though not a test that any government of to-day will accept until it is compelled to do so by public opinion and therefore a test that cannot be applied—is simply this: an aggressor nation is a nation which makes any preparation, display or use in peace or war of military weapons. Here is a definition which is at least in accord with the facts of international relations, even if international *realpolitik* will not permit aggression thus to be defined in practice.

No imperialism can long endure without the implements of war; and while they are retained, small nations are not safe. Thanks (?) to the bombing plane, the days of seventy-six are long since past, and probably forever. Freedom from the imperialist yoke cannot be purchased in our times by open or guerrilla warfare. The Aguinaldos and Sandinos of the future can be but advertisers of a cause.

Society must mobilize not against an actual aggressor but a threatening nation, a nation armed and ready for a war; just as it stamps out communicable diseases by defining as dangerous anyone who has the malady and by applying antisepsis. A pacific nation is a disarmed nation, a coöperating nation, a nation creative, constructive, trusting the processes of peace. Any other if tested practically, is an aggressor, a constant menace to the world's well-being.

I advocate no literal non-resistance. None of the non-resistants ever lived it: they resisted, though not by violence. The Quakers did not practice it; nor do the very ones to-day who use the term for want of a better. To justice we owe a debt as well as to peace.

No one to-day would urge a supine acceptance of the invader's terms, irrespective of their appeal to his sense of fair play and his intelligent estimate of their good or harm to the future of humanity. An increasing number, however, would advocate the substitution, for military defense, of active good will accompanied by non-coöperation with wrong or injustice. They would adduce, as partial evidence that such an attitude is practicable, the long history of the Quakers, in Pennsylvania and elsewhere; or, it may be, in recent times the Chinese boycott of Japanese goods which ultimately had much to do with the restoration of Shantung; or the non-coöperation campaigns in South Africa and India under the leadership of M. K. Gandhi.

They would have to admit, however, in deference to truth, that these and similar experiments have not been unmixed with hate and violence on the part of those not yet sufficiently self-disciplined. And the discipline required for successful non-violent resistance, especially an unyielding resistance in the spirit of good will, is infinitely greater than that imposed by stern officers for military morale.[16]

In his *Non-Violent Coercion*. Clarence Marsh Case, after pointing out all the dangers from within that such a method of resistance must face, is still able to say:

It is plain that, if persuasion and non-violent coercion must fall short of realizing the largest hopes of aroused and eager social crusaders, it is still more clearly demonstrated that the methods of *violence* offer infinitely less of permanent good.

If no more than that were true, it would be incalculably worthwhile for a nation, if ever truly a defender, to try non-violence and "applied good will." The nations of the world have heard about loving their enemies and about heaping coals of fire; but they have thus far practiced such tactics against no enemy whatever. To do so would be risky; lives might be lost, property destroyed, and civilization shaken. But with war what it is in this modern era and in a conflict of magnitude, dire loss in terms of property, life, and civilization is not a problematical speculation as an outcome of the military method; it is an absolute certainty.

However untried and unsure is the way of pacifist defense, even so reticent a scholar as Professor Case is compelled to concede that

In actual operation as described, and also in theory, these methods seem capable of producing effects upon economic and political affairs, without entailing the bitter and irremediable after-effects that spring up in the paths of violence.

Security—From What?

Lured, however, by this baseless idea of defensive war, the nations of the earth through their spokesmen at Geneva and wherever an international assemblage occurs, join frantically in an inept search for a basis of security.

"Men's solicitude for self-defence," rang the words of truth from the lips of Samuel Whelpley in 1818, "adds nothing to their security."

No nation can be assured of security without assurance on the part of every other nation of its own insecurity. A country absolutely secure guarantees the insecurity of every other. Under the war-on-the-aggressor compacts, it is a certainty that war anywhere means war more and more nearly everywhere;

that no nation is secure against war. And security against war is the only security which truly matters.

Real security from war can come only when we have killed the willingness of people in every country to make war, to such an extent that by the presence of dependably recalcitrant minorities, the war-making power of governments is hamstrung.

Paradoxically, but truly none the less, security can be obtained only by the achievement of total military insecurity. History shows that a bully among the nations is in the long run insecure; it shows that whenever nations have built up armaments for security these armaments have had to be used. We may be obliged to learn from another world conflict, waged in the name of law and order, that threats of punitive war constitute just one more guarantee of insecurity.

Without security, statesmen say, there can be no disarmament. Without disarmament, retort the peace forces of the world, there can be no security. This circular argument has rolled like a hoop across the century just passed. It will stop with a bump when statesmen find the peace forces ready to do something more than talk; when they cease to handle the gods of war with deference.

The peace movement has followed such a deferential policy for over a hundred years. The more radical view has not prevailed. Not because of this alone, but because of it in part, it was possible for a War Department *Manual of Citizenship Training* in 1927 to say, with unintentional irony:

America has never fought a war of aggression. She has always endeavored to maintain peaceful relations with other nations. Yet practically every generation has been compelled to take up arms in defense of the Nation or the principles set forth in her Constitution.[26]

It is not, you can hardly fail to realize, for the Nation quite so frequently as for our principles. And when you analyze that down, it resolves into just what has been previously said—our national interest.

How often we have "been compelled" to take up arms is indicated by the fact that in our national history—exclusive of the Revolution—we have fought five major wars, sixty-seven Indian campaigns, and have carried on an almost continuous fanfare of minor engagements.

The *Historical Register and Dictionary of the United States Army,* published in 1903, contains an interesting chronological list of "battles, actions, etc., in which troops of the regular army have participated." This list extends only from 1790 to the middle of June, 1902, and does not include naval engagements or marine actions at all. Yet it enumerates no fewer than 3292 separate engagements of sufficient importance to justify a record. The records become more interesting still when you discover that if the war years of the War of 1812, the Mexican War, the Civil War and the War with Spain are taken out, 2328, or approximately seventy-two per cent of these engagements, are accountable to years of "peace."

A more detailed record is the *Alphabetical List of Battles,* compiled by Newton A. Strait from official records and published as a government document in 1909. This reference book lists nearly nine thousand battles and important skirmishes in the War of 1812, the Mexican War, the Civil War, the Spanish-American War and various minor military excursions. Violence and combat seem to have been something of a steady diet, even in this supposedly pacific country.

As a deterrent from conflict, as a means to security from war, the concept of "defensive" war seems to have been more than a little wanting.

CHAPTER VI

TOWARD UNION OF THE WORLD

In Rome, the notion of international obligation was very strongly felt. No war was considered just which had not been officially declared; and even in the case of wars with barbarians, the Roman historians often discuss the sufficiency or insufficiency of the motives, with a conscientious severity a modern historian could hardly surpass. The later Greek and Latin writings occasionally contain maxims which exhibit a considerable progress in this sphere. The sole legitimate object of war, both Cicero and Sallust declared to be an assured Peace.—LECKY, *History of European Morals.*

CHAPTER VI

TOWARD UNION OF THE WORLD

IT has been the fashion for writers on world organization, arguing by precedent, to trace the idea of an international confederacy from earliest times.

There is indeed a certain similarity among the old-time plans; but it would be stretching facts out of proportion to assume primarily an unselfish, pacific motive for all such projects.[1]

The Amphictyonic leagues of ancient Greece, named after King Amphictyon, were bound fraternally in an economic, religious and political alliance, the one best known, centering in Delphi, comprising a union of twelve states. But behind each fraternal family lay a menace from the others—economic and military; and each confederacy existed as much for the safeguarding of its own power as for the beneficent motives often ascribed to the amphictyonies by their press agents in the peace movement. Even among themselves the member states were not held back from wars, and they sometimes made war on other groups to carry out their purposes.

Essentially the same is true of the Lycian League of twenty-three cities in ancient Asia Minor prior to the sixth century B.C., and the Achæan League of the Grecian peninsula in the second and third centuries B.C.

Dante, and Marsilius of Padua, in fourteenth-century Italy, and the Abbé Honoré Bonnor in France of the same century, promulgated the idea of a federation of states under the rule of a single monarch; but these were to be as much concerned with military strength and safety as with peace in the real sense of the term.

Podiebrad, King of Bohemia, sought to establish a pacific European empire in the fifteenth century; but its function, as he saw it, was to draw the teeth of the threatening Turkish tiger, ever ready to forage from the eastward jungles on the territories of the righteous.

At the end of the fifteenth century a scheme was agitated for a congress of kings at Cambrai, by William of Ciervia (in all probability an Italian town) and John Sylvagius, Chancellor of Burgundy—the latter influencing Erasmus to write *The Complaint of Peace.*

Erasmus in 1516 proposed a kingdom of all Europe. The ambitious Cardinal Wolsey for a time maneuvered to the same ostensible end in order that his liege, King Henry VIII, might head the federation; while others coveted that honor for the Pope. Few indeed were the plans for anything in those days— days not unique in that respect—conjecturable apart from political intrigue.

A French savant, Éméric Crucé, published in 1623 a project for a congress of ambassadors to represent every nation of the world, to meet continuously. This plan would probably have split, if attempted, on the rock of precedence, which he assigned in the following order: the Pope, the Sultan, the Emperor, the King of France, the King of Spain, etc.

The Grand Design of the Duke of Sully and France's King Henry IV, launched about 1600, is one of the most famous plans for a republic of European states, embracing France, Great Britain, Sweden, Spain, Lombardy, Denmark, the Papal See, the Holy Roman Empire, Bohemia, Hungary, Poland, Switzerland, the Netherlands, Venice and Central Italy. Religious liberty and free trade, along with arbitration through a joint judicial body, were major planks in Henry's platform. The French dreamer might have made headway with the project, for Queen Elizabeth was greatly interested in it; but his career was peremptorily cut short by the blade of the assassin, Ravaillac. Henry's grandiose Christian league, however, like that of Podiebrad, contemplated the subjugation of the Turk by force of combined military power.

The great work done for international law by Hugo Grotius in his *De Jure Belli ac Pacis* was supplemented by proposals for arbitration courts and congresses; but Grotius' mind was primarily obsessed with the hope of regulating and humanizing war.

A "society of sovereigns" was suggested in 1666 by a German prince, Ernest Landgrave of Hesse-Rheinfels (or Hessen-Rheinfels or Hesse-Cassel), and von Pufendorf in 1672 followed with a similar proposal in his *Law of Nature and of Nations.* Again this scheme was hardly of unalloyed pacific implications.

Even William Penn, after demonstrating by his "holy experiment" in Pennsylvania that the impossible can be done, brought out at the end of the seventeenth century his *Essay Towards the Present and Future Peace of Europe By the Establishment of an European Diet, Parliament, or Estates,*[2] and provided therein for the sanctions of force:

. . . before which sovereign assembly should be brought all differences depending between one sovereign and another that cannot be made up by private embassies before the sessions begin; and that if any of the sovereignties that constitute these imperial states shall refuse to submit their claim or pretensions to them or to abide and perform the judgment thereof, and seek their remedy by arms, or delay their compliance beyond the time prefixed in their resolutions, all the other sovereignties, united as one strength, shall compel the submission and performance of the sentence, with damages to the suffering party, and charges to the sovereignties that obliged their submission.

A few years later, in 1713, the Abbé Charles Irénée Castel de Saint-Pierre, stirred by the War of the Spanish Succession, published in Utrecht where he was secretary to one of the French plenipotentiaries at the peace settlement his *Projet de la Paix Perpetuelle*. Saint-Pierre's scheme was set forth in great detail, centering in a Senate of Europe, made up of twenty-four delegates representing the adhering nations. It wielded a great influence on political thought; Rousseau was greatly moved by it and borrowed many of its ideas for his own works. But Saint-Pierre was concerned not merely with the preservation of peace within the federation, but with its power, if necessarily exerted, against outside states or combinations.

Though less a scheme for organized peace than a set of principles by which mankind might outgrow war, the peace essay by Immanuel Kant published in 1795 was far more radical in many respects than anything of a similar character ever issued in the past. At an inn Kant had seen one time a sign depicting a cemetery, and over it the words *Zum ewigen Frieden,* "To Eternal Peace." In Kantian irony, the philosopher seized on this title for his essay. It was a highly idealistic work, envisaging a state of peace toward which the human race would be driven inevitably by the logic of progress from the natural to the directive condition of society. Though clinging still to "sovereignty"—or what he called *majestät*—Kant declared that peace must be based on three principles : first, every nation to be republican (though not necessarily a republic) with a body of responsive representatives of the people; second, a federation of free states—later, in 1796, defined as a "continuous congress of nations"; third, the rights of any nation in any other to be limited to the rights of hospitality.

Though not published until 1839, a Plan for a Universal and Perpetual Peace was written by Jeremy Bentham, the proponent of utilitarianism, between 1786 and 1789. Bentham's project embraced a diplomatic conference or diet, with two deputies from each member state, to act as a tribunal for the settlement of all disputes. All decisions were to be enforced by public opinion, or, that failing, by political and economic ostracism of the offending country. All colonies were to be freed, and armaments were to be drastically reduced by common agreement.

Kant's outspoken, daring essay and the non-military project of Bentham make a natural transition from their war-tinctured predecessors to the Congress of Nations and High Court proposed in the United States by the pioneers of the peace movement. There was in these no war sugar-coated as "enforcement of peace," "restraining the aggressor," or "war for law."

The sanctions were the strength of publicity, public reproach, international ostracism; in short, that public opinion which, said William Ladd, no army, no fortress, can withstand, which "reaches the tyrant on the throne, and the conqueror on the field of battle, and stings through the folds of purple and the coat of mail."

It is only in these latter days, under the influence of leaders who dare not take both feet at once out of the bogs of the war system, that the peace movement has been swinging back to the sanction of military force, to the war to end war, to that curious fire protection which seeks to put out a conflagration by drenching it in gasoline.

The "American Plan" of 1828-40

A man of such stature as William Ladd needs no excessive adulation; but he has received it, naturally enough, from the Society that he founded, and sometimes to the confusion of the facts. It gives no adequate comprehension of historic development to say, as the American Peace Society has said repeatedly, "The founder of the Society, William Ladd, was the first to propose a Congress and High Court of Nations." Having outlined in his own project some of the schemes referred to above, he would hardly make such an unqualified claim. Even so, however, Ladd himself reveals in his writing an extraordinary unfamiliarity with the literature of the peace movement prior to his personal entry into the struggle.

In 1840, after the breakdown of a prize contest for essays on a Congress of Nations—a subject dear to the heart of Ladd and his cohorts since 1828—the splendid persistence of the intellectual ex-sea-dog rescued the best of the essays from loss. Ladd secured enough subscribers to warrant their publication in a large volume, *Prize Essays on a Congress of Nations*. Five essays by contestants are included, one of them under the authorship of Thomas C. Upham. The sixth and last essay was the work of Ladd, and was the second longest in the collection—a fact which hardly warranted him in chiding the others for prolixity! He states that out of the thirty-five essays not published, he has selected and adapted the best thoughts, adding to them his own ideas.

The author has endeavored to comprise all the thoughts on a Congress of Nations contained in the rejected essays, worth preserving. He differs from all the other essays, either accepted or rejected, in dividing the subject into *two parts*, viz., a *Congress* of Nations, for the purpose of settling the principles of international law; and a Court of Nations, for the adjudication of cases submitted to it by the mutual consent of two or more contending nations.

Undeniably true; but the student of to-day is at a loss to explain the following statement of Ladd's about the Massachusetts Peace Society:

There is nothing in the publications of the Massachusetts Peace Society which favors the idea that the plan for a Congress of Nations ever engaged the attention of the Rev. Noah Worcester, D.D., the venerable founder of that institution and the only editor of "Friend of Peace," the organ of that society, or of any one of its members; nor do we find any mention of the plan in the publications or proceedings of any other peace society in America prior to the organization of the American Peace Society.

From the context it is clear that Ladd referred, not to his own specific plan, but to the general concept whose evolution he had been tracing. Yet in Noah Worcester's *Solemn Review*—the very pamphlet responsible, along with the influence of President Appleton who also had been moved by it, for Ladd's conversion to the peace movement—the stocky crusader of Boston had said:

If the eyes of people could be opened in regard to the evils and delusions of war, would it not be easy to form a confederacy of nations, and organize a high court of equity, to decide national controversies? Why might not such a court be composed of some of the most eminent characters from each nation; and a compliance with the decision of the court be made a point of national honor to prevent the effusion of blood and to preserve the blessings of peace?

He had written in *The Friend of Peace* for August, 1819—

nine years before the American Peace Society was formed—a three-page article about the value to humanity of a High International Tribunal, with public opinion to enforce its decisions, citing as the example of such a court the Supreme Court of the United States, still one of the most common arguments used to-day by proponents of the outlawry of war.

In April, 1820, Worcester reprinted from a British peace periodical a "poem" written in 1813:

A Remedy for War

What could secure the earth from future wars
So fully as a mutual compact made,
THE BASIS OF THE PEACE, that future wrongs
Of realm and realm should finally be judged
As those between the subjects of one king?

And in *The Friend of Peace* for July, 1820, he spoke in no uncertain terms to the very point Ladd says he never mentioned. Witness:

. . . we may suggest some means for improving the condition of men, relieving them from unnecessary burdens, preserving peace between different nations, and tranquillity under the several governments. We shall, however, attempt only an outline of a plan of improvement, in a few propositions:—

1. That the several powers of Christendom should agree on a General Congress to be held at the most convenient place, composed of authorized delegates from every government which may be disposed to unite in the general object.

2. That the real and avowed object of the Congress be, to devise and adopt means for improving the condition, preserving the peace, and promoting the general welfare of all nations.

In particular:—

To organize a High Tribunal for the adjustment of disputes between the several powers, and thus to prevent the crimes and miseries of war.

To agree on reciprocal terms for the reduction of standing armies and navies, that the burdens of the people in each country may be diminished, and that national revenues may be applied to more useful and benevolent purposes than the destruction of mankind.

To form a solemn compact, that in future no armed force by

sea or land shall be employed by any one nation for the annoyance of another—nor for any purpose, except the legal suppression of piracy, the slave trade, insurrection, and outrage. . . . Something analogous to the plan now proposed has been suggested by writers of great respectability.

The plan for a Congress of Nations and a World Court had been "in the air" for centuries. Through the suggestions of Worcester, Upham, and others, and the tremendous driving energy of William Ladd, it was laid before the American people persuasively, in detail, with an erudition born of the keen minds whose scattering shot of argument Ladd had fused into a rifle bullet of conviction.

As early as 1830, an enthusiast whose labors are shrouded with anonymity, went about among the citizens of Boston purposely neglecting the peace societies and the "aristocracy," and secured many signatures (unfortunately no exact number is reported) to the following declaration:

We, the undersigned, convinced of the great advantages and blessings which *an abolition of war,* and the reference of all international disputes to a *Court of Nations,* would confer on mankind, heartily concur in recommending a suitable reference of this subject, by the peace societies, to the attention of Congress, as soon as such a reference shall be found practicable and convenient.*

Nine out of ten, when offered this document, so says the sponsor of it, signed without hesitation, and even the minority of non-signers praised its main idea.

Encouraged by this symptom of public hospitality, no doubt, the warriors on war let no grass grow under their feet. They went out to capture support in high places. Chief Justice John Marshall's response was rather typical. To Ladd he wrote, September 12, 1832, from Richmond:

The human race would be eminently benefitted by the principle you advance. The religious man and the philanthropist must equally pray for its establishment. Yet I must avow my belief that it is impracticable.*

But faith burned strong in the sturdy souls of Ladd and his

fellow pacifists. By February, 1835, they had indeed made headway. William Ladd and Thomas Thompson, Jr., had addressed a petition with several thousand signatures to the Massachusetts Legislature, had induced the Honorable Sidney Willard to present it to the Senate, and on the sixth of that month experienced the pleasure of knowing that for the first time in our history an official body was considering a definite plea for international peace—though a plea not as yet crystallized into any specific scheme. A special committee of three soon rendered a favorable report, which was adopted by a vote of nineteen to five; the only appreciable opposition coming from a "gentleman who, needlessly," as Ladd remarked, "acknowledged that he had never examined the subject."

Two years passed by; years occupied by a multitude of arduous duties, not the least of which was the preparation of further petitions. A pair of strong appeals were made in 1837 to the Legislature of Massachusetts, which were referred to a joint committee; and to the elation of the peace societies, the committee's report was highly favorable, specifically inviting the attention of the President to the subject and recommending "a negotiation with such other governments, as in its wisdom it may deem proper, with a view to effect so important an arrangement"—the arrangement being nothing less than an International Congress! By a vote of thirty-five to five in the State Senate and a unanimous vote in the House, this historic report was adopted.

The petitioners fared less well in Maine and Vermont; but even there, as in most of the states where peace societies had taken hold, many individuals and religious bodies were manifesting an active interest. The time had come for a more ambitious drive; and the campaign was shifted from the banks of the Charles to the more difficult shores of the Potomac.

This time the New York Peace Society got away to a quick start, with a half-dozen petitions signed by 609 more or less influential citizens of the then respectable Manhattan Isle. The other peace societies fell in line: 540 petitioners in Maine, 144 in Vermont, even 136 members of the Massachusetts Legislature, totaling altogether nearly 1500 signatures. Not a great number, indeed; but as Ladd reports, "more attention was paid to the respectability than to the number of subscribers."

Congress, however, refused to be impressed though the petitions were heralded by the liquid speech of John Quincy Adams in the House. As Adams wrote to Ladd, "The Chairman of the Committee of Foreign Affairs manifested a strong inclination to have it laid on the table." These petitions had made the unfortunate tactical error of being concrete instead of general; in short, they actually meant something, suggesting Mexico as a natural country with whom to start the process of amicable settlement by arbitration; and such a step as that was quite too much for the constitutions of many good brethren on Capitol Hill, who saw lurking behind the proposals the looming demon of abolitionist sentiment against the expansion of slave territory.

This experience, reënforced by an illuminating journey of Ladd's to Washington, convinced the man from Maine, as the peace movement has always been convinced every few years only to forget it again, that "if the rulers in representative governments are to be induced to adopt any new measure of public utility, it must be through their constituents. In such purposes application must be made chiefly to those in whom the sovereignty is established—to monarchs in monarchical governments, to the people in popular governments, and to both in mixed governments. . . . Before either the President or the Congress of these United States will act on this subject, the sovereign people must act, and before they will act, they must be acted upon by the 'friends of peace.'"

For a span of eighty-eight years the "friends of peace" have been "acting on" the people, usually, however, neglecting the masses and concentrating on the well-known worthies, and periodically descending on a well-nigh impregnable Washington.

On January 16, 1849, the Honorable Amos Tuck introduced into Congress a resolution for the institution of arbitration treaties and the establishment of a Congress of Nations. The

American Peace Society was still pushing for this program after the Civil War, and after the Spanish-American War was calling for a World Parliament. Arbitration especially, but also a World Court and Congress of Nations were supported by the more radical Universal Peace Union from its organization in 1866 to its disappearance, for all practical purposes, with the death of its founder and pulmotor, Alfred H. Love, in 1913. In fact, the project has won its way to an increasing status in the public opinion of the United States, despite our non-adherence to the present League. In view of what happened between 1914 and 1918, chronic isolationists may look back on our history and derive what joy they can from William Ladd's despairing and rather savage cry in August, 1840:

> The glory of this movement I would fain have my own beloved country receive; but I should not be surprised if the King of Prussia should send in his adhesion to the plan before we can get our own rulers to move in its behalf.

The Outline of Ladd's League and Court

Ladd's *Essay on a Congress of Nations, for the Adjustment of International Disputes, and for the Promotion of Universal Peace, without Resort to Arms*—those last four words are worthy of especial notice—was circulated by the author among the crowned and uncrowned leaders of national life all over the world. Like Worcester's *Solemn Review* its influence was out of all proportion to the numerical magnitude of the movement from which it grew.

The zest with which United States citizens have been prone to generalize from their own institutions must seem to other nations rather naïve. But we thus generalize to-day, and Ladd was doing so in 1840. Here is the threefold U.S. pattern:

> I consider the Congress as the legislature, and the Court as the judiciary, in the government of nations, leaving the functions of the executive with public opinion, "the queen of the world."

I trust I have not succumbed to the appeal of one-hundred-percent Americanism when I state, however, my belief that Ladd may not have been as groundlessly overconfident as appears at first sight when he declared,

> This division I have never seen in any essay or plan for a congress or diet of independent nations, either ancient or modern; and I believe it will obviate all the objections which have been heretofore made to such a plan.

The Congress, according to Ladd, would create and codify international law, thus laying a basis of order and procedure; the Court would adjust international differences, thus interpreting and applying the law. In his conception of the organization of the Congress and its method of operation, he went further than most proponents of international federation go to-day; but in his conception of the Court he was just about as advanced as the most conservative Court advocates now are, providing for the consideration of disputes submitted only by both parties. In the present Permanent Court of International Justice forty-three nations have already agreed to the principle of compulsory jurisdiction by signing, though in most cases with reservations, the so-called optional clause; of these signers twenty-nine have ratified (August, 1930). Unlike the present Permanent Court (I am not referring here to the earlier Hague Tribunal of Arbitration) which provides for both summary and advisory opinions, Ladd's court stopped with the latter. In his ideas of the kinds of cases to be handled by such a court, as also of the questions of law with which the Congress should concern itself, Ladd was still too close to the war system and the "regulation" basis of Grotius, Vattel, and the elder von Martens—whose works on international relations engrossed the attention of most early scholars in the American peace movement.

It is the importance ascribed by William Ladd's composite program to the police power of public opinion which gives it distinction. Said he:

> . . . if we look into the condition of man in a state of civilization, it will be found that where one man obeys the laws for fear of the sword of the magistrate, an hundred obey through fear of public opinion.

We who are for the present League of Nations, when hard pressed by its critics in respect to the sanctions of Article XVI, customarily point out a gradual reduction in the use of force and an increasing emphasis by the League on public opinion. Such arguments are on the whole but specious. Too little time, by far, has yet elapsed for anyone to say with sound support in fact, that the sanctions of armed force have fallen into a blessed coma of innocuous desuetude; else why all the talk in recent years of an overwhelming force to be hurled against an offending and dangerous "outlaw" member? The authorization is there, ready for instant reference when the frantic crisis comes. And it is on that Gibraltar of might, bristling with guns, however veiled by the mists of diplomatic verbiage or caverned in diplomatic silence, that the ship of peace, builded by patient and hopeful hands, will smash next time the international seas are lashed to fury.

All men not utterly blind to the consequences of the League's failure must hope for its success; but what realistic observer can doubt the gravity of its inability to disarm, or the extent to which it is interwoven with imperialism, or its sanction in the last analysis of military might? If it is unable to purge itself of these basic dangers, it may appear to our descendants not as an instrument of peace at all, but an agency of militarism, of oppression, of deadly conflict—a larger but no less execrable Holy Alliance.

In fact, there is an ironic lesson in the circumstance that for a time the exertions of the early peace movement everywhere were diverted from the ultimate formation of a real peace Congress, to labors of hope on behalf of the now unsavory "Holy League."

The Holy League of Long Ago

When Napoleon Bonaparte had flung his troops in one final unavailing effort against the Allies, and militarism was crushed in Europe (so said the optimists) the Emperor of Russia, Alexander I, made a visit to London. While there he attended a religious service of the Society of Friends which greatly impressed him. Shortly afterwards, he was interviewed by William Allen and Stephen Grellet, another famous Friend of saintly, strenuous life. He carried Friends' books to Russia with him when he left, after assuring Grellet and Allen that "these are my sentiments also." Afterward, the two Quakers made a venturous trip to St. Petersburg, where, with Daniel Wheeler, a Friend authorized by Alexander to undertake a huge drainage project, they besought his influence for world peace.

Meantime, from the United States, Noah Worcester's *Solemn Review* was on its tortuous way to the pious monarch's desk. To the Massachusetts Peace Society, Alexander's Prime Minister, Prince Galitzin, expressed the Emperor's sincere interest and agreement, by a letter courteously written in English.

Who can weigh the effect of seemingly futile gestures? How important a factor these influences were in Alexander's dreams of a peaceful Europe no one can positively say. Though the Tsar had exhibited interest in international coöperation as early as 1804, the evidence is ample, in my opinion, to warrant the conclusion of the peace movement in this country and the Friends in England, often expressed, that these bold efforts at persuasion were responsible in no small measure for his newer actions. Certainly another element was the Emperor's conversion by that strange mystical fanatic, the Baroness von Krüdener.

Suffice it to say that the Congress of Vienna, ending in June, 1815, "a war settlement" as much in terms of the future as of the past, was followed in November by the formation of the Holy Alliance of Austria, Prussia, and Russia. No combination of states before or since was ever announced by so exalted an Act of Alliance, containing that memorable passage:

> The sole principle of force, whether between Governments or between their subjects, shall be that of doing each other reciprocal service, and of testifying by unalterable good will the mutual affection with which they ought to be animated, to consider themselves all as members of one and the same Christian nation; the three allied Princes, looking upon themselves as merely delegated

by Providence to govern three branches of the one family, namely
Austria, Russia, and Prussia, thus confessing that the Christian
world of which they and their people form a part, has in reality
no other Sovereign than Him to whom alone power really belongs,
because in Him alone are found all the treasures of love, science,
and infinite wisdom, that is to say, God, our divine Saviour, the
Word of the Most High, the Word of Life. Their Majesties consequently recommend to their people, with the most tender solicitude, as the sole means of enjoying that Peace which arises from
a good conscience and which alone is durable, to strengthen themselves every day more and more in the principles and the exercise
of the duties which the divine Saviour has taught to mankind.

What a pity that the zealous Baroness could not also have
converted the wily Austrian conspirator, Metternich, who
called the Alliance a "loud-sounding nothing!" Under his
"master mind" it soon gave a most sinister application to the
Treaty of Chaumont, which formed the real basis of this Holy
League and which had not overlooked the object

. . . of assuring the repose of Europe by the reestablishment of
a just equilibrium . . . and of maintaining against all attacks
the order of things that shall be the happy outcome of their
efforts.

In short, the Alliance became the guardian of the *status quo*,
forbidding change for the better as well as change for the worse,
denying the rights of the smaller nations to genuine expression,
and invading ruthlessly wherever liberal, democratic, or revolutionary ideas threatened to jeopardize the rigidly fixed system by which the "fixers" were to profit and to maintain power
and prestige.

But in the calmer air of Massachusetts the paper bearing the
Tsar's fine phrases and the League's sublime ambitions crackled
with electrifying hope. Said the fifth issue of Noah Worcester's *Friend of Peace:*

Another signal event of this auspicious era, adapted to arouse
attention, and to stimulate activity, is the unexampled compact
lately formed between three of the greatest monarchs of Europe,
the Russian, Austrian, and Prussian; a compact, which they solemnly swear has no other object than "to show, in the face of the

universe, their unwavering determination to adopt, for the only rule of their conduct, both in the administration of their respective states, and in their political relations with every other government, the precepts of the Christian religion, the precepts of justice, of charity and of peace; which, far from being applicable solely to private life, ought, on the contrary, to influence the resolutions of princes, and to guide all their undertakings, as being the best means of giving stability to human institutions, and of remedying their imperfections." Meanwhile they invite "all powers who shall wish to profess the sacred principles," which dictated the measure, "and to acknowledge how important it is to the happiness of nations, too long disturbed, that these truths should henceforth exercise upon human destinies all the influence which belongs to them," to join in "this holy alliance." Thus, in the face of the universe, have these three mighty potentates erected the standard of peace, and invited all nations and all people to rally round it, and combine their influence for the permanent tranquillity and happiness of the world. Only let the principles here solemnly proclaimed be universally adopted, and carried into effect; and wars will cease unto the ends of the earth, the spear will be cut in sunder, and the chariot will be burned in the fire.

The argument for the League proceeded as the great hope grew. In the following number of Worcester's paper we read:

Since the fifth number of this work was published, it has been stated in the newspapers that Sweden, Holland, Denmark, and Switzerland have acceded to the "Holy League," which was formed between Russia, Austria, and Prussia. If this intelligence be correct, SEVEN European governments are now allied for the preservation of peace. May we not hope, that our government will not be the last to accede to the pacific alliance?

Was there a hint of penetrating doubt in the same magazine, next issue?

Let those who formed the "Holy League" but adhere to its principles, and all the nations of Europe will abandon the savage custom.

There was no doubt, however, in the mind of the Honorable Thomas Dawes, one of the Massachusetts Peace Society's most widely known leaders, when he stated to the Society on the occasion of its second anniversary, 1818:

The Holy League of august sovereigns, in which the Emperor of all the Russias has taken so conspicuous a part, is a strong indication of the future prevalence of the cause of Peace. Jealous politicians may have doubted the motive. Oh, familiar words! But they had not then read the undisguised answer of that illustrious man to the Corresponding Secretary of this society.

Inclined to overemphasize the influence of single personalities in the destiny of nations, and therefore to overemphasize the mental state of a ruler who could not, without renouncing his kingdom, step out of the war system in which he was enmeshed no less than those of more evil intent, the "friends of peace" in the United States were hard to convince of lurking wrong. Said Worcester again, early in 1819:

Little reason, it is believed, has been given by their public acts to support the suspicions which were entertained of intrigue and insincerity. But since that period, many have been the acts of Emperor Alexander, which afford reason to believe that he was sincere in professing a desire to prevent the recurrence of war. It has been repeatedly stated in our public papers as a fact, that since the year 1814, he has discharged from the Russian service no less than four hundred and fourteen thousand men; and in his Ukase for establishing the Society of Christian Israelites, he has expressly exempted the whole society from "military services" and from liability to have soldiers quartered upon them.

And shortly after:

When this society was formed, with what a gloom it was surrounded! except when it looked up to the Father of lights, or into the Gospel of his son. . . . Not a syllable had reached our country respecting the pacific league of the three sovereigns; and nothing, perhaps, was more remote from expectation than such a phenomenon. It was, indeed, a formidable objection in the minds of many that nothing of the kind was known to exist in Europe. But now this objection is obviated; the gloom which accompanied the dawn is dispelled, and the SUN OF PEACE is above the horizon.

A little time and the passage of certain concrete events; and then the chill of doubt had struck more deeply.

Admitting the possibility, and even the probability, that the alliance for the preservation of peace will be violated, and that there will again be wars in Europe, prior to the happy day when the nations shall learn war no more—still the Holy League may be of vast advantage.

And what was that advantage? Do not these words ring with a striking familiarity on the ear of those who hark to uncritical enthusiasts for our present League?

It is calculated to call the attention of the people, of all classes, to the destructive character of war. It opens a door for a free discussion of its nature and principles. . . .

Nevertheless, the inexorable outgrowths of policies that the "pacific" alliance would not relinquish, were such as to justify Sebastiani, Minister of Foreign Affairs in a somewhat chastened France, when in 1830 he declared that

the Holy Alliance has made its own the principle of intervention which annihilates the independence of small nations.

And even seven years before that, on November 7, 1823, President Monroe in the presence of John Quincy Adams, his Secretary of State; John C. Calhoun, his Secretary of War; and Samuel L. Southard, his Secretary of the Navy (his other two cabinet members were absent), laid in these words the corner stone of his historic doctrine:

We learn now with great concern that the Holy Alliance is planning to send armies to America to aid Spain and Portugal. This reactionary body, formed to restore the despotic system which existed in Europe, prior to the French Revolution, has undertaken to stamp out liberty in Europe. . . . The Holy Alliance denies the sovereignty of the people, abhors representative government, and has declared war on the freedom of the press. In short, gentlemen, it is the enemy of all that we hold sacred.[5]

It was soon the enemy of all that the peace societies held sacred. By 1832 the Massachusetts Peace Society, in its annual report, was complaining:

That we do not report the rise of more Peace Societies on the Continent of Europe is because the despotic character and jealous political policy of their governments do not permit them to be openly established with safety.

The fruit had rotted on the tree! But at last the peace movement could work, once more, for a congress of nations after its own heart: a league conception which was indeed a weak and ill-fed infant, yet able to grow with the passing years, free from the leprous taint of military imperialism in its veins. To grow thus free, that is, until, through a nostrum, the poison of war was sent into its blood stream under the dubious offices of an organization known by the world's record-breaking homeopathic title: the League to Enforce Peace. Long before it, Thomas Hobbes had said: "Covenants without the sword are but words." That, exactly, was the L.E.P. idea.

Give them credit. Few organizations have ever won in such brief time so many dignitaries to a banner. Possibly that was one of the things the matter with it. Ex-President William Howard Taft became its president when it was organized on June 17, 1915; and under the energetic support of such men as Theodore Marburg, Hamilton Holt, and others it flourished. Its essential idea was endorsed by Aristide Briand, von Bethmann-Hollweg, Viscount Grey, and President Wilson, whose famous speech before the League's membership in May, 1916, betrays what inroads the "force without stint or limit" of a later day had made even then upon his mind, under, of course, a supposititious service to world order. "Mere agreements," said Mr. Wilson, "may not make peace secure. It will be absolutely necessary that a force be created as a guarantor of the permanency of the settlement so much greater than the force of any nation now engaged or any alliance hitherto formed or projected, that no nation, no possible combination of nations, could face or withstand it."

During the World War the peace movement, under whose auspices we were rushed into the conflict, stated often that the Allies were in effect organized as that very force; that the War in actuality was simply a campaign to safeguard peace against a marauder. Casting one eye over the utterly discredited idea of Germany's sole guilt, and the other at the kind of struggle another such campaign would surely be, a skeptical observer may be excused for reminding himself of the candidate for a

civil service position who was asked what to do to stop a nose-
bleed, and who answered, "Put a tourniquet around the neck."

But it is just this sort of "martial logic" that inspired the
Covenant's Articles X and XVI. It underlay the proposed
Draft Treaty of Mutual Assistance; the proposed Geneva Protocol; it underlies the Locarno treaties; it was not really forbidden by the Pact of Paris (soon to be considered); it is implicit if not explicit in substantially every project launched by
the orthodox peace movement since the League to Enforce
Peace took the peace forces on its back and mounted up with
wings (and claws and beak) as of eagles.

The core of the question is to be found in Article X; and
the best illustration of how pivotal is the idea of military force
in the League of Nations is in the numerous attempts, long
drawn out and uniformly fruitless, to arrive at a common understanding of this Article.[*] From the time when Canada requested its elimination soon after the League was organized,
committee after committee, composed of eminent jurists, have
tried to find out what responsibility for the use of armed force
rests upon member states of the League who have declared
under Article X, that

The Members of the League undertake to respect and preserve
as against external aggression the territorial integrity and existing
political independence of all Members of the League. In case of
any such aggression or in case of any threat or danger of such
aggression, the Council shall advise upon the means by which
this obligation shall be fulfilled.

It should be noted that the Council, under the Covenant,
does not decide whether or not a violation of the Covenant has
occurred. Rather, it merely expresses an opinion and the member states do not have to concur; but as a practical procedure
a sharp disagreement with a group of such powerful nations as
those on the Council would be none too likely.

Also, as declared by the Commission of Jurists on Article X
in September, 1921:

The members are not obliged to take part in any military action.
It is true that Article XVI alludes to joint military action to be

organized, on the recommendation of the Council, by the several Governments concerned; but, in general, the members are not legally bound to take part in such action. . . . The Committee wishes to point out that there can be no doubt that the Council, under the terms of this Article, can only advise as to the means to be employed; it cannot impose them.

This interpretative trend had its latest official showdown in the Fourth Assembly, when a resolution on Article X definitely declared that the measure in which each member was bound to use military forces was a matter for the authorities of that state to determine, though "the recommendation made by the Council shall be regarded as being of the highest importance and shall be taken into consideration by all the members of the League with the desire to execute their engagements in good faith." Twenty-nine nations, including England, France, and Italy, voted for this resolution; Persia was the only country to vote against it. But twenty-two nations did not vote at all, and the resolution was accordingly declared neither adopted nor rejected! This may be taken as evidence, however, that the non-sanction school within the League is powerful and that happily it by no means has abandoned its campaign to persuade the countries still wedded to the notion of "enforcing" peace.

The plain truth is that nobody knows—nobody in the world —what the legal obligations are and are not, for the use of force when ordered by the Council. As for that, the question doesn't seriously matter; for the Council possesses within itself —excepting Soviet Russia and the United States—about all the real military and economic power there is to use.

Under the influence of the Pact of Paris and the liberalization of British policy under the Labor Ministry, the danger in the situation has been most hopefully modified through the signature of the new powers to the Optional Clause of the World Court, whereby they submit to "affirmative" or, substantially, compulsory jurisdiction. Hitherto only small nations, except Germany, had signed; but at the League Assembly of 1929 this forward step was taken by most of the great nations within the League.

There is incalculably dangerous international anarchy in an irresponsible aloofness on the part of the United States; on the other hand, the continued existence of international anarchy within the League must not be underestimated, even though it is definitely decreasing. And even though we have not joined, the influence of the Kellogg Treaty has been great on League policy and has symbolized a growing rapprochement between the League process and the viewpoint of this country.

An exhaustive bulletin of the Foreign Policy Association [7] excellently summarizes the kinds of wars which are allowed to League members by the Covenant:

1. Wars to enforce judicial decisions, arbitral awards or recommendations of the Council.

2. Private or duel wars, e.g., wars which may arise when the Council fails to reach a unanimous agreement.

3. Punitive wars directed against a state which is guilty of a breach of the Covenant.

Illumination on the moot question of military sanctions in the Council of the League was shed by an exchange of correspondence late in 1927 between the British Prime Minister, Mr. Baldwin, and the present Lord Ponsonby, who had sent the government a Peace Letter signed by 128,770 persons declaring in advance their refusal to take part in another war. Said Mr. Baldwin:

Article 16 of the Covenant lays upon the Council the duty to "recommend to the several Governments concerned what effective military, naval and air force the members of the League shall severally contribute to the armed forces to be used to protect the covenants of the League." How can we honour this undertaking without armed forces? Clearly we could not do so. We should be obliged to leave the League. . . . The complaint which has been heard in the Assembly of the League is not that the armaments of Great Britain are excessive or that they menace the peace of the world. It is that these forces are not placed more unreservedly at the disposal of the League for the enforcement of its decrees.

M. Briand, in his first negotiations with Secretary of State Kellogg in late 1927 for a Franco-American treaty outlawing war, declared that France could not sign a treaty barring war altogether because of her commitments to the League's force sanctions. Thus a great League power felt it could not consummate a treaty prohibiting war, though able to sign military treaties freely—as, for example, the treaties between France and Belgium, or Poland and Roumania (with France as a third party).

If force is not an essential in the League, why need any League nations persecute their war resisters? In some of the countries belonging to the League, even in times of peace those who refuse military drill and army service for conscientious reasons are often treated with ruthless severity worse, if anything, than that accorded common criminals.

One hundred and eleven resolutions on armaments, Professor William I. Hull pointed out, in 1928, were "adopted by the Assembly and Council of the League of Nations in forty-four of their sessions; fourteen of the League's Commissions have debated disarmament in 120 sessions." The hope of the future is the establishment of pacific bases for the international structure that will not only stand pressure but will tend to push the League steadily away from reliance on force.

War and peace cannot live in the same house and abide with safety. The lamb may lie down with the lion under such an arrangement; but in the cold gray dawn of the morning after it seldom if ever gets up again.

In the long run, the most important test of the League as a force for peace and as an aid to justice—for the two cannot be separated—will be this: can it provide the machinery, if its present machinery proves too rigid, and can it summon a sufficiently generous mood on the part of the great powers, to make possible without resort to arms, the necessary changes in the *status quo?* No major test of this kind has yet confronted the League. Soon or late the terrifying test will come.

On the eve of the World War, a profound student of international relations and a believer in peace—albeit a conservative—described the nature of that test in words scarcely less true in this day of an organized League than in the pre-War period of international anarchy:

If we study the map of the world, it is impossible not to be struck with the fact that national boundaries, even in Europe, are still in the highest degree "artificial." The function of a new international confederation would again be, like that of the Holy Alliance, to protect these artificial boundaries; to attempt, that is to say, to stereotype political systems with which, certainly in many cases, the people who live under them are not content. The attempt would be even less likely to succeed now, when the spirit of nationalism is strong, than a hundred years ago when it was in its weak beginnings. . . .

The new Holy Alliance, then, like the old, would find itself face to face with revolutionary forces which it would have to repress, save in the very probable event of its being willing to conciliate them by conceding their extreme demands: the satisfaction of every nationalist aspiration, and the universal establishment of pure democracy under unimpeachable republican forms. In any case conflicting ideals would, sooner or later, struggle within it for mastery, and in the end it would not bring peace but a sword.*

As against this disturbing prophecy, stand the Irish Free State, autonomous Iceland, Soviet Russia, Czechoslovakia, Poland, Esthonia, Latvia, Lithuania, the conglomerate Kingdom of the Serbs, Croats, and Slovenes. Yet with the exception of the first two examples of "self-determination," these arbitrary and often reasonless dispensations of territorial control contain as many seeds of future conflict as did the pre-War explosives by which they were propelled into their present precarious existence. As an illustration of the turbulent minority problems which threaten Europe's future peace, the observer's attention is invited to the accompanying map.

Against the pre-War international anarchy consider the critical conflict of capitalist and communist ideology as exemplified in Mussolini or France contrasted to the Soviet Union; against the defiance of decency in the pre-War secret agreements, the present flouting of League ideals and procedure by its own members, openly and by secret compacts; against Imperial Russia and Imperial Germany, the post-War dictatorships of varying ruthlessness in Italy, Russia, Greece, Persia, Spain, Lithuania, Turkey, Poland, Hungary, Bulgaria, Roumania, Jugoslavia, and heaven hardly knows where not.

From a confidential report which recently came to hand
from a group of travelers and observers, men of balanced judgment and acquainted with many sorts of people from labor and

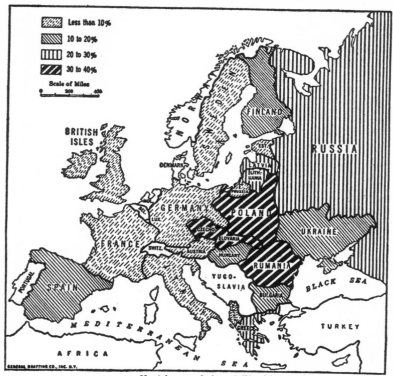

Used by permission of The Literary Digest, New York.

EUROPE'S NATIONAL MINORITIES

religious groups to political leaders, one can derive nourish-
ment only for well-grounded concern. Of the region throughout North Central Europe and around the Baltic they say:

Amongst all the minorities with which we came into contact,
the conviction reigns that the existing boundaries are not final.
Everywhere is to be found a really mystical belief that some event
not yet foreseen, a successful revolution or a new war, will and

must alter the present frontiers. There is a general distrust of the
League of Nations, from which nothing is expected; hopes are
laid for the most part on violent solutions.

The majority peoples on their part find it in their interests that
the present frontiers should remain as they are and they rely on
the League of Nations, powerful armaments, "security" treaties
with the Western Powers, and partly on an unwise and violent
treatment of the minorities. This situation makes international
disarmament impossible.

Some twenty-six treaties providing defensive alliances have
been registered with the League since the end of the World
War. Most of these treaties have been arranged between nations victorious in the War, who depend on the new alliances
to safeguard advantages, mainly territorial, gained in the conflict. It is not without significance that these treaties have continued to come into effect regularly, over a period of ten years.
As lately as 1926 the greatest number were signed of any
single year.°

A test? A tidal wave of trouble! Yet, if the League cannot
meet the trouble when it comes, war is absolutely certain, war
impossible to segregate; and to posterity this League will be
another "Holy" Terror.

If, however, it can rectify injustice, if it can gracefully relinquish old feuds, if it can grant ever-increasing equality of
status to the exploited races and peoples, if it can hold a Mussolini back from incitement to war and prevent a line-up of
capitalistic states bent on demolishing revolutionary Russia—it
will be a boon the like of which seers long have hoped for.

The present outlook for such a performance is neither bright
nor hopeless. The United States has remained outside from a
mixture of motives, provincial, pacific, good, bad, indifferent.
Yet with us in or out, until the League is definitely and completely disassociated from the principle of preserving peace by
throwing fear of war into a possible offender, it will never be
a real League of Peace at all. The dogs of war are not safe
guardians for the house of peace. When once let loose, they
bite without discrimination.

A peace movement that starts out to keep peace by allowing

war-to-end-war and which continues to tolerate the threat of legalized conflict as a central feature, suffers a tremendous handicap. To remove the sanctions of military force now endangering the League's future and the safety of civilization, is the first responsibility of all believers in the value of pacific world organization.

And even then, a League alone would be far from enough. More is required, a different approach, a much more vital guarantee of peace. In the war on war, organization is essential; but beyond organization, we have to fight. The how and when and what of that high struggle remains for consideration later on.

CHAPTER VII
ARBITRATION'S LONG CAREER

*What an amazing way of trying controversies! What must man-
kind be, before such a thing as war could ever be known or thought
of upon earth? How shocking, how inconceivable a want must
there have been of common understanding, as well as common
humanity, before any two Governors, or any two nations in the
universe, could once think of such a method of decision?*—JOHN
WESLEY, *The Doctrine of Original Sin according to Scripture,
Reason and Experience.*

CHAPTER VII

ARBITRATION'S LONG CAREER

THE human race has never tasted peace. War has at times been limited; yet chiefly checked, however, by the nations' inability to fight. The interregnums in the bloody rule of Mars have not been years of peace, but only breathing spells. As the *Encyclopedia Britannica* (13th edition) puts it, in discussing peace, "its sense in international law is the condition of not being at war."

A catalogue of mankind's wars would take a volume. The prevalence of conflict up to the birth of the organized peace movement is strikingly shown by the wars between France and England only. In the following table the years when war broke out are given in the left-hand column; each war's duration is stated at the right.[1] In Europe there are two distinct periods known as the hundred years' wars.

War Began	Continued, Years
1110	2
1141	1
1161	25
1211	15
1224	19
1292	5
1332	21
1368	52
1422	49
1492	1 month
1512	2
1521	6
1549	1
1557	2
1562	2

War Began	Continued, Years
1627	2
1665	1
1689	10
1702	11
1744	4
1756	7
1776	7
1793	9
1803	12

Twenty-four wars, occupying 265 years out of 705, and between these two nations alone! Wars with other powers excluded; civil wars left out; and yet between two countries, allies in the last great spree, hate and slaughter amounting to more than 37½ per cent or three-eighths of their total intercourse!

Between the Napoleonic Wars ending in 1815 and January 1, 1930, the nations of the world precipitated at least 252 conflicts, classified roughly as follows: Wars of Great Magnitude, 9; Smaller but Large Scale Wars, 49; Other Conflicts, 194. This averages well over two new outbreaks every year. (See Appendix I.)

All this time the idea of arbitration has been known; and it has solved a multitude of minor questions. Could you chart the difference between the additional wars mankind might have summoned means to carry on, and the wars stopped by some form of arbitration, you would find the area far too meager for your satisfaction.

Most of the early schemes for peace contained the arbitral idea.

Fénelon, writing in 1699 his *Adventures of Telemachus,* advised a young prince to seek arbitration rather than carry out what he alone deemed best. Came back the olden, modern query: "Am I not a sovereign Prince? And is a sovereign to leave the extent of his dominions to the decision of foreigners?"

The answer is symbolic; for on the reef of sovereignty, quintessence of nationalism, plans for arbitration have more than one time foundered. That stalwart Episcopalian, the late Admiral Mahan, well knew the fact, and fairly reveled in it.

"It is possible," he said, "that we have before us a period of transition, wherein the strong sentiment of nationality may prove simply the conservative force which by delaying shall steady the onward movement toward the logical consummation of arbitration without finally preventing it. . . ." [2]

Steady the onward movement? Let those who can, show where the progress of peaceful international relations has been "steadied" by that "pooled self-esteem," as Clutton-Brock once called it, [3] we know as nationalism; but which is known to militaristic minds as "independent nationality, which has played so great a beneficial part in the history of European civilization for the past four hundred years." [4]

Back in the misty origins of ancient Greece, King Amphictyon and the amphictyonies relied on arbitration. Arbitration likewise was a practice of the Achæan and Lycian Leagues. King Darius of Persia (who ruled 521-486 B.C.) decided a contest between Artabazanes and Xerxes; after his death, the issue not being entirely cleared by his decision, Artabanus or Artaphernes, uncle of the two pretenders, acted as arbitral judge, deciding in favor of Xerxes. Another Artaphernes, Satrap of Sardis, following a defeat of the Ionians, made the deputies of the conquered cities sign an arbitration compact to settle controversies by law instead of arms.

Among themselves the Greeks also employed arbitration, mainly in reference to religious or territorial questions. Solon (born 638 B.C.?) brought about an arbitration, under five judges, between the Athenians and the Megarians over the ownership of the Island of Salamis. The Cimolians and Melians engaged in a dispute over certain islands, settled about 416 B.C. by arbitration. A boundary dispute between the cities of Melite and Pera in Thessaly was arbitrated by the Ætolians. A similar issue between the Corcyreans and the Corinthians was arbitrated by Themistocles (who died about 460 B.C.). The city of Mitylene, when appointed arbitrator by King Antigonus (who died about 301 B.C.), resolved a contest between the inhabitants of Teos and people of Lebedos who had recently settled there. A very important case, disobedience in which was responsible for a disastrous war, was the arbitral judgment of five hundred talents granted by the Sicyonians to the Oropians against the Athenians.

Thucydides, in his history of the Peloponnesian War, quotes Archidamus, King of Sparta, who said: "It is impossible to attack as a transgressor him who offers to lay his grievance before a tribunal of arbitration." Pontarcus, famed as a wrestler, arbitrated an issue between the Eleans and the Achæans; and Pittalus, winner of the Olympic games, judged a dispute between the Eleans and the Arcadians. Simonides, the poet, is said to have prevented a war between Hiero of Syracuse and Theron of Agrigentum. The Oracle of Delphi several times arbitrated differences. A treaty between Argos and Lacedæmonia contained a clause providing for arbitration of contentions. Similarly the cities of Hyerapytna and Priansus provided between them definite arbitral machinery.

The Romans, on the other hand, were less interested in arbitration, though there are records of many appeals to the arbitrament of the dictator-emperors, or of the Roman senate. For a time, outside nations ventured to resort to the pomp and power of Rome as an arbitrator of their differences; but they soon learned the unwisdom of that course. In one instance, Rome decided a dispute over possession of certain territory between the Aricians and the Ardeans by grabbing the land for itself. Again, about 180 B.C. a dispute between Nola and Naples was "settled" in the same expeditious manner.

In the "barbarian" world, arbitration appears to have been common. The Gepidæ, a Germanic tribe, once offered arbitration to the Lombards; Theodoric, King of the Ostrogoths (about 454-526 A.D.), invited the Kings of the Herculians and Varnes to join in a proposal of arbitration to Clovis, King of the Franks, and his enemies the Visigoths—a move that was successful.

The Popes were often asked to serve as arbitrators in the Middle Ages, their pontifical dignity and overlordship lending prestige to the decisions. Most of these settlements were of minor, personal, or local significance; but occasionally there loomed up grave intersectional crises. Wars of some magnitude were prevented or at least delayed. A well-known case of settlement is the imaginary line drawn from Pole to Pole by Pope Alexander VI (who ruled 1492-1503) to divide the newly found lands in the Western Hemisphere between Spain and Portugal. Also possessing a power generally thought to be derived more directly from on high than that of temporal rulers, Bishops often were requested to arbitrate. The emperors of the Holy Roman Empire sought to exercise a similar power but were involved in too many intrigues to be often trusted. Feudal lords were often chosen to arbitrate between their vassals. Cities, though rarely, were asked to judge between other contending cities, and the parliaments of France occasionally settled disputes between foreign rulers. Sometimes a commission of arbitration would be set up by the disputants, and once in a while some internationally famous jurisconsult would be sought out as a referee. Arbitration was a practice of the Hanseatic League.

In a treaty of alliance, 1235, between Venice and Genoa, one article reads:

If a difficulty should arise between the aforesaid cities, which cannot easily be settled by themselves, it shall be decided by the arbitration of the Sovereign Pontiff; and if one of the parties violates the treaty, we agree that His Holiness shall excommunicate the offending city.

With the relative decline of the Papacy's power and with waves of war sweeping relentlessly over Europe, arbitration fell out even of such fashion as it had been in.[5] It continued to hold only casual favor until the end of the nineteenth century. De Bustamente, in his book on *The World Court,* lists the following table of arbitrations throughout the world, taken from a French compiler:

From 1789 to 1840, there were 23 arbitrations, or 1 every 2 years.
From 1841 to 1860, there were 20, or 1 a year.
From 1861 to 1880, there were 44, or 2 a year.
From 1881 to 1900, there were 90, or over 4½ a year.

In 1794 John Jay, our Secretary of State, negotiated with Great Britain a treaty of amity, commerce, and navigation which drew world-wide comment.

Needless to say, it attracted attention in the new United States. One-hundred-per-cent Americans burned Jay in effigy, and killed any chance of his landing in the White House.

In the first petition to Congress, 1837 (referred to in Chapter VI), the petitioners asked not only for steps toward a Congress of Nations and a World Court, but arbitration: arbitration in general; and in particular, arbitration of the pending disputes with Mexico.

The petition was turned down flat by the Committee on Foreign Affairs, which discovered, among other things, a danger from the Holy Alliance, long so jubilantly hailed by the peace societies, and praised even less than a year before (1836) by *The American Advocate of Peace* and the Windham County (Connecticut), Peace Society. Was ever a more typical urbane rebuff handed to any group of non-political humanitarians? The Committee concluded

by recommending to the memorialists to persevere in exerting whatever influence they may possess over public opinion, to dispose it habitually to the accommodation of national differences without bloodshed.

To the House it moved

that the Committee be discharged from the further consideration of the subject referred to them.⁶

And that—you can almost hear them rubbing their hands—was that.

It was. But the flood of petitions did not cease. From that time forward, the busy warriors on war kept matters hot for the timid men at Washington.

Again the Legislature of Massachusetts was faithful to its vision. In 1844, in reply to a single petitioner, it took a stronger stand for peace than hitherto. After roundly condemning war and declaring that "if any method can be devised for the set-

tlement of national controversies without the evils of war, the
adoption of that method is a consummation devoutly to be
wished," it expressed the opinion that

. . . the peace societies formed in this country and in Europe
within the last twenty-eight years and enrolling some of the purest
and most gifted minds in either hemisphere, have poured the light
of reason and revelation upon the practice of war, until multi-
tudes have come to the conclusion, that a custom so fraught with
evil, and so hostile to the first principles of religion, *cannot be
necessary.* It begins to be extensively acknowledged, that *individuals* and *communities* are subject to the same divine authority,
and are bound to conduct their affairs and regulate their mutual
intercourse on the same principles; and therefore, that legal adjudication should take the place of physical force, for the maintenance of national rights and interests, as it has already with regard
to those of a personal and domestic nature. . . .

We regard arbitration as a practical and desirable substitute for
war in the adjustment of international differences.[7]

Meantime William Jay, gracious son of an illustrious sire,
and President of the American Peace Society, had been campaigning for "stipulated arbitration." In 1842 he said:

Suppose in our next (commercial) treaty with France an article
were inserted of the following import—"It is agreed between the
contracting parties that if, unhappily, any controversy shall hereafter arise between them in respect to the true meaning and intention of any stipulation in this present treaty or in respect to any
other subject, which controversy cannot be satisfactorily adjusted
by negotiation, neither party shall resort to hostilities against the
other; but the matter of dispute shall, by a special convention, be
submitted to the arbitrament of one or more friendly powers; and
the parties hereby agree to abide by the award which may be given
in pursuance to such submission."[8]

Not even the august prestige of William Jay nor the forceful
benignity of his oratorical efforts, however, so much as dented
the crusty exterior of Congress. Still struggling manfully,
Jay and the more radical laborers who were coöperating in
the common fight, were obliged to watch impotently, for the
time being, while the slave-holding South won the reactionary
Polk to open war with Mexico.

Nevertheless, at the close of that disgraceful buccaneering raid, in the Treaty of Guadalupe Hidalgo signed in 1848 an article (21) was inserted not as a sop to arbitration sentiment but to secure Mexico's more willing adherence.⁹ Though Article 21 may have inspired the minor arbitration settlements of 1868, 1897, and 1902, nevertheless when United States-Mexican relations were strained in 1927 almost to the point of war (from this side of the border), the government of our country ignored the expressed willingness of Mexico's Secretary of Foreign Affairs to resort to a mixed commission, and substantially declared with an almost contemptuous disdain that there was nothing to arbitrate.

In so doing, this country did not violate the treaty, which does not make arbitration mandatory. In 1914, President Wilson had ignored a similar suggestion from Huerta's spokesman, and sent our troops to Vera Cruz.

Up to the Civil War, in all, the House denied three resolutions appealing for arbitration, and the Senate two.¹⁰

The Free Soil Party in 1852 adopted a plank which read:

We recommend the introduction into all treaties hereafter to be negotiated between the United States and foreign nations of some provision for amicable settlement of difficulties by a resort to decisive arbitration.

In February, 1853, the Senate Committee on Foreign Affairs adopted a resolution reading:

Resolved, that the Senate advise the President to secure, whenever it may be practicable, a stipulation in all treaties hereafter entered into with other nations, providing for the adjustment of any misunderstanding or controversy which may arise between the contracting parties, by referring the same to the decision of disinterested and impartial arbitrators, to be mutually chosen.

That got no farther. But on June 5, 1854, a treaty was consummated between Great Britain and the United States laying down the limits of fishing grounds. There was in this treaty an arbitration clause:

The Commissioners shall name some third person to act as an arbitrator or umpire in any case or cases on which they may themselves differ in opinion.

The high contracting parties hereby solemnly engage to consider the decision of the commissioners conjointly, or of the arbitrator or umpire, as the case may be, as absolutely final and conclusive, in each case decided upon by them or him respectively.

As the poisons of bitterness, intrigue, oppression and unreason swept the country on to that dread schism of 1861, peace work slowed up, peace sentiments were hushed, peace principles were pocketed—as usual, "for the duration of the war."

In 1871, however, with the favorable award, by arbitration, of the Alabama claims against Great Britain, once more the public's open-mindedness revived; revived also the hope and working energy of the movement for world peace.

Ever since May 31 of the "Alabama year," Charles Sumner had labored to get an arbitration resolution through the Senate. He could not do it, influential though he was. On March 11, 1874, he died. And then on the final day of the session, June 23, the Senate passed a resolution consisting of nothing but the third point in the more thoroughgoing Sumner resolution, and failed to consider a resolution passed by the House, also more meaningful. The House's resolution read:

Resolved, by the Senate and House of Representatives [the resolution was to be concurrent], That the President of the United States is hereby authorized and requested to negotiate with all civilized powers who may be willing to enter into such negotiation for the establishment of an international system whereby matters in dispute between different governments agreeing thereto may be adjusted by arbitration, and if possible, without recourse to war.[11]

So far, this was the high-water mark of official arbitration sentiment. It never became law, but it did fill the movement with renewed good cheer when encouragement was sorely needed.

It was not until the electoral campaign of 1876 that arbitration made any impression, since 1852, on the platform builders of the parties. In that year the Prohibition Reform Party, forerunner of the Prohibition Party—and, incidentally, inaugurator of many progressive planks adopted later by the larger parties—declared for

The introduction into all treaties hereafter negotiated with foreign governments of a provision for the amicable settlement of international difficulties by arbitration.[12]

Blaine, the Republican candidate in 1884, was supported heartily by the peace forces; for he had declared himself a believer in arbitration. *The Messenger of Peace,* a journal of the Friends, then published at New Vienna, Ohio, called

the attention of all the Christian people . . . to the great importance of their encouraging the Republican Party . . . in the glorious and greatly needed work of binding all the nations of the earth as soon as it can be done in bonds of peace by the reasonable and philanthropic power of arbitration.

At the great convention of "Friends, Tunkers, Mennonites, and Advocates of Peace and Arbitration" at Mystic, Connecticut, in August, 1884, the Reverend Dr. R. McMurdy, Corresponding Secretary of the National Arbitration League, aroused no little public comment by a ringing endorsement of Blaine.

But the Reverend Dr. Burchard's outburst about the Democrats as the party of "rum, Romanism, and rebellion," along with a strong Democratic war chest, floored Blaine forever, as a presidential candidate.

Prompted by an appeal from the French Society of the Friends of Peace to all civilized countries, a new wave of arbitration endeavor rolled up, especially in this country and in England. Under the persuasion of Andrew Carnegie a delegation from the British Parliament memorialized President Cleveland in favor of arbitration treaties and Mr. Cleveland replied with a response undeniably courteous and open-minded, but vague, tradition-bound, and clearly none too hopeful.

Let Mr. Carnegie tell the story of what followed as he recounted the stirring events of the period in his letter of 1910, transmitting $10,000,000 to the trustees of the Carnegie Peace Foundation. Responsibility for the spelling I hasten to place on the author of the missive, who was an advocate not only of peace but of orthographic reform as well:

I call your attention to the following resolution introduced by the Committee of Foreign Relations in the First Session, Fiftieth Congress, June 14, 1888:

Resolved by the Senate (the House of Representatives concurring), that the President be, and is hereby, requested to invite, from time to time, as fit occasions may arise, negotiations with any government, with which the United States has or may have diplomatic relations, to the end that any differences or disputes arising between the two governments which cannot be adjusted by diplomatic agency may be referred to arbitration and be peaceably adjusted by such means (Resolution not reached on calendar during session, but reintroduced and passed: Senate, February 14, 1890; House, April 3, 1890).

This resolution was presented to the British Parliament, which adopted a resolution, approving the action of the Congress of the United States and expressing the hope that Her Majesty's Government would lend their ready cooperation to the Government of the United States for the accomplishment of the object in view (Resolution of the House of Commons July 16, 1893, Foreign Relations, 1893, 346, 352).

Here we find an expression of the spirit which resulted in the first international Hague Conference of 1898; the second Hague Conference of 1907; and eighty treaties of obligatory arbitration between the great nations of the world, our own country being a party to twenty-three of them.

It was my privilege to introduce to President Cleveland in 1887 a Committee of Members of the Parliament of Britain, headed by Sir William Randal Cremer, in response to the action of Congress, proposing a treaty agreeing to settle all disputes that mite arise between America and Great Britain by arbitration. Such a treaty was concluded between Lord Pauncefore and Secretary Olney in 1897. It faild of approval by the necessary two-thirds majority of the Senate by only three votes.

And "faild," the man of steel and peace might well have added, after some of the most pitiful exhibitions of jingoism ever indulged in by a war-wed Congress. A House, for example, whose Foreign Relations Committee rendered a lukewarm, defeatist report damning arbitration with faint praise; and also a minority report expressing the noble conviction that

we will be purblind if we relax our attitude and accept a paper guaranty of peace in place of the moral and military forces that are the supreme elements of strength in our splendid Republic.[18]

Notoriously the Senate has been for years the graveyard of pacific international agreements. It would require more space than this chapter can preëmpt to tell the whole story of arbitration's experiences on the threshold of that mortuary. In the *Annals of the American Academy of Political and Social Science,* July, 1928, Professor Philip C. Jessup has just about "told all"—even to quoting a pungent comment by John Bassett Moore after the Senate had cantankerously asserted its prerogatives in regard to the treaties following the 1907 Hague Convention: "The result of this action is that, so far as the United States is concerned, it is now in actual practice more difficult to secure international arbitration than it was in the early days of our independence."

We have often said No to appeals by other countries that disputes to which we were a party be settled by arbitration. Our war with Mexico followed such a refusal. Our war with Spain followed a refusal to arbitrate the question of who was responsible for sinking the *Maine* in Havana Harbor; and we followed the war by a refusal to arbitrate the question of the Cuban debt and our possession of the Philippine Islands. We refused Colombia's request that we arbitrate our seizing of Panama. We refused to arbitrate the passport controversy with Russia in 1911, and in 1913 we refused to arbitrate with Great Britain the question of the Panama Canal Tolls Act. We would not arbitrate with Huerta in 1914 our demand that the Mexican president salute the Stars and Stripes. In 1917 we refused to arbitrate our right to make the Bryan-Chamorro Treaty with Nicaragua, which was held invalid by the Central American Court of Justice. Professor J. W. Garner, in his excellent work on *American Foreign Policies,* after considering our record, asks whether, "until we catch up with the procession and show by our acts our faith in arbitration and judicial settlement, we can continue to claim a leadership which no longer belongs to us. . . ."

The First Hague Conference of 1899 broke the ice of national isolation; but it amounted to little in terms of peace; its labors were primarily devoted to making war polite. At this Conference the United States rejected the ban on poison gas. All disarmament proposals—first in order on the agenda of the Tsar whose rescript brought about the meeting—failed utterly. The Conference did, however, promote the procedure of mediation, conciliation, and inquiry, and established the Hague Tribunal—a court not totally devoid of usefulness, but which between its inception and the outbreak of the World War handled only cases of extremely minor character.

Though the Second Hague Conference of 1907 brought into its sessions all the countries of the so-called civilized world except Honduras, Costa Rica, and Abyssinia, nevertheless as stated by Charles A. and Mary R. Beard,

. . . the fatal animus of the powers was clearly manifest at the second conference when practically the only points on which concord could be reached were new rules for "civilized warfare," legal rules which were soon to be treated by them all as mere scraps of paper, incapable of restraining armed forces facing each other.[14]

Yet so sure of their accomplishment were the peace forces, so jubilantly certain that war was on the run, that they seized with glee a skeptical bit of newspaper verse which illustrates, as Edward Everett Hale was saying in 1905 before the second Conference, "what was thought of the Hague Tribunal *for a while*":

A soldier of the powers was on picket in Algiers,
(Or China—any place you choose that finds a rhyme for tears);
The battle had been bloody and the rival armies lay
On gory blades, preparing for another one next day.
A figure from the darkness crept, a figure stern and grim,
Approached the watchful picket where he stood, and spoke to him:
"I pray you bear this message to the powers, where they lie,
For I'm the Hague Tribunal, and I've come to say good-bye!

"Pray, Soldier, drop a tear for me, and bless me ere I go;
I tried to take your job away, but you'll forgive I know.
Men petted me and cherished me, and cried me for a boon,
But now I see that I was born a century too soon.

We part and may not meet again; I bid you my farewell,
And when again you see the powers, soldier, you may tell—
Tell them—" his voice was broken and he smothered a great sob,
"Just tell them when you saw me, I was looking for a job!" [15]

Between the 1905 of Hale's exultant assurance and the 1914
of the verse's vindication, arbitration treaties had been negotiated by the United States with other powers: by Elihu Root,
as Roosevelt's Secretary of State, twenty-five treaties, of which
three were never fully made effective, and eleven of which were
permitted to lapse; by Philander C. Knox, as Taft's Secretary
of State, two treaties with Great Britain and France respectively; by William Jennings Bryan, Mr. Wilson's Secretary of
State, twenty-one. [16] Some of these were not put into operating
condition. Mr. Kellogg assiduously promoted the signing of a
great many new treaties all of a rather weak character, and he
also reconstituted the Bryan commissions for conciliation. In
the Pan American Arbitration Congress which closed on January 5, 1929, the United States delegates signed a treaty which
could doubtless prove of real value in Latin American relations, and which goes further toward compulsory arbitration
than any previous commitment. If ratified by the Senate, this
treaty would mark a noteworthy forward step.

Yet the fact is, not a single treaty to which the United
States is committed binds us to arbitrate *all* questions, and in
the last analysis, only such treaties matter very much.

We do not lead: we lag. Even prior to 1917, a half dozen
bilateral treaties actually banning war *over any dispute whatever* were in force in Europe and Latin America; since the War
two dozen or more such thorough treaties have been effected. [17]

Not one of our treaties, however, fails to provide some loop-
hole whereby arbitration may be dodged. Either by invoking
our sacred and inviolable "honor" or by simply declaring, as
with reference to Mexico in 1927, that there is nothing to arbi-

trate, we can reduce—we have reduced—these treaties to the level of mere gestures. We believe in them when they apply to minor matters—but do not choose to heed them when the issues really count. About seventy-five times we have been party to such small-stake arbitral negotiations, some of the machinery being established outside of treaties.[18] While it is possible that these matters might have led to war, it is probable that few if any of them would. And in that same period of time, we have also had war and war and war and war.

Is arbitration useless? Only when it deceives with false assurance. As a means of educating popular opinion for internationalism; as a stimulus to further international regulations to tie up war-makers and make their alibis a little harder to concoct; as a written expression of an international morality and world responsibility felt by increasing numbers of the people, treaties of arbitration, conciliation and mediation have a genuine part in peace.

But they are not enough. Arbitration by itself is a precarious safeguard. Something more potent held in reserve; something less easily circumvented by inept and cynical men in foreign offices without detection by the people until it is too late; some power that speaks peremptorily to war and says, "No further shall you come!" is still required.

CHAPTER VIII
HUMAN NATURE VS. HUMAN NATURE

From whence come wars and fightings among you? Come they not hence, even of your lusts that war in your members?—APOSTLE JAMES, iv. 1.

CHAPTER VIII

HUMAN NATURE VS. HUMAN NATURE

"There is no animal so strange as man," says the dour Carlyle in his *French Revolution*. Strange indeed! for mingled with man's defiant egotism, his courage to risk his life in combat, his ceaseless conquest of natural forces, is a strain of abject self-depreciation.

Toward many of his problems man's attitude has been defeatist; but toward none so much as toward himself. He has scaled mountains, flung himself through air and burrowed for desired objects deep through layered rock; but in his own weak nature he has often seen one thing not to be conquered, too unregenerate for hope.

The doctrines of infant damnation and total depravity had their day, as pseudo-Darwinian ruthlessness and Freudian demonology have been having theirs. Far back in the primitive glories of Israel the songster twanged his lute and queried dolefully, "What is man, that Thou art mindful of him?" And they did not estimate then, as we do now, that the earth is no less than 250,000,000,000,000,000 miles away from the center of our universe!

There need be scant wonder that in the efforts of war-scarred peoples to discover why violence cursed the world, they should seize on that naïve explanation: human nature. No single quotation from Scripture was used in the literature of the early peace movement with such continuous reiteration as the lugubrious analysis of the Apostle James. It figures in almost every speech, article, tract, or book. Again and again the warriors on war gathered about the camp fire to begin their incantations with James' stern warning of lusts, though to end on Isaiah's bright prophecy of pruning hooks and plowshares.

Most certainly there is no warrant for the fairly common assumption that the current interest in the psychological basis of war is new. The approach is often different to-day and, of course, the terminology. The old-time inquirers did not probe man's behavior in the laboratory manner; nor did they write about "neuroses of the nations." It is absolutely incorrect, however, to say that the founders of the peace movement were not seeking to discover and eradicate the causes of conflict in the make-up of man.

It was easy when men sang glumly, "Oh! what a worm am I," to see an obvious cause for war in human nature. It is a little more difficult to see why so simple an explanation should continue to command respect to-day. The influence of those truculent high priests of the survival of the fittest—Treitschke, Bernhardi, Cramb, and Roosevelt—has been discredited in biology and social relations. Even the single-track psychologists have moved on far from the uncritical adaptations of Freud, and man, if not a subject for rhapsody, need not be cause for absolute despair.

Neither chronic dyspepsia nor the widening influence of Mr. Mencken's cynicized minority are adequate grounds why estimable people should evade the complexities of war causes and take refuge in such an easy simplification as human nature. The reason, it seems to me, is to be found perhaps in the overwhelming reluctance of these moderns to make basic social readjustments; rather than change social customs and institutions radically, they prefer to stagger along, putting the blame on the devil. In olden garb or new, the devil is always a comforting symbol to the conventional-minded.

Says General J. G. Harbord:

Permanent universal peace still remains as an ideal lost in inaccessible distance, until envy, malice, lust and avarice have disappeared from the human heart.[1]

The late Judge Elbert H. Gary voiced the lament of the prosperity worshiper:

Human nature is selfish and apt to forget what is really for the best interests of every country—that is, to maintain peace is the thing that encourages, maintains, and sustains prosperity.[2]

It is obviously a great deal simpler for General Harbord to ascribe the blame for war to the human heart than to renounce war and refuse further to take part in it. It was also simpler for Mr. Gary to lambaste human nature than refuse to make munitions or to attack the use of military forces, say, for the safeguarding of foreign investments.

I find it difficult, however, on any other ground than sheer disillusionment to account for Mr. John Carter's attempt, in *Man Is War*, to share the cynical view of human nature enjoyed by the best minds of all ages among the militarists, profiteers, slave drivers, and inventive theologians. Mr. Carter only a few years ago wrote in defense of youth. And now? Says Mr. Carter:

The heart of man begot the Roman legion and the Roman law, the Christian ethic and the Spanish Inquisition, the instrument of commercial credit and the practise of commercial war. Men have fathered the theory of liberty, equality, and fraternity, the guillotine and the Cheka. Man has created the frescoes of the Sistine Chapel and mustard gas. For everything begotten of man shares the nature of man and is as apt to destruction as to creation.

The world will escape the blight of war when man has ceased to be human. The world will find peace when man is extinct.[3]

This last paragraph is a neat little epigram which the first paragraph proves to be all too neat and simple. The Inquisition is behind us; the church that forced Galileo to recant and denied the Copernican astronomy, whatever else may be said against it, now maintains expensive astronomical observatories and alone among religious bodies keeps abreast of new discoveries in the visible skies. The score of mankind's newer foolishness would make a large book; but not so large as the old follies long since laid aside. The golden age of man may lie far off in dim futurity; but as Mr. Carter would agree, it assuredly never existed in the pain-filled past.

One thing is certain about the relation of human nature to war; and that is, that peace has not yet been effected by sentimentally low ideas of human capacity, that victories are not born of defeatist states of mind. Neither man as incorruptible angel nor as devil all depraved is a stimulating concept. Disillusioned humanitarians as well as cynical traditionalists have harped on the theme of fallen man for a century or more, but with little helpful effect for peace.

Grotius had declared man "a creature most dear to God." But David Low Dodge, touched by the icy finger of Calvinism, felt less enthusiastic. "An inspired apostle," said he, "has informed us whence come wars and fightings. They come from the lusts of men that war in their members. Ever since the fall, mankind have had naturally within them a spirit of pride, avarice, and revenge." [4] The Reverend Benjamin Bell in a fiery denunciation of the War of 1812, delivered in 1813, enumerated the causes of wars as follows: 1. Pride, 2. A covetous spirit, or an inordinate love of the world, 3. Revenge, 4. Idleness, 5. Debtors who try to overthrow governments by war talk, thus escaping their financial obligations, 6. Desire in rulers for increase of power and influence. [5]

Noah Worcester thought very differently. In his *Solemn Review* he said:

That there is nothing in the nature of mankind, which renders war necessary and unavoidable—nothing which inclines them to it, which may not be overcome by the power of education, may appear from what is discoverable in the two sects already mentioned. The Quakers and Shakers are of the same nature with other people, "men of like passions" with those who uphold the custom of war. All the difference between them and others results from education and habit. The principles of their teachers are diffused through their societies, impressed on the minds of old and young; and an aversion to war and violence is excited, which becomes habitual, and has a governing influence on their hearts, their passions and their lives.

Nurture versus nature, the olden conflict stated in terms refreshingly alien to psychological laboratories. There were not many to agree with Worcester, even in the loyal ranks of the peace societies, still less outside. Thomas Williams in 1815 pulled an over-vertical face still longer and anticipated General Harbord by a century and more:

It is certain, that war will exist, so long as the nations of the earth retain that character with which the human race are born into the world.[6]

John Jay, who ought to have known better, wrote to Noah Worcester from Bedford, New York, on November 12, 1817:

Until the Gospel shall have extensively corrected the hereditary depravity of mankind, the wickedness resulting from it, will in my opinion, continue to produce national sins and national punishments; and by causing unjust wars and other culpable practices, to render just wars occasionally indispensable.[7]

Thomas Dawes later in the same year answered back, however, in his speech before the Massachusetts Peace Society:

Though wars and fightings arise from the passions of men, they are not therefore always inevitable. The same apostle who asks "whence came they" answers his own questions and prescribes the remedy. He exhorts the twelve tribes then scattered abroad to cleanse their hands and purify their hearts.[8]

William Ladd in 1823 was writing papers for *The Christian Mirror* (as "Philanthropos") some of which indicate a lively interest in the causes of war: "Warlike Ambition or a Love of Military Glory," "The Present System of Education a Cause of Warlike Ambition," "The Militia System a Cause of War," "Preparation for War Often the Cause of It," "The Influence of the Female Sex Often Exerted in Favor of War." In 1828, the "Apostle of Peace" focused all these, perhaps because of his close contact with naval seamen and the militia encampments of Maine and Massachusetts, on one central cause: "The love of military glory is a cause of war, greater than all others put together."[9]

In 1834, the Reverend C. S. Henry of Hartford told the Windham County (Connecticut) Peace Society:

The causes of war exist in the corrupt passions of human nature.[10]

Stephen Thurston in 1838 delivered himself of this analysis:

The lust of dominion, the lust of wealth, the lust of power, the lust of fame or glory, and the lust of revenge, have ever been the most prolific causes of war.[11]

On and on, thus went the argument, up to the appearance of the *Origin of Species,* from which time *homo sapiens* seemed a constitutional roughneck, and to Prince Kropotkin's *Mutual Aid a Factor of Evolution,*[12] George W. Nasmyth's *Social Progress and the Darwinian Theory,*[13] and the impact of the new science of psychology on the strait-laced biology of the non-gay 'nineties. Beecher, shocked at the Franco-Prussian War, turned fierce oratorical irony upon a mentally squirming congregation, saying:

War is not an acute disease which can be cured by special remedies. It is a constitutional disorder. It belongs to human nature. It is the remnant in man of that old fighting animal from which Mr. Darwin says we sprang. One might find some presumption in favor of this theory from the fact that there is so much of the animal left in us yet. It has been supposed that we sprang from monkeys; and there has been an inquisition to see if there has not been a caudal appendage rubbed off. Nations have been explored to find a man who had a tail, as a monkey has, or some traces of one. You are looking in the wrong place. Look inside, and you will find resemblances to the monkey, the lion, the tiger, the bear, and the hog, all of them.[14]

Toward the end of the last century Guy de Maupassant, remembering his ten years at clerical work in France's navy department, and touched even then perhaps by the depression which was later in accentuated form to drive him into lunacy and early death, reached the acme of despair over docile, stupid human beings:

The most surprising thing is that the whole of society does not rise up at the very mention of war.
We shall therefore continue to live under the burden of the old, repulsive customs of criminal prejudices, of the wild conceptions of our barbarous forefathers. We are therefore animals and shall continue to be animals, who are governed by our instincts, and whom nothing can change.[15]

No one can prudently fail to admit that if peace depends upon this interpretation of human nature, and if human nature cannot be changed, we are in for scientific roughhouse forevermore. Nor can one rationally deny that there is something in human nature that isn't as good as it might be.

Even human nature can see that. And because it observes the folly of the race, it proves itself not purely foolish.

Anyone can see that Ladd was right, for example, in ascribing war in part to a love for military glory, even though he gave it overemphasis. As familiar a student of war as Brevet Major General Emory Upton, whose work on *The Military Policy of the United States,* written almost half a century ago, has been reprinted four times and still serves as a sort of Old Testament to army gospel, commented thus on the rewards of military success, which serve, of course, as a constant example to the ambitious:

> Our own people, no less than the Romans, are fond of rewarding our military heroes. The Revolution made Washington President for two terms; the War of 1812 elevated Jackson and Harrison to the same office, the first for two terms, the latter for one; the Mexican War raised Taylor and Pierce to the Presidency, each for one term; the Rebellion has already made Grant President for two terms, Hayes for one term, while the present Chief Magistrate, Garfield, owes his high office as much to his fame as a soldier as to his reputation as a statesman.
> Long wars do not reward the highest commanders only. After the Revolution Knox, Dearborn and Armstrong rose to the office of Secretary of War; Hamilton was Secretary of the Treasury; while Monroe, first Secretary of State, was finally elected President for two terms. During the Rebellion nearly 150 regular officers rose to the grade of brigadier and major general who, but for the four years' struggle, would have been unknown outside the military profession.
> Since the war, distinguished officers of volunteers have filled nearly every office in the gift of the people. They have been elected chief magistrates of their States, and today on both floors of Congress they are conspicuous alike for their numbers and influence.

The Spanish-American War raised up its Roosevelt and the World War delivered itself of Dawes. Must we blame this on human nature? Every last one of these beneficiaries, in all probability, sincerely considered himself as a Moses for his people; nor have the leaders of peace movements always been teetotally ambitionless. No greater mistake could be made, even if it were not sublimely pharisaical, to assume that the soldiery, from the humblest private down to swashbuckling admirals, are ruled on the whole by any other than laudable motives. Most of the hideous deeds perpetrated by human beings, for that matter, from the Inquisition to the sanctimonious lynchings in our Southern states, have been inspired by the *shrecklichkeit* of righteous but miseducated impulse.

Human beings do not wage or foster war because they are depraved. Increasingly, men will not fight except for causes that can be made to appeal to their ideals, however misdirected those ideals may be. No longer do armies of mercenary troops pillage alien lands for the whim of an equally alien employer; it takes conscription to drive men into war, and the passionate appeal of nationalism or the lure of a world ideal to reconcile them to their slavery.

The term "human nature," as generally used, means all sorts of things. It may mean original nature, that is, man's inherited psychological equipment; or it may mean his cultural, standardized, group ways of acting—which many people thoughtlessly confuse with so-called original nature.

In reality human nature consists of both elements. The cynics find little justification in such a view as that of Professor Charles H. Cooley, a respected student of human nature:

By human nature we may understand those sentiments and impulses that are human in being superior to those of lower animals, and also in the sense that they belong to mankind at large, and not to any particular race or time. It means, particularly, sympathy and the innumerable sentiments into which sympathy enters, such as love, resentment, ambition, vanity, hero-worship, and the feeling of social right and wrong. . . .

Human nature is not something existing separately in the individual, but a *group nature or primary phase of society,* a relatively simple and general condition of the social mind. It is something more, on the one hand, than the mere instinct that is born in us—though that enters into it—and something less, on the other, than the more elaborate development of ideas and sentiments that makes up institutions. . . . Man does not have it at birth; he cannot acquire it except through fellowship and it decays in isolation.[16]

Professor Dewey crisply declares, "Those who argue that social and moral reform is impossible on the ground that the old Adam of human nature remains forever the same, attribute however to native activities the permanence and inertia that in truth belong only to acquired customs."[17] And going still further, Professor Hocking states that "To any one who asserts as a dogma that 'human nature never changes,' it is fair to reply, 'It is human nature to change itself.' "[18]

Human nature can be changed. Further and further away from the idea of immutable instincts grows psychology; if behaviorism errs in wiping instinct altogether away, the trend of other schools is uniformly in the same direction even if they do not go so far. In biology, environmental factors receive increasing emphasis, even the older, orthodox eugenics having acquired in recent years an attitude of sullen resignation. A breezy publicist issues a book addressed to the human race, impertinently declaring, of human nature, *You Can Change It (Though You Won't)*.[19] Another, suggesting how humans are subject to change by the pressure of circumstances even writes about *Man the Puppet*.[20]

Not all at once can we change it; we need have no illusions on that point either. It was a bold, but somewhat unanchored speech made in 1826 by Don Manuel Lorenzo Vidaurre, Minister from Peru to the Pan American Congress at Panama, in which he said, soaringly (the italics are his):

Human passions will always operate and can never be extinguished; nor, indeed, should we wish to stifle them. Man is always aspiring, and never content with present possessions; he has always been iniquitous, and can we at once inspire him with a love of justice? *I trust we can.*[21]

No; not at once. Only by painfully slow degrees, and not, perhaps, in time to prevent the next war or the next half hundred. Those wars, however, are not inevitable. They are not inevitable simply because war can be eliminated without changing human nature much, if any. Human nature, as Montaigne long ago concluded, consists of so general and constant a variety that any individual and even the entire kingdom he might chance to live in could seem only as a pin's point in comparison.

As a matter of concrete experience it is no easy thing in these days to whip up a population to a state of war. The people have to be lied to, and lied to so persistently that huge machinery must be put into operation; machinery of censorship and suppression on the one hand and of lying propaganda on the other. And finally, relentless conscription must be resorted to in order to bring out the necessary troops and regiment the human war-units behind the lines. Observation does not support what Noah Worcester called "the unfounded and bewildering opinion that wars are inevitable from the nature of man."

Even during the Revolution many men of fighting age had to be dragooned by force and more by short enlistment policies. In Maine, for example, when Colonel Jonathan Mitchell was preparing for his Expedition of 1779 (so it was brought out by a subsequent investigation), Adjutant General Jeremiah Hill reported that

the troops were collected with the greatest reluctance so that I commanded martial law. Some were taken and brought by force, some were frightened and joined voluntarily, and some skulked and kept themselves concealed.

General Thompson had chortled:

If they will not go, I will make the country too hot for them.

While Brigade Major William Todd narrated how he marched to Casco Bay, July 14, with one hundred and thirty York County men, "several of which were brought with force of arms." **

Says Professor Van Tyne, in his book on *England and America:*

. . . in a country containing something like 700,000 men of fighting age, there was never, even on paper, over one-eighth their number in state militia and Continental army together, and Washington was never able to gather for any one battle over 20,000 men.

In England, according to the same writer:

So great was the dislike of serving abroad, the horror of the brutal practices in the army, and the aversion to the war on America, that not twenty thousand soldiers of the English breed were available in 1776, and recourse was had to mercenary soldiers from petty German states.

In securing the soldiers of British nativity every device was tried between 1775 and 1781. Having exhausted the expedient of voluntary enlistment with the lure of bounties, North did not scruple to offer pardon to malefactors on condition of joining the army. From that his ministry resorted to impressment and inducing justices of the peace to give over to the recruiting officers idle or indigent men.

In the War of 1812, it was no easier to sweep up all the available lads from the farms into the military hopper grinding out its cannon-fodder. The War with Mexico, our vilest conflict, brought forward more volunteers than could be used, but even then largely because of the brief enlistments permitted. Though volunteers were numerous in the Civil War, they were utterly inadequate for the task, and conscription was employed on a considerable scale.

Desertion during the Civil War, a most reliable book by Professor Ella Lonn, published in 1928 by the Century company, gives some startling figures about the hold which the war cause had on the rank and file of the troops (see Chapter XV, below, on "The Fight for War"). "Buried," she states, "in the *Official War Records* lies a perfect mine of evidence of an overwhelming amount of desertion in the Confederacy, revealing the important part this factor played in the ultimate failure of the South to achieve independence. Appalling in the Southern armies, it was even worse in the Northern regiments. . . . The reader will learn that there can be no cause so just or beloved that war in its behalf will not be attended by desertion among its defenders when a conflict waged on so high a plane as was the Civil War could not be free from it."

The War with Spain was less a war than a preliminary skirmish of imperialism with a great deal of *opéra bouffé* about it: as General Funston called it, "a sharp and short little war, with its sequel in the form of a more protracted and far bloodier struggle in the Philippine Islands." [22] The Philippine campaign was waged principally by regular army troops.

In the World War, from the severance of diplomatic relations with Germany up to the start of the draft, enlistments were astonishingly few in view of the strenuous efforts exerted by the President, the army, and organizations of zealous war patriots. During February the army took in only 4852 recruits; even Recruiting Week, boomed by Mr. Wilson's persuasive eloquence, netted only 9043, though it was everywhere realized that enlistment brought certain privileges of choice hardly to be expected under the impersonal distribution of tasks rosily but unsuccessfully heralded as selective "service." Mr. John Kenneth Turner, who gives these figures, points out that the entire period from the first of April to the first of July, 1917, produced only 133,992 enlistments even under an appeal of special privilege, honor, and social prestige. [24] Says he, "The impulse for America's war certainly did not come from the common people."

The case is very strong, though not so strong as this. The War Department's figures, which I consider authoritative and trustworthy on this point, give for army enlistments for April, May and June 301,693; furthermore there is no reason to confine ourselves to army figures. For army, navy and marine corps the grand total for those revealing three months comes only up to 410,750. At that rate it would have required nearly thirty-three months to raise the 4,412,553 men who were inducted by November 11, 1918. But even that rate was entirely artificial. Says the *Second Report of the Provost Marshal General* (1919):

. . . the selective draft, at certain stages, stimulated voluntary enlistment. . . . Enlistments ran high in April, May, and June, 1917, and then gradually but emphatically dropped to 25 per cent of the highest figure, in the Navy in July and in the Army in September. In the Army this change was apparently influenced by the announcement of the order numbers of the draft in late July; for thereafter the certainty, implied by high order numbers, of not being liable to early call in the draft, removed for many persons the motive to enlist. . . .

In short, the selective draft, in the varying stages of its indirect compulsory influence, was an effective stimulant of enlistment. In spite of the general popularity of the selective service system as such, there persisted always—for many, at least—the desire to enter military service (if needs must) by enlistment rather than by draft—that is, to enter voluntarily in appearance at least. Thus, whenever the prospect of the draft call seemed near, enlistments received the benefit of the dilemma thus created. This indirect effect of a selective draft in stimulating enlistment must be reckoned as one of its powerful advantages.

Though the evidence is less overwhelming, when it is all considered, than Mr. Turner's incomplete use of it would indicate, it is full enough to vindicate his ultimate conclusion. The draft was proof positive that in 1917 there existed no overpowering popular desire to fight.

"England, of course," said a military enthusiast in 1916, "did the same thing at the outbreak of the war as we did at the outbreak of the Civil War, viz., call for volunteers. And the thoughtful, generous-souled, and the patriotic answered the call by thousands. But when the Government wanted tens of thousands, and hundreds of thousands, and millions of course such an appeal broke down." [15] Human nature did not seem very warlike! To this ardent conscriptionist it did not seem very noble; yet what becomes of the thesis that human nature rushes governments into warfare?

When war is on and battle is suspended, one of the worst foes of military ardor is that terrible danger to morale, stigmatized as "fraternization." Brotherhood, after all, bites deeper than bullets. Soldiers at numerous points on both the

Western and Eastern fronts, especially the latter which had suffered most heavily early in the war, had to be shifted about. Germany had to ship troops, on occasion, all the way from one front to the other, because they had grown altogether too kindly disposed to their enemies—with whom, of course, they had more in common than with their own commanders.

Well might the military leaders fear that spirit which occasionally flared up in secret as revealed by Stephen Graham, who tells of finding on a pillar the bayonet scratches of a lone sentry, which read, forebodingly:

> Roll on the Duration
> Roll on Peace
> Roll on the Revolution.[26]

If human nature has changed enough to account for the tremendous social transformations of the past, we need not be too pessimistic over war. If it has not been modified and never can be modified, still those social changes cannot be effaced from the record.

The constructive elements in human nature have conquered over the destructive elements sufficiently for society in general to rid itself of such "habits" as marriage by capture, human religious sacrifice, infanticide, chattel slavery, the duel, prolonged religious wars. Blunder though it may, the race moves on to the new customs and institutions essential to survival. It may not move away from war; but that it *can* so move, what student of societal evolution ventures to doubt?

CHAPTER IX
THE BATTLEGROUND OF ECONOMICS

Consider this, beloved, that on account of private possessions exist lawsuits, enmities, discords, wars among men, riotous dissensions against one another, offences, sins, iniquities, murders. On account of what? On account of what we each possess. Let us therefore, brethren, abstain from the possession of private property or from the love of it if we may not from its possession.
—ST. AUGUSTINE, Commentary to Psalm CXXXI.

CHAPTER IX

THE BATTLEGROUND OF ECONOMICS

THE pioneers in the peace movement did not roll off glib phrases, however meaningful, about world markets, surplus values, imperialism, and the internationalization of raw materials. Modern industrialism had not developed sufficiently, machine production was still too primitive, to start the great movement of modern imperialistic penetration that from 1875 to 1914 was to partition Africa, turn Asia into a hunting ground for European invaders, and bring South America to the verge of an aggressive United States hegemony. Imperialism there had been, indeed, since the gold quests of the ancient Pharaohs; but when imperialism had behind it the roar of machine production, it was driven forth as if that roar came from a mighty cataract of capital pouring from the centers of industrialism over the rest of the planet.

It was not until 1867 that Karl Marx outlined the future course of industrialism as he saw it, in *Das Kapital*.

In new America, neither Dodge nor Worcester could have foreseen such a social pattern. They were eager, however, for light on the causes of war, Worcester in particular, for he had never succumbed to the orthodox simplicity of the "human nature" preoccupation. He and Channing and a group of others in the Massachusetts Peace Society determined to find some factual basis for their pacific operations. Accordingly a committee of highly competent investigators was entrusted with the complex task of finding the causes of past wars. Competent, that is, according to the rather naïve standards of social investigation in their period, but not wholly trustworthy to-day. Yet their summary has much value even now.

A formidable mission! Yet one's admiration is awakened by the workmanlike manner in which they conducted the inquiry' and rendered their report. No trace of any similar investigation since that time have I been able to discover.

The fact that this study seems practically unknown, and the absence of any thorough modern investigation to supplement it and make necessary revisions, is one of the reasons, possibly, why the air is filled with a multitude of prophecies, each stoutly voicing the one and only cause of war.

Examined in the light of existing economic conditions, this astonishingly detailed study reveals a strong cognizance of economic factors, though again the terminology is not that of the modern.

The committee's report was rendered in 1820. It was confined to "wars in which civilized nations have been engaged since they became Christian," or "since Constantine assumed the reins of the Roman Empire," omitting "a great number of petty wars in small nations of antiquity—temporary insurrections or trivial hostilities—and a multitude of wars which have been carried on between Christian and savage nations, such as the aborigines of Asia and America." The report relates to "286 wars of magnitude, in which Christian nations have been engaged." These wars were classified under ten heads. The summary is given in Appendix II.

Briefly tabulated, the conclusions of the committee were reported as follows:

Cause	Number
Plunder or tribute	22
Extension of territory	44
Retaliation or revenge	24
Disputed boundaries	6
Points of honor or prerogative	8
Protection or extension of commerce	5
Civil wars	55
Contested titles to crowns	41
Pretense of assisting allies	55
Jealousy of rival greatness	23
Religious wars	28
Defense	0
	286

Any such classification, of course, must of necessity be limited in value, for few wars have a sole and simple cause. Clearly, however, the motives here are chiefly economic. Even though civil wars have sometimes had no economic motive, the preponderance of revolutions is significant; let it be noted by those whose approach to war leaves class struggle entirely out of consideration.

The economic roots of war were perceived rather generally by the early spokesmen of peace, and were discussed in the moral terms of selfishness and possession—not far from the emphasis that St. Augustine fell into for a time. "Philadelphus," the Reverend Samuel Whelpley, wrote in 1818 in connection with war:

> The intense ardour with which many professing Christians pursue wealth, the luxurious purpose for which they employ one part of it, and the adamantine gripe with which they hold the other, and the desperate means they will take to defend even what is superfluous, are contrary to the laws of Christ, and I fear that they are Christians only in name.[1]

Acting on the fallacious assumption that mere increase of human contacts promotes peace, there were those who saw the end of war as a result of growing commerce. Colonel Lindbergh's hope of peace from airplane communication is only a modernized version of the peace optimism engendered by the invention of the steamboat. Tyler Bigelow, at the Massachusetts Peace Society's eighth anniversary celebration in 1824, prophesied that

> The interests of science and of commerce have become so identified with social order, and the peace of the world so much the common property of all nations, that no single nation dares compromit them, without attempting to conciliate, in form at least, the opinion of the world. . . . Commerce, agriculture, and manufactures, considered as the great and leading interests of the many, are the growth of modern times. They are essentially the friends of peace.[2]

John Stuart Mill in 1848 wrote of international trade as "the principal guarantee of the peace of the world," and in words the like of which we have been hearing often in recent years, "It is commerce which is rendering war obsolete. . . ."

Not by the early nineteenth century, however, had the great nations outgrown the views stated earlier by John Evelyn in England. All of them in varying degree shared in practice his blunt belief that

A spirit of commerce, and strength at sea to protect it, are the most certain marks of the greatness of Empire. . . . Whoever commands the ocean, commands the trade of the world, and whoever commands that, commands the world itself.[3]

John Jay, in his *Miscellaneous Correspondence,* had also written down a rather different impression gained from first-hand experience when on his mission of peace to England in 1794. France and England were then at war, and the common people of Britain, as of France, would gladly have welcomed a settlement. At a dinner of two hundred British merchants, interested in the promotion of American trade, Jay offered upon request a toast, and one he considered tactful and neutral: *to a safe and honorable peace to all the belligerent powers.* "You cannot conceive," he says in his correspondence, "how coldly it was received, and though civility induced them to give it three cheers, yet they were so faint and single, as most decidedly to show that peace was not the thing they wished. *They were merchants.*"[4]

Yet John Jay's son, "Judge William," out of a mellow optimism befitting his high social position, stated before the American Peace Society, afterwards, that "various causes have contributed to the existing pacific state of the world," and led off his list with "the extension of commerce and the consequent distribution of private property in foreign lands."[5]

Jonathan Dymond would have agreed with Jay the elder. Said Dymond:

Wars are often promoted from considerations of interest, as well as from passion. The love of gain adds its influence to our other motives to support them, and without other motives, we know that this love is sufficient to give great obliquity to the moral judgment and to tempt us to many crimes. During a war of ten

years, there will always be many whose income depends on its continuance; and a countless host of commissaries, and purveyors, and
agents, and mechanics commend a war because it fills their
pockets.[6]

William Ladd did not hesitate to speak boldly on this point:

A great obstacle to the progress of pacific principles is avarice.
Many men in this country, and more in Europe, get their living
and acquire splendid fortunes by war, while the people, to use the
language of Dr. Johnson, "are recompensed for the death of mul-
titudes and the expense of millions, by contemplating the sudden
glories of paymasters, agents, and contractors, whose equipages
shine like meteors, and whose palaces rise like exhalations." No
wonder such men, like the silversmiths of Ephesus, applaud a custom which enriches them, for by this *craft* they have this wealth.
But the wonder is that the silly multitude should join them in
their *hurras,* for *they,* at last, must pay the cost, which is wrung
from the hard hand of labour, and filched from the mouth of poverty, to increase the wealth of the rich and the poverty of the
poor.[7]

Do not overlook the fact that these are not the words of a
modern World War socialist dissenter, many of whom were
mobbed and jailed for saying less with more politeness. This
is the language of the Reverend William Ladd, respected
churchman, founder of the American Peace Society which said
recently it remains true to his ideals, while indulging in all sorts
of thrusts at "economic radicals."

There is a certain kinship, if only partial and separated by
many decades of economic change, between the outspoken
Ladd and the tall old man whose trial for a speech made at
Canton, Ohio, in 1918 sent him to Atlanta Penitentiary. During his arraignment the unflinching Debs took the same train
of thought as Ladd—of whom he had probably never heard—
and carried on it a store of current socialist ideas. "War," he
said, "does not come by chance."

War is not the result of accident. There is a definite cause for
war, especially a modern war. The war that began in Europe
may readily be accounted for. For the last forty years, under this
international capitalist system, these various nations of Europe
have been preparing for the inevitable. And why? In all these

nations the great industries are owned by a relatively small class. They are operated for the profit of that class. And great abundance is produced by the workers; but their wages will only buy back a small part of their product. What is the result? They have a vast surplus on hand; they have got to export it; they have got to find a foreign market for it. As a result of this these nations are pitted against each other. They are industrial rivals—competitors. They begin to arm themselves to open, to maintain, the market and quickly dispose of their surplus. There is but the one market. All these nations are competitors for it, and sooner or later every war of trade becomes a war of blood.

Debs went to jail. And less than one year later, while still refusing to release him, the President who sent him there was saying, in St. Louis:

Why, my fellow-citizens, is there any man here, or any woman —let me say, is there any child here—who does not know that the seed of war in the modern world is industrial and commercial rivalry? . . . This war, in its inception, was a commercial and industrial war. It was not a political war.[8]

Military and naval men, as well as socialists, ascribed the War to the same chief cause. A year before its actual beginning Professor H. C. Emery of Yale had expounded to the Army War College the economic basis of modern life which brings on hostilities. Professor R. M. Johnston, of Harvard and the War College, in 1915 stated that "economic ambitions are behind the greatest war in history." Senator Harding, later of the White House on Pennsylvania Avenue and Little Green House on K Street, openly differed with President Wilson's idealistic interpretations of 1918. But the Senator from Ohio did not go to prison. After the War, the late Admiral A. P. Niblack avowed the conviction that "greed is the ultimate cause of nearly all wars through the selfish national policies pursued."[9]

Repeatedly, spokesmen of the army and navy express in public identical opinions. Economists of radical and conservative views substantially coincide on the importance of commercial policies as the taproot of war. The outstanding difference rests simply in the unwillingness of the conservatives to sacrifice the economic policies for the sake of peace; by conservatives meaning, of course, the commercial groups who are served by the retention of the present industrial and imperialistic policies that are wrapped up in what is called, with a somewhat inexact succinctness, "the capitalist system."

Dignify these economic practices by propaganda regarding "incentives," "prosperity," "the full dinner pail," "the full garage," and blend with them the overwhelming sanctification of nationalism, and you have a war-breeding combination positively guaranteed to keep the world in constant threat of what Sherman (imitating Napoleon who knew vastly more about it) termed inadequately "hell."

A list of thirty-two world industrialists who "by virtue of corporate positions and their tremendous moral influence upon the rank and file of their respective industries, control the disposal of the raw materials without which war cannot be waged," was given out in late 1929 by Edward N. Hurley, wartime Chairman of the Shipping Board, with the suggestion that these men use their combined power to prevent all wars. His suggestion immediately inspires the question of how secure the world really can ever be while its destiny remains in the hands of a small group of industrial magnates.

"Many a man," says Norman Thomas in *The Challenge of War*, "without six feet of earth in which to be buried is swollen with pride because his country 'owns' an empire." The three strands of economic imperialism in present-day terms, as summarized by the same writer, are

(1) desire for investment markets for surplus capital;
(2) need for raw material outside the national boundaries;
(3) demand for new markets for manufactured goods.[10]

Many socialists—and most communists also—do not stop with demonstrating that war has economic roots, and that some wars may be prevented by eliminating the underlying economic causes. They go on to contend that by eradicating the economic causes of war, the whole war system will be overthrown and lasting peace brought to the world. Impatient are some whose emphasis rests primarily on economic causes, of all who unlike them do not lose sight of psychological factors. Do away with the capitalist system; pull up the economic roots of war, and war is thereby done for.

Perhaps this too is oversimplification. It was not a disciple of Wall Street but a British socialist, Bertrand Russell, who flung some deadly potshots at this theory a little while ago:

Many socialists contend that modern war is due to capitalism, and would automatically disappear if capitalism were abolished. The first and obvious objection to this theory is that war existed before capitalism. Modern wars are not so entirely remote from ancient wars as to make it certain that their causes are utterly different. Nor do we find that the most capitalistic nations are the most warlike; in fact, America is the least warlike of the great powers, while France, the most warlike, is the least industrial. The little countries of Southeastern Europe are intensely bellicose, but mainly agricultural. Czarist Russia was by no means pacific, though 85 percent of the population were peasants. We find, of course, that capitalism, like every other political force, becomes connected with the forces making for war wherever such forces exist; but it is a wrong analysis to suppose that capitalism generates these forces.[11]

Where does Mr. Russell seek these forces then? In the realm of the emotions!

Fear, rivalry, love of dominion, and love of excitement are the chief emotions which make the ordinary man not averse from war.

Are we back, after all, at Professor James' "moral equivalent"? Not exactly. But we are up against the fact that causes which sometimes lead to war in certain circumstances do not always eventuate in hostilities when the circumstances are not the same. Since the World War, partly because of exhaustion and partly because governments have not been able to rely with assurance on their populations 'for war service, numerous occasions for war have passed unseized, although beside them the assassination of an Archduke seems trivial in comparison.

Also we are face to face with another fact so obvious as hardly to need stating. Causes of war revolve with the eternal wheels of time. Old causes disappear, as feudalism, chivalry, and chattel slavery have vanished from the picture. New causes rise to plague the earth, born out of man's mechanical inventions largely, and fostered by his need of furthering them—as, for a modern instance, the world-wide race for rubber and oil. Nor are war causes always easy to dissociate from war's results. Few great treaties of peace have not contained the materials for wars that may have been postponed for centuries. As Dymond came to see, "what was originally an effect becomes a cause, and what was a cause becomes an effect," until, at length, "it is difficult to detect them in all their ramifications, or to determine those to which it is principally to be referred."

We are up against a third important fact: namely, that men will throw their lives away—their dearest possession—after all other possessions have been sacrificed, for the sake of some driving emotional conception of right or duty or "honor." Whatever be the case with governments, peoples go to war not for gain nor for glory but for what they think is to be justice. "Men will fight," says a student of the "national honor" concept, "not so long as they feel it is profitable, but so long as they feel it is right." [12] Conversely, they will cease to fight, or refuse to take part in war, when they feel it is distinctly wrong —or stupid.

Here come to grips the two chief motives for the fact of war: the economic and the psychological. I see but one conclusion to be drawn. War is grounded in numerous complex causes, the chief of which are probably economic. These causes, however, are not static nor the exclusive property of this present period; were they removed, other causes would soon grow to danger-strength. To eliminate the causes of war, therefore, will not eliminate war itself. If we are to wipe out war, it will have to be through a method which makes it impossible for nations to fight even though the most potent causes of war exert the maximum of pressure.

Numerous projects to render war less likely despite disputes have been discussed in earlier chapters: international organization, world court, arbitration along with varying machinery for inquiry, negotiation, mediation, and conciliation. Chapter X will survey briefly a newer proposal in the outlawry of war. While every one of these plans and processes may be made extremely useful, alone or working smoothly all together they would not be enough. We have to seek a procedure that will make war as utterly inconceivable the world over as a scourge of yellow fever would be now in the Panama Canal Zone.

There is one cause for war, rooted in custom and until recently never attacked by any vociferous portion of public opinion: the willingness of people to do their government's fighting. Here is one indirect but genuine cause of war, assuredly, which if removed makes war impossible to wage.

Labor and the War on War

"The forces for peace in the United States," writes an outspoken critic, "when compared with the forces in England, are insignificant as to numbers and ineffective as to methods. There can be no controversy regarding this fact. The only point worth discussing is why the situation exists. The time has come for a frank study of the present status of the peace movement in the United States.[18]

Why, however, need there be any difficulty about discerning the reason for England's superior status? The answer is obvious. England has a strong labor movement with which the peace movement is nearly though not quite synonymous. Most of the social idealism in England centers in the British Labor Party. There is no such divorce there, as here, between political and trade union activity. American labor has not only been politically conservative; it has lost ground seriously even in the number of workers organized in unions. And while labor in the United States has promoted Latin American friendship, its views on peace are amazingly backward. Toward the problems of international political organization it has turned consistently a cold, disdainful shoulder.

The American Federation of Labor's officials give their blessings to the Citizens' Military Training Camps. They chum around with reactionary hundred-per-centers and lend themselves to the government's program of industrial preparedness. Whereas British labor cursed Ramsay MacDonald for his wartime pacifism only to make him Prime Minister six years later, American labor has not yet recovered from the shock of the pacifism of American socialists—the only socialist party among the belligerents not to surrender its principles on demand. And American socialism, even after the communist exodus, is still less pacifist in tactical theory than British socialism. In Britain pacifism is found chiefly in labor groups and secondarily in religious bodies; in this country it resides primarily in the churches and religious groups and is conspicuous for its absence in labor circles. Not only is American labor utterly indifferent to pacifism; it is almost equally unregardful of the more conservative peace movement.

And why? If the peace movement has made little impression on labor, it is partly due to the lack of interest in labor's problems on the part of the peace forces. The two movements run along side by side but at scarcely a single point do they meet. The only effort to aid the cause of labor comes from a small—though steadily increasing—number of people in the radical pacifist societies, and on the part of the pacifist student movement. And it must be frankly confessed, labor has thus far revealed no growing interest in pacifism.

Most of the radicalism, the alertness to new social ideas in general, has been confined to unions preponderantly Jewish in make-up, for example the Amalgamated Clothing Workers. On the other hand, the only peace groups which have manifested any keen interest in the labor cause have based their pacifism on the ethical teachings of Jesus—for instance, the Fellowship of Reconciliation and Christian undergraduates. Thus no general *rapprochement* has been possible as in England, whose No More War Movement takes in thousands of workers irrespective of religious or anti-religious predilections.

From the left of labor to the right, and the "right" of the peace movement to the pacifist "left," there is no common ground. Labor's leadership is working-class, but inclined to ignore the values of organized peace effort; the peace movement is "high-hat" or upper middle-class when not positively blue-blooded, caring apparently little about the great labor struggle and, when caring, frustrate from its own internal sectarianism. Religious peace groups make few or no attempts to enlist labor in the peace enterprise, concentrating almost entirely on the ministry and the churches; the military forces pay labor assiduous attention. Given such conditions, what else could sanely be expected?

Though interested, as we have discovered, in the economic causes of war, in the relation of greed and private possession to national ambition, the peace movement has never felt the justice of labor's struggle enough to share it. The peace groups have never been able to understand that economic injustice and oppression within a nation prevent any true world peace fully as effectively as any international tyrant striding over the backs of prostrate countries.

It must not be forgotten that the score of years from 1820 to 1840, which was a stressful and important period for the early peace pioneers, was also, as Professor John R. Commons has called it, "the awakening period of the American labor movement." Unions had been formed, as for example those of the New York printers, as early as 1786; but, says Professor E. L. Bogart, "the real labor movement did not begin until 1827, when the Mechanics' Union of Trade Associations was organized in Philadelphia." [14]

Instead of being merely ameliorist in character the early trade union movement was often militantly reformist, calling again and again, as one of its spokesmen put it, for "gradual but fundamental changes in the *whole organization of society*." [15]

When the Massachusetts Peace Society was stirred to jubilant enthusiasm over the receipt of a letter from Russia's Tsar, Lowell mill girls were working an average of ten hours and ten minutes a day, and many of them twelve hours and a half, with 30 and 45 minutes allowed for breakfast and dinner respectively.

The Windham County (Connecticut) Peace Society grew laudatory over the introduction of organized charity, but exhibited no interest in the efforts of workingmen for better conditions. In its report of 1832 it hailed approvingly the charity organizations because they would "lead the rich to feel a deeper interest in the welfare of the poor, and cause the poor to rejoice in the abundance of the rich," suggesting vaguely the good old hymn of Dr. Watts:

> Though I am but poor and mean,
> I will move the rich to love me,
> If I'm modest, neat and clean,
> And submit when they reprove me.[16]

Garrison, in his declining years, declared that "we must more and more look into the causes of war, and do all that in us lies to remove them, or our abstract peace testimonies will amount to little or nothing," [17] yet he could not be persuaded, though numerous attempts were made by his friends, to show regard for the organized labor movement or to modify, by cooperative sharing, the tactics in it to which he took exception. Toward the relation of economic justice to world peace he maintained a persistent blind spot. With extreme illogic, he seemed to consider the ballot, which he thought it wrong to use, an all-sufficient remedy for labor's ills.[18]

The benevolent and elderly Whittier, rightly concerned about slavery in all parts of the world and moved by the steps taken to wipe out the slave trade in Africa by the British General, "Chinese" Gordon, wrote a letter filled with extravagant praise, entirely overlooking the imperialistic butchery to which the famed fighter had given himself. A realistic leader of the American peace movement was stirred to remind those likely to be influenced through the Whittier communication, that "Gordon, sent out on a pacific mission, forgetting his duty began to call the Arabs 'rebels,' and to send accounts of the number he had slain. March 23, he reported three hundred and fifty killed and wounded; June 30, two hundred rebels killed. Yielding to his military instincts he was writing to Sir Evelyn Bar-ing to deplore that with his 'lovely Krupp guns' he could do so little execution on the natives, for though firing into masses of them, he had succeeded only in killing forty men and wounding sixteen." [19] A parallel might be found in some of the latter-day saints among the Quakers, a few of whom approved our war of 1927 in Nicaragua and who consistently refuse to heed the moral challenge of modern economic issues.

No application to our own class problems was thought of by the peace movement of the 'thirties, in which great interest was aroused by Lafayette's remarks on the future of peace in Europe:

As on this side of the Atlantic aristocracy and despotism are in incessant war with the rights of nations and of men, I do not see how a peace making system may be obtained until that fundamental warfare is put to an end—then indeed good sense and self-interest will suffice to remove the chances of war. [20]

Of course, the heady young Republic, determined to cash in on its vast resources, had no deep fear by then of aristocracy here, in the strict sense of the term. And yet, it was of these early times that the *Illinois Miner* recently asserted, with pardonable force:

They worked us eighteen hours in their slimy burrows. They killed us by the thousands beneath their rotten tops. They blew us skyward from the muzzles of their grassy shafts. They paid for sweat and blood and broken bones with wormy beans and rancid fat. They forced us to go begging crusts of bread from brothers as poor as we, displaying stumps and blinded eyes as our right to beg. They kept us in their stinking camps behind barbed wire and stockades like prisoners of war—like convicts doing time. And scarcely had the last clod hit our coffins when they drove our loved ones from their company shacks—to scrub and wash, to beg or steal, or starve or rot. And then we met in the dark of the night, in culverts, caves, and deserted shafts, to find a way from woe and want, from slavery and misery. Thus the union was born. How we struggled, how we fought and bled for that puny union babe! Oh, the tears we wept and the blood we spilled and the lives we paid to raise that precious child! We, too, had our Valley Forge, where we slept on frozen ground, with shivering limbs and empty guts. We, too, left the tracks of bleeding feet in the snow of many a camp. [21]

Charles Sumner, in his address on *The Duel Between France and Germany,* cites with satisfaction some radical European working-class declarations against the Franco-Prussian War. The General Council of the International Working Men's Association on the War stated in London their conviction that "whatever turn the impending horrid war may take, the alliance of the working classes of all countries will ultimately kill war." The Paris Branch of the Association even ventured to send out an appeal, "Brothers of Germany! . . . our division would only bring about the complete triumph of despotism on both sides of the Rhine." At Chemnitz a gathering of delegates representing fifty thousand workers of Saxony replied: "We are happy to grasp the fraternal hand stretched out to us by the workingmen of France." A working-class body in England asserted that "without us war must cease. . . ."

Elihu Burritt, as we shall find, worked directly to build up among labor bodies a strong will against war, and in England at least was conspicuously successful.

Yet so far as the United States is concerned, generally speaking, the anti-war voices of labor have been raised to sing of peace as soloists; for the peace movement has rarely chimed in with them to make the performance a duet.

Time after time the peace movement, in a wholly praiseworthy effort to prevent conflict, has found itself embarrassingly wrecked on a dilemma which, natural history to the contrary notwithstanding, possesses three definite horns. There are times when harmony may be purchased by a compromise between two sides of a conflict, leaving one party impaled on the sharp point of injustice.

Through their zeal for arbitration, for example, the peace societies in the 'eighties all but canonized Secretary of State William M. Evarts for his arbitration pledges, though beyond a hearty handshake at Washington these amounted to little. They were still lauding him as an example of a pacific statesman years after he had announced a certain foreign policy of great historic significance, seen with more and more clarity nowadays to be a breeder of that injustice which leads all too frequently to war. That policy, aimed at Mexico for an example, gave an official precedent for all our subsequent acts of armed imperialist intervention. It ran as follows:

The first duty of a government is to protect life and property. For this, governments are instituted, and governments neglecting or failing to perform it are worse than useless. Protection *in fact* to American lives and property is the sole point upon which the United States is tenacious. So far, the authorities of Mexico, military and civil, in the vicinity of the border appear not only to take no step effectively to check the raids or punish the raiders, but demur and object to steps taken by the United States. The pretense that the United States are plotting or executing invasions for conquests in Mexico is fallacious and absurd. No American force ever goes over the Rio Grande except in pursuit of "invaders" who have already "invaded" the soil of the United States and are escaping with their booty. The United States have not sought the unpleasant duty forced upon them, of pursuing offenders who, under ordinary usages of municipal and international law ought to be pursued and arrested or punished by Mexico. Whenever Mexico will assume and efficiently exercise that responsibility, the United States will be glad to be relieved from it.

And this, oh ye peace workers unstirred by economics, was offered by Mr. Calvin Coolidge as the chart of our sacred duty when we nearly made war on Mexico, and did intervene in Nicaragua in the brave year, 1927!

Though as far as any awareness of the labor movement is concerned, the American Peace Society after the Civil War might just as well have operated on the Blessed Isles of Greek fancy, the Universal Peace Union early in its career saw that if peace was worth while in the dealings of nations, it was desirable in the realm of industry. Arbitration everywhere was its hobby, and Alfred H. Love, its prime motive power, served as an arbitrator in a number of industrial disputes, with almost uniform success and satisfaction to all parties. The U.P.U., for example, settled a dispute in 1880 between the Brotherhood of Locomotive Engineers and the Reading Railroad Company.

However, judging by present labor standards, the neutrality

of the Union was of questionable service to true justice. If justice cannot be obtained by such instrumentalities of adjustment, the waste of strikes is sure to follow, and after the repeated failure of the strike, violent revolt, in the long run, almost inevitably. The specific arbitral program of the Union called for the maintenance of the open shop, regarded by labor, whether camouflaged as the "American Plan" or not, as a foe to organization, and by labor students as the foe of a responsible unionism. In the great steel strike of 1901 the appeal of the U.P.U. was on behalf of harmony and settlement, and the claims of the striking workers—now seen to have been comparatively conservative—were given scant consideration. The same thing was true during the coal strike of 1902.

Nor was there in evidence, at first, any vision beyond the profit motive. "We must especially represent and appeal to those who are aggrieved and disposed to strike," said the peace society, "to remember that they may some time become employers." [22] On the wage scale permitted there appears to have been a rather slender chance of such a consummation! And how shortsighted was such an emphasis is plain now, when it is the despair of discriminating humanitarians that labor, in this country no less than capital, refuses to work toward social control and production for use rather than for profit.

From its contact with actual labor questions, however narrowly motivated, the U.P.U. was awakening to a new interest in economic issues as a whole. More than the peace societies of to-day, for the most part, it examined open-mindedly even so militant a phenomenon as Debsian socialism. In the late 'nineties and early nineteen-hundreds, socialism was finding its way into the staid pages of *The Peacemaker*. Debates were staged over the contribution of socialism to social peace. Said Alfred Love:

Don't you do us an injustice after all these years of radical and earnest action, through opposition and persecution? Don't you see we not only assume but assert the equal rights of employer and employed?

To which his opponent, Dr. H. A. Gibbs, responded in hopeless resignation:

Nowhere do I find any intimation but that the strife [industrial strife, of course] must go on interminably, and the most we can do is to act as a buffer between the contending parties.[23]

Officials of the U.P.U., however, ventured now and again to enter socialist meetings, eager to understand the implications of the movement. Mrs. Mary A. Livermore, famous as abolitionist, suffragist (and as a means of leading Northern women to accept the Civil War), wrote to *The Peacemaker* in her eightieth year to say:

. . . to me socialism . . . is only "applied Christianity," and will prove as fundamental in the work and business and social affairs of life, when fully tried, as the law of gravitation in the physical world.[24]

And to-day? Between the bulk of the peace and labor-socialist movements—exactly opposite to the situation abroad—stands an abyss that few dare try to span.

What is the reason? Why do so many in the organized peace movement hasten, when pressed, to disclaim any connection with socialism or even to breathe the word; that so many who in their hearts honestly believe in the soundness of its major tenets avoid it as they would the plague? Is it because socialism has grown appreciably less pacific? It cannot be, for the left-wing split took away the prophets of violent revolution. No, the reason, in my opinion, is precisely because the movement in the United States *did* stand true, officially, to its professed internationalism in the test of 1917.

Also, of course, because any effort to reorganize the economic basis of our society brings contest, brings insistence on justice, brings endless struggle; and struggle is the one thing that the dilettante peace movement of the United States abhors with all its soul. The struggle for a better economic order, a society based on a true industrial democracy, even though waged only by ballot, personal sacrifice, and public demonstration, means heavy casualties to entrenched respectability. And until the recent opposition of the superpatriotic Paul Reveres, no movement in our history had ever become more excessively respectable.

It is symptomatic of our condition that a person may be an "absolutist" conscientious objector and receive scarcely more punishment in war than the same objector in time of "peace" is likely to experience if he asserts an equally devoted interest in the struggle to emancipate the toiling masses.

And so while war will not pass away when its economic causes are uprooted, the alliance of the peace forces and the labor movement—a movement probably destined to preëmpt the social history of the twentieth century—cannot with wisdom be delayed. It is the workers who will be the raw material out of which the rebellion against war must come; it is they who have the most to gain from war's eradication. If labor cannot be placed in back of the push for a warless world, the peace movement may as well give up at once. For a hundred years it has practically ignored labor and the working millions. Toward the abolition of war it has made slight progress if any. There are many reasons for that failure, but surely this is one.

CHAPTER X

WAR AS AN OUTLAW

There are some who say, "We are skillful at marshalling troops; we are skillful at conducting battles." They are great criminals. —MENCIUS (died about 289 B.C.), in *Tsin Sin.*

CHAPTER X

WAR AS AN OUTLAW

THE period which witnessed the birth and early growth of the peace movement was strongly dominated by moralistic criteria. If a practice was considered to be morally defective, it was speedily labeled "unlawful." By "unlawful" or "criminal" was meant something which was unsanctioned, not by the legal but by the moral code.

So it was with war in the thought of the peacemaking reformists. Hundreds of examples, literally, of such references to war could easily be adduced. The Reverend Benjamin Bell was interested in showing precisely on what occasions "only it is lawful to go to war." [1] All of the more prominent leaders commonly referred to war as "unlawful" or as "a crime." The Reverend Howard Malcolm, President of the American Peace Society from 1861 to 1878, once published a pamphlet on *The Criminality of War*. Yet the old-time poet was right:

> When high are piled
> Mountains of slain, the large enormous guilt,
> Safe in its size, too vast for laws to whip,
> Trembles before no bar. [2]

Noah Worcester, as exponents of the modern movement for the Outlawry of War will recognize, had caught in 1819 at least a glimmering of the ideas actuating Mr. Salmon O. Levinson to launch his Outlawry project in 1918. Public opinion, Worcester said, would be enough when enlightened to compel the decrees of a High Tribunal under whose jurisdiction should come the complex problems of international relations. Just as duelling had been brought to a defensive place by public opinion, so would war come to occupy the same position on the

moral defensive. A High Tribunal could as successfully enforce its decrees internationally as had the Supreme Court in
the United States. The Founder of the Massachusetts Peace
Society further said:

> In many instances a change in public sentiment has paralyzed
> an absurd or inhuman law, years before it was repealed by legis-
> lators. When public opinion changes in regard to the necessity of
> a sanguinary law, it first becomes difficult and afterwards impos-
> sible, to carry the law into execution. . . . As a change in public
> sentiment can thus enervate an absurd or cruel law, so it can
> enforce one which is humane and wise; and as it can enforce
> humane laws, so can it give effect to humane compacts and deci-
> sions. Therefore, should such a Tribunal as has often been pro-
> posed be organized by a compact between the rulers of different
> nations, it will stand in no need of armies to enforce its decrees.
> An enlightened public sentiment in its favor will be infinitely pref-
> erable to all the military and naval establishments in the universe.[3]

Feeling his way along the same dim corridor, Andrew Preston Peabody in 1843 allowed an unwonted note of hard realism
to creep into his speaking:

> So long as war is deemed lawful, its deeds and heroes will be
> painted in attractive colors, and held forth for the admiration and
> praise of mankind,—its anniversaries will be a nation's gala-days,
> —its glories will crowd the page of history, inspire the tragic muse,
> and float on the breath of song. . . .
> The evils of war, that are usually spoken of, are such as occur
> only in a state of actual warfare; and it is, perhaps, not an uncom-
> mon idea, that, were permanent peace cemented among the leading
> powers of Christendom, in whatever way such a result was brought
> about, the friends of peace would have nothing left to demand or
> desire. I think very differently. Were actual warfare suspended,
> from motives of policy, for any indefinitely long period, yet, were
> the lawfulness of war still recognized, were the associations of
> glory connected with martial progress left untouched, war, in a
> spiritual aspect, would be hardly less a curse upon mankind than
> it is during a time of actual warfare. In the Peace Reform, as in
> all religious reformations, a merely outward change is of little
> avail.[4]

He was thinking primarily, as the context makes clear, of
the need of organizing the moral sentiment in the Christian

world for the utter repudiation of war. Referring to a change
in the policy of the American Peace Society in 1837 to a radical pacifist basis, he says:

It is for these reasons that our Society has of late years dismissed its old argument for peace on the ground of expediency
and policy, has based the cause of peace on Christian grounds and
has aimed chiefly to produce a state of sentiment conscientiously
opposed to war under any and all circumstances.

As was natural, he therefore passed over the legalistic under-
cutting that his logic had led him up to, and went straight on
to an even deeper-lying factor in the fight for peace.

Elihu Burritt toyed with the phrase but gave it the "reverse
English," writing on "Christianity Outlawed by War." [5]

It was on March 9, 1918, that Mr. Salmon O. Levinson, a
Chicago attorney, proposed in *The New Republic* that the
nations delegalize war. Later that month, in the same journal,
appeared an article of comment by Professor John Dewey. In
1919 Mr. Levinson formulated his idea specifically, in collaboration with Senator Knox, and the issue for December 29,
1921, of *Unity*, edited by John Haynes Holmes, first published
the text in full, with comment by numerous early proponents
of the scheme. A resolution for Outlawry was introduced in
the Senate on February 13, 1923, by Senator William E. Borah
of Idaho. From that time to this, discussion of the Outlawry
plan has steadily grown in volume. Its most noteworthy advocates have been Senator Borah, the late Senator Philander C.
Knox, Professor Dewey, the Reverend John Haynes Holmes,
Judge Florence Allen, Colonel Raymond Robins, the Reverend
M. V. Oggel, and, conspicuous for his fidelity to the cause and
his great aid in giving the project wide publicity, Dr. Charles
Clayton Morrison, editor of *The Christian Century*. Dr. Morrison's book *The Outlawry of War*, published in 1927, is the
most comprehensive and authoritative statement of the ideas
underlying the Outlawry movement.

So much attention has been paid to the Pact of Paris that a
false emphasis is easy to give. Whatever its proponents may
say in their enthusiasm, the Pact does not signalize the

final achievement of Outlawry; rather, it constitutes the first great stage. Hence it may be well for the sake of clearer perspective to postpone for a moment any consideration of the Pact, and take up briefly the original aims of the movement for Outlawry and its later development.

The proposal to outlaw war, in comparison with the older projects, came as a youngster; its aim was almost revolutionary in its approach to war, but its tactic was a peaceful revolution along legal channels of procedure.

War, it declared, is an institution, and cannot successfully be eradicated by the policy of taking "next steps" for peace within the war system. The war system must be outlawed by the nations. So long as war remains legal, hope for a real peace is only visionary.

The process of outlawing the war system required a fourfold program: (1) the denunciation of war as a crime by international agreement, preferably at a conference of all the powers, large and small; (2) creation and codification of a body of international law; (3) establishment of a world court with affirmative jurisdiction, that is, competent to handle cases upon the appeal of a single nation; (4) enforcement of international law and agreements only by the pressure of public opinion.

The procedure of the original plan is indicated by the draft printed in *Unity* under date of December 29, 1921, as formulated in 1919 by Mr. Levinson and Senator Knox:

A Conference of all Civilized Nations to be called for the creation and codification of international law; the code to contain, among other things, the following provisions, with which all the other provisions of the code must not be in conflict:

1. The further use of war as an institution for the settlement of international disputes shall be abolished.
2. War between nations shall be declared to be a public crime, punishable by the law of nations.
3. War shall be defined in the code and the right of defense against actual or imminent attack shall be preserved.
4. All annexations, exactions or seizures, by force, duress or fraud, shall be null and void.
5. An international court with affirmative jurisdiction over purely international disputes shall be created modelled as nearly

as may be on the jurisdiction of the United States Supreme Court over controversies between states. All purely international disputes as defined by the code shall be decided and settled by the international court sitting as a judicial body, which shall be given jurisdiction over all parties to a dispute upon the petition of any party to the dispute or of any signatory nation.

6. All nations shall agree to abide and be bound by and in good faith to carry out the orders, decrees and decisions of such Court.

7. One nation cannot summon another before the International Court except in respect to a matter of international and common concern to the contending nations, and the jurisdiction of the court shall not extend to matters of governmental, domestic or protective policy unless one of the disputing parties has by treaty or otherwise given a country a claim that involves these subjects. The classes of disputes excluded from the jurisdiction of the international court should be specifically enumerated in the code and not be left open to the flexible and dangerous distinction between justiciable and non-justiciable controversies.

8. The court should sit in the hemisphere of the contending nations; and if the disputants live in opposite hemispheres, then in the hemisphere of the defendant nation.

9. National armaments to be reduced to the lowest point consistent with domestic safety and with the necessities of international requirements.

10. Abolition of professional soldiery and the substitution of a potential army through citizen soldiery on the Swiss model.

11. All nations shall make public report once each year setting forth fully their military and naval armaments, structural and chemical. These reports to be verified by authorized committees.

12. The doctrines of military necessity, retaliation and reprisal which are open to such flagrant and abhorrent abuse, shall be eliminated.

The Levinson-Knox-Borah plan suffered not a little from the confused use of the term "outlawry" which followed upon a seizure of the word by agencies with other schemes to float. The phrase, of course, was not copyrighted or trade-marked, and strictly speaking could be applied to other methods. Since, however, a definitely organized American Committee for the Outlawry of War had been functioning in Chicago under Mr. Levinson's leadership and since the idea emanated from him, it seems not only fair but wise for the sake of clarity to let the term remain attached to this specific project. In any case, the brilliant strides ahead made by the idea in a remarkably brief period, appear to have settled this point beyond dispute.

What are the special advantages to world peace in the Outlawry proposal and its rapid development?

First, it is free from the responsibility for maintaining the World War settlements. In this its advantage over the League of Nations is tremendous. The League's roots are still caught in the World War, the iniquitous Treaty of Versailles, and a complex of arbitrary territorial adjustments—such for example as the exploitation of mandated areas, the creation of buffer states along the Russian border, the separation of East Prussia, and the ever-troublous question of national minorities.

The court and law visioned by the Outlawry movement would be comparatively free from such commitments—though less free perhaps, nations still being what they are, than some outlawrists have recognized. As far back as 1889, Edward Everett Hale preached a sermon in Washington on "The Twentieth Century," uttering a prophecy which shows how far we are from the real aims of the world court movement of pre-war vintage:

The twentieth century will apply the word of the Prince of Peace to international life. The wisdom of statesmen will devise the solution, which soldiers and people will accept with thankfulness. The beginning will not be made at the end of a war, but in some time of peace.

A reordering of international law uncompromised by the emotional states and economic disturbance of war conditions would be, indisputably, a more pacific instrumentality.

Second, Outlawry does not contemplate the joint use of force as a sanction. Not merely because force engenders force, not only because force, even though reserved ostensibly for violators of international agreements, has its inevitable corollary in fear instead of real security; but also because force sanctions are almost invariably to be found in defense of "law and order," that is, the *status quo,* and against just and necessary social change—for this reason in particular. Outlawry's repudiation of military sanctions has an important advantage over previous ideas of international law enforcement. In this respect Outlawry is in accord with the far-sighted William Ladd; and it stands as a constant challenge to the older European concept of sanctions.

Third, Outlawry seeks to undercut the prevalent idea of war as a last resort. If delay fails; if conciliation, arbitration, diplomatic compromise leave issues unsettled and contention unreconciled, war is still as criminal as ever. While injustice may be done in some such cases, Outlawry says boldly that war is no remedy, not even in extreme cases, but is itself the worst injustice in the world. It anticipates the settlement of controversies up to the *n*th power without a punitive war on an offending nation.

And fourth, Outlawry reverses the traditional relations of warmakers and peacemakers by giving the pacific elements of the world recognition as law-abiding citizens while stigmatizing the jingoes and patrioteers as outlaws, guilty not only of indiscretion but of illegality. A conscientious objector, were Outlawry an established fact, would have behind him the force of law and, ultimately, public sentiment; while otherwise, he must suffer the handicap of an obstructionist status. Given Outlawry, the tables are turned: colleges, churches and other respectable institutions would not have to summon all their courage and tolerantly permit the presence of peace speakers while welcoming perforce the brass-buttoned dignitaries of slaughter; instead they would have to be persuaded—oh, sweet vision of Topsy-turvyland!—by tolerant pacifists to hear the well-meaning but, of course, misguided General Stalwart decry the passing of the good old days when men were men.

Let not your awakening, however, be too long delayed! Unfortunately the Outlawry plan, despite its magnificent promise, contains some points of danger.

For one thing, it puts too much reliance on the force of law. Outlawry is an American plan; and Americans characteristically fail to distinguish between legislation and social accomplishment. As Felix Frankfurter and James M. Landis put it in *The Business of the Supreme Court:*

> To an extraordinary degree legal thinking dominates the United States. Every act of government, every law passed by Congress, every treaty ratified by the Senate, every executive order issued by the President is tested by legal considerations and may be subjected to the hazards of litigation. Other nations, too, have a written Constitution. But no other country in the world leaves to the judiciary the powers which it exercises over us.

Naturally enough, the idea of Outlawry lends itself to over-emphasis. Spokesmen for Outlawry as, for instance, Senator Borah in his resolution, cite the example of our Supreme Court, which is "a practical and effective model for a real international court, as it has specific jurisdiction to hear and decide controversies between our sovereign states."

So little sovereign have our states become, however, that even the Constitutional right to maintain a genuinely separate militia has been practically abrogated without protest, for State and Federal forces have been dovetailed by the creation of the National Guard, and it has become increasingly common, though not without early protests, for Federal troops to enter a state for police purposes.

During Jackson's administration South Carolina all but seceded from the Union over the tariff favoritism shown to the North; and her spokesmen openly flaunted the power of the Supreme Court. It was Congressional action, coupled by Jackson's retreat, that saved the country from armed rebellion. And saved it for a few years only, for when an issue became joined between the whole South and the North, the Supreme Court was powerless to do a thing to check the drift toward the Civil War.

Another analogy drawn by those who advocate Outlawry is that between war and the duel; both, as they say, specific social institutions. "War," says Dr. Morrison, "is dueling on an international scale"; and further, "The outlawry of the institution of war will have precisely the same effect in international relations as the outlawry of the duel had in individual relations." Says Mr. Levinson, "Finally, the simple discovery was made that the way to get rid of dueling was to condemn it by law,—to call it by its right name, murder, and thus to outlaw it. Thereupon, dueling as an institution ceased and codes of dueling became museum exhibits."

Prohibition, however necessary, seems often laggard in prohibiting, whatever be the custom outlawed. The analogy between dueling and war breaks down, like most analogies; for in practical working out, it matters infinitely less to the future of the human race whether dueling go on than it does whether outlawed wars break out, for war to-day may actually mean the extinction of our culture.

As a matter of fact, the outlawry of dueling did not stop the practice, though unquestionably in the long period before dueling ceased to be common the point of view of the law exercised an influence on popular opinion. Still, dueling lingered for many years. In Europe it even now is far from totally extinct. As Kirby Page has pointed out:

In such countries as France, England and Germany dueling continued for nearly three hundred years after it became illegal. In France dueling became a capital crime, punished with death, as early as 1602. Yet within the following decade two thousand nobles were killed in affairs of honor. One authority tells us "that the private duel though much practised during the medieval period of English history, was never legalized, and was denounced and prohibited by a royal edict of James I in 1613 and by a decree of the Star Chamber in 1614." Yet dueling survived in England till the middle of the last century.[6]

In fairness to Outlawry, however, it must be said that one of the chief reasons why dueling continued so long was due to the severity of the punishment which made the law a paper statute only, respected by no one. By the change to a more reasonable code as was suggested by Bentham in 1789, dueling was soon frowned upon; and it is worthy of note that in this respect Outlawry's reliance upon a general disapprobation is considerably more advanced and efficacious than, for instance, the League's authorization of punishment by war.

Nevertheless, it was a gradual relinquishment of the prerogatives of outraged "honor" that gave dueling its death blow in most places. According to one of our historians writing of the period 1830-1850, in the United States:

This product of chivalry had in the preceding generation prevailed in all sections except New England and Pennsylvania, but had been made illegal. The law, however, had little effect upon the practice. It is popularly supposed to have received its death blow when Burr so killed Hamilton. It is possible that this was so but in that case the blow must be considered as having very lingering effects. Twenty years later one of the most advertised of American duels took place between Clay and John Randolph Roanoke—the West against the South. Nor did the duel die out during the lifetime of this generation.[7]

And Clay wrote to his former constituents in Kentucky, of dueling, "Its true corrective shall be found when all shall unite, as all ought to unite, in its unqualified proscription."[8]

The Burr-Hamilton encounter had taken place at the foot of Weehawken cliffs, beside the Hudson, in the sultry early morning of July 11, 1804. A monument to Hamilton was erected on the spot, but so prone to the heroics of the *duello* were brave young bloods afterwards that the memorial had to be removed, since it encouraged others to go and fight out some issue of honor where so distinguished a citizen had fallen. As *The Calumet* explained in 1831:

Instead of serving as a beacon to warn others away, it would be taken as an excuse or justification for engaging in the same mad conflict—in fact as a sort of lure to duelling.[9]

It was not law that replaced the duel, as stated by Professor William Macdougall:

The practice of duelling has declined only in proportion as men have been assured of redress for their injuries at the hands of the courts of justice.[10]

A common but a false conception! The questions over which duels were chiefly fought lay not in the realm of legal but of "non-justiciable" concerns, involving redress for insults of all degrees from those of serious political magnitude to the pettiest trivialities of the dance floor, the moonlit aisles of courtship, or the grogshop.

The real manner in which the duel passed away was by the

refusal of men in increasing numbers to sanction or engage in it, no matter what the provocation or how stern the challenge. Washington was challenged but contemptuously declined to participate in what the early peace movement used to classify as "private war." Again and again the daring ones who pooh-poohed the sacred claims of "honor" added more to their numbers, until at length an institution even so deeply rooted in centuries of custom was "outlawed" by a public opinion increasingly determined not to heed the call of the personal ordeal-by-combat.

Another early weakness of the Outlawry movement was its insufficient reliance on political action. It is not correct to criticize Outlawry, as numerous League advocates have done, for chronic isolationism; Outlawry, too, takes cognizance of the need for world organization. Nevertheless, throughout the Outlawry movement ran for a time a depreciation of the need for increasing international political union, and an unwarranted trust in juridical processes. Yet some of the gravest challenges to peace issue out of problems entirely political in character. Without a gradual lessening of the significance of artificial boundary lines, without a growth toward *bona fide* political federation, a world court however competent judicially, though a lighthouse to mark the shoals of international relations, will be a beacon built on stilts instead of solid rock.

In one additional respect the Outlawry program has been dangerously confused and weak. This weakness is the tolerance, as a rule not explicit, of defensive war. Uncritical partisans of Outlawry stoutly contend that this is not so, that the right of self-defense is inalienable and can never be taken away by law, and that the right of self-defense and defensive warfare are not at all the same thing. This is a subtle distinction which can exist in theory but never in practical affairs. The source of this distinction appears to be not the founders of the movement for Outlawry themselves, but no less a jurist than John Bassett Moore. Writing in *Unity* for September 4, 1924, Mr. Levinson declares:

In 1920 John Bassett Moore suggested to the writer a change in the wording of the Outlawry plan, saying: "When you once outlaw war do not use the word 'war' any more. Do not attempt to make a distinction between aggressive and defensive wars. The right of self-defense is inherent and must be preserved, but is not war."

Resorting to the antique analogy between individuals and nations—an analogy responsible for as much muddled thinking as any ever used in world relations—Dr. Moore goes on to say, according to Mr. Levinson:

Self-defense by an individual makes the defender neither a murderer nor a duellist.

What kind of defense has been contemplated by the proponents of Outlawry, who declare that defense is not "defensive" war? Do they propose non-violent resistance, non-cooperation, or any pacifist technique? What they mean is clearly indicated. In comments published together with the original plan, Mr. Levinson stated explicitly that "An international agreement based on the foregoing . . . would preserve the Monroe Doctrine, our tariff and revenue policies, our right to repel invasion. . . ." The plan, as quoted previously, provides for the reduction of national armaments *to the lowest point consistent with domestic safety,* and calls for the *abolition of professional soldiery and the substitution of a potential army.* When Mr. Coolidge toward the end of his term stated that there was no relation between the Pact of Paris and the plan to increase our cruisers, he was giving voice to Yankee cynicism, perhaps, but nevertheless he was not so far afield as some of those whose loyalty to the Outlawry movement has resulted in a self-hypnosis that blinds them to the existence of patent facts.

Dr. Morrison, for example, is forced to the acme of metaphysical subtlety, and asserts that the whole question of self-defense is irrelevant to Outlawry:

If the danger of omitting such clauses from the draft treaty and the resolution consists in the possibility that an ultra pacifist interpretation may be read into the outlawry proposal, the danger of including such clauses consists in the likelihood that some people will not really read what the words say. The words do not say that self-defense is approved; nor do they say that self-defense is condemned. The words say that self-defense is neither *involved in* nor *affected by* the outlawry of war. Outlawry absolutely has no point of contact with the question of the right of self-defense.[11]

In my opinion, it had better have! Suppose we are to outlaw war in general, but neither condemn nor approve it; it is a monstrously absurd undertaking. Then why the same impossible treatment of defensive war, which, in national practice, unless definitely named and definitely renounced, will be the concrete expression of the evasive "self-defense." If Outlawry cannot forthrightly renounce warfare as a means of defense, it has slender warrant for criticizing the League's tolerance of war against an "aggressor" nation.

In his message to Congress on December 4, 1929, President Hoover gave what must be accepted as an official view of our responsibility through the Treaty. "Under the Kellogg pact," he said, "we have undertaken never to use war as an instrument of national policy. We have, therefore, undertaken by covenant to use these equipments [i. e., our armaments] solely for defensive purposes."

Interestingly enough on the twelfth of December, 1927, Senator Borah reintroduced his resolution with the section allowing defensive war deleted. Officially, at least, one of the chief weaknesses of the project was thus corrected. But the correspondence regarding the Paris Pact has shown quite plainly where the nations stand. In any public discussion the great bulk of its backers may confidently be relied on earnestly to testify that the program is not pacifist and has no relevancy to pacifism.

It has, of course; unless pacifism be considered merely as an individual, purely personal witness against war, intended not as a war preventive but as surcease to one's soul or conscience. Such an interpretation of pacifism is unwarranted. Though some pacifists and conscientious objectors, it is true, have manifested just that kind of individualistic non-conformity, the great bulk of pacifists regard their movement as a challenge to the war system, directed squarely toward the purpose of mobilizing opposition to war—minority opposition to be sure, but by a minority sufficiently numerous and sturdy, so braced for propaganda and for punishment as to tie the itching hands of Mars.

Such a pacifism—which *is* pacifism to-day—is not only relevant to Outlawry, but at the heart of it. Squirm away as they will, all other movements to abolish war must reckon with it. Pacifism is no panacea; in fact, the pacifist movement is all but unique in recognizing the valid necessity for many complementary approaches to peace. By ignoring it, however, the other movements leave out the policy most central to any genuine abolition—instead of the mitigation, reduction or postponement—of armed conflict.

Regarded as a magnificent first step toward Outlawry the Paris Pact, if lived up to sincerely, would open the way for a peace program impossible before this to achieve. No document of such a character has ever been agreed on in all history. Considering the difficulties in the way, its signing is alone a splendid tribute to the real value of Outlawry, as well as to the energy and devotion of its proponents.

It will now be possible to set up a new code of international responsibility, to penetrate the folk-thinking of peoples with a new conception. So much hangs on the Pact that a clear appreciation of its nature is essential. What it does is apparent in the text (which will be found as Appendix III); it renounces war as an instrument of national policy, and it pledges settlement by pacific means of all disputes of whatever origin or nature.

Could these provisions be taken at face value, everything conceivable in the way of war renunciation would thereby be accomplished. Unfortunately, by a series of notes exchanged prior to the signing of the Pact, it was made clear that certain interpretations are held binding by such powers as France, England and the United States. While not technically reservations, these interpretations are tantamount to the same thing.

The Pact does not renounce all war, but only war "as an instrument of national policy." Exactly what these words mean nobody knows although they are generally understood to refer to unprovoked wars of conquest or aggression. "Defensive" wars allowed by Outlawry are permitted under the

Briand-Kellogg treaty. What has been stated earlier about "defensive" war points straight to the conclusion that the Pact renounces all wars except the wars we are most likely to have.

"War as an instrument of national policy" will be defined not in advance of a test but under the impact of concrete crises. That a final decision does not exist is clear from the efforts made by publicists to explain the term, especially in the writings of its coiner. In his book *War as an Instrument of National Policy and Its Renunciation in the Pact of Paris,* Professor Shotwell brings the matter back finally to the attempt to define an aggressor on the formula of refusal to arbitrate. Though this idea is basically far from adequate, it is at least more practicable than the idea of territorial defense implicit in Outlawry, which Professor Shotwell in an address before the Academy of Political Science thus handled:

The categories of defense extend beyond the action of the defense of an invaded soil. Especially since the airplane has come, this is absolutely clear to anyone who is familiar with the phenomena of war. The only adequate defense against the airplane, speaking realistically and as the wars of the future would be fought, is to attack the airplane before it leaves the ground. There is no adequate defense for an invaded city or land once the airplane with its heavy bombs is above the point of destination.

That is mere incident, however, for the whole treatment of defense must rest upon another distinction than the place where the war is fought. In parenthesis the claim of Britain to have fought anything like a defensive war in the last war is, of course, in point here, because it fought on the Plain of Flanders and in France. Not *where* a war is fought, but *how* or *under what conditions,* constitutes the category of defense which we shall have to detach from the commitment of this treaty.

But it can hardly be too strongly emphasized that the interpretation of "war as an instrument of national policy" finally rests with the great powers among the nations of the world. Only time will tell what governments mean to do about it. They have tried to tell what it is not; but they have been mute or vague regarding what it is.

Each nation signing the Pact is to decide for itself when it thinks another signatory has broken the Treaty, and although a joint punitive use of force is not authorized, each nation is free thereafter to take whatever action it desires, military or otherwise. Thus the Pact does not get down to the roots of international anarchy, but leaves the principle of "sovereignty" just about where it is. And sovereignty, the right of a nation to be a law unto itself when it feels such a course essential, is a primary contributor to war.

The Pact does not rescind the force provisions of existing treaties of military defense, treaties that reach across all continental Europe.

The adherence of the United States to the Pact can at any time be repealed by the treaty-making powers—President and Senate. The ratification of the Pact has done nothing appreciable to change the armament situation, anywhere in the world. War resisters, objecting to conscription, are nowhere handled better than before; as H. Runham Brown, Secretary of the War Resisters' International, recently stated, "Tell the peoples of every nation that the solemn renunciation of war through the Pact of Paris has made no difference in the treatment of those who take it seriously and who outlaw war by refusing to prepare for it." The United States still denies citizenship to radical pacifists.

Further, in certain large and important areas of the world the Treaty is held not to apply. Such is the case with places essential to Britain's imperialist strategy, as revealed by the British notes and declarations prior to signing the document. Similarly, our own interventions in Latin America escape denunciation because they are not deemed to be war. Charles Sumner, when upholding our own sovereignty sixty-five years ago, declared in ringing tones, "Armed intervention is war and nothing else." [12] But when it becomes our policy to intervene in the affairs of other states, we do not call it war and thereby expect for it immunity under a document banning wars "of whatever nature or of whatever origin they may be."

Chiefly in respect to its failure to authorize punitive war, the Pact is a great advance over the League's mechanics. It will have an increasing influence on the development of the League in this particular.

From the very inception of the Outlawry movement it came

into sharp conflict with the basic assumption of the League of Nations, and in my judgment rightly so. The contrast has not been so much as one hundred per cent in favor, however, of the Outlawry proposal. Born in days when the League's worst features were so painfully obvious as to obscure what good was in it; fathered politically by leaders unfree from the taint of habitual isolationism, Outlawry's reaction against the League process was extremely sharp. Time has wrought changes on both sides and a new note of better mutual comprehension has crept into League and Outlawry circles, and in both groups a note of greater realism.

Clear has it become that unless the League is soon plunged by a war into the limbo of unpleasant memories, it is not going to abdicate, even to suit so potent a gentleman as Uncle Samuel. That the League should deliberately bore a hole in its own hull seems a preposterous notion. The chances are that for the twentieth century, at any rate, it is this League or none.

Looking backward upon the age-long effort to accomplish any kind of semi-comprehensive world *rapprochement,* realizing the immensity of the task, what sane person can hope for the break-up of the League in war? Or even for its gradual ossification? There is no such thing as innocuous desuetude; in any realm of life desuetude is not innocuous but rather filled with potencies of danger. The small nations which suffer under mandated exploitation and groan beneath the imperialism of the great powers cling desperately to the League machinery. Economic radicals, however far to the Left, are encountered by the presence of Russia as an observer in League affairs, using the very process of League discussion for publicity regarding her strictures on the League's controlling policies. Better by far that the League, modified by danger as its good points are, be subjected to attempts at drastic modification before it is given up. So long as it exists, for better or for worse, no fresh effort at comprehensive international organization is conceivable.

Some such considerations as these, perhaps, induced Mr. Borah to publish in the *New York Times* of February 5, 1928, a discussion of the Briand-Kellogg negotiations in the course of which he said, not that under no circumstances would the United States enter the League, but that (italics mine)

the United States now stands ready to coöperate and *identify itself with* a system based upon pledges not to wage war.

"It seems to me," declared the Senator also, "as Lord Thompson has said, 'If war were outlawed, the League would be far more firmly founded than it is to-day.' " This comment signified a turning point. A new coöperation with the affairs of the League is increasingly evident on the part of outlawrists; and on the other hand the European diplomats have ceased to sneer at Outlawry. There is no basic conflict between the two which should prevent a developing service to each other.

On the part of American outlawrists, any realistic program toward the League would doubtless include an effort for the inclusion of defensive war in the war to be outlawed (by dropping the "war" clause in the Preamble) and an express willingness to join the League provided specific changes are made in the Covenant and Court looking toward the final consummation of Outlawry. On the part of the League a start toward a really vital peace instrument would be continued by abandonment of the war sanctions; by completing the force of the Optional Clause in the Court, a step toward which tremendous gains have been made; by the recodification of international law on the basis of outlawed war; and, particularly, to avoid the perpetual schism in which so much war danger still lurks, the admission of Soviet Russia (a signer of the Pact) into the League, the only test of that country's fitness being a desire to enter.

Are such developments as these impossible, incredible, fantastic this side of the millennium? To many they will seem just that. And yet it is scarcely unrealistic to suggest action that may not be taken; it is unrealistic to seek the goal of peace through means that are less than adequate.

Both the concept of Outlawry and the concept of world organization are valid and essential. Neither can stand still. Together they must go forward, adjusting themselves to new world needs.

CHAPTER XI

ARGUMENTS OF THE FIGHT FOR PEACE

In hilly New England the settlers discovered that the best way to build a barn is to set the foundation in a hillside, keep the animals in the basement and drive the wagons from the uphill side into the second floor on the level. When their descendants emigrated to the flat prairies of Illinois, they continued to build barns in the only way they knew. Having no hillsides they built the barn first, built a plank hillside running up into the barn and then got stalled trying to haul loads of hay up this hill! . . .

In an early day in the level West the practice struck root of laying out roads on the section lines. Later the gridiron plan was adhered to even in rough country where it would have been more economical to lay out the roads according to the contour, so that they would follow the water courses or the water partings. Today millions of loads are needlessly hauled over hill after hill on their way to market and thousands of hillside roads are washed away every season because men blindly follow precedent.—EDWARD A. Ross, in *The American Journal of Sociology*, March, 1920.

CHAPTER XI

ARGUMENTS OF THE FIGHT FOR PEACE

THE traditionalism of military minds is axiomatic. That other minds run the same human danger becomes clear as we examine the historic ideology of the peace movement. Along with the major approaches to a warless world a set of typical arguments have been adduced over and over again to win the support of public opinion.

Like a squirrel in his wheel the peace movement for more than a century has run over the same pleas again and again; and like the squirrel it gets nowhere by that route. Not that these ancient arguments are unsound; merely that they are side issues, nothing but skirmishes in the real fight for peace.

There may be profit in examining them, one by one. They have a contribution to make to the ultimate victory; but a view of them in perspective will serve to fix their true relationship to the whole peace struggle.

War's Cost in Life and Treasure

Very much as a man who, fighting drunk, has run amok and slaughtered madly becomes appalled when sober at the swath he has scythed through his innocent victims, so a war-mad world when its spree is over settles down in horror to count the cost.

Said a conservative pro-war newspaper, five years after the World War was over:

Let us visualize a march of the British dead down Fifth Avenue. At daybreak they start, twenty abreast. Until sundown they march . . . and the next day and the next. For ten days the British dead pass in review. For eleven days more the French dead file down the "Avenue of the Allies." For the Russians it would require the daylight of five more weeks. Two months and a half would be required for the Allied dead to pass a given point. The enemy dead would require more than six weeks. For four months men actually killed in the war, passing steadily, twenty abreast. . . .[1]

A gruesome motion picture? But that is only one part of the cost of war. Though on a smaller scale, of course—mankind being less skilled and civilized in days gone by!—it has always stricken post-war populations.

One of the early issues of *The Friend of Peace* sought to convey a graphic estimate of the cost in lives of Napoleon's famed campaign against the Russians:

From the time the French crossed the Niemen in June, to the time the survivors recrossed it in December, was 173 days. Admitting the whole number that perished to be 500,000, the average *daily* sacrifice was 2,890; which amounts to 20,230 per week and more than 80,000 per month. It was equal to 120 every hour, or *two* every minute during the 173 days. That we may have a more impressive view of this dreadful waste of human life, let the numbers before us be compared with the census of the United States in 1810. The average *daily sacrifice* exceeds the whole population of Londonderry in N. H., or Haverhill in Mass., or Windsor in Conn., or Windsor in Vermont.

Dr. McMurdy, of the Arbitration League, was quoting figures he had picked up about 1883, which purported to show that war destroyed annually, on an average (the date when these figures began is not given!) 2,333,333 human beings, or 194,444 per month, 6181 per day, or 270 per hour.

But war destroys, too, man's hard-gained goods in money and material possessions. As far back as 1783 Benjamin Franklin put a pious exclamation point—now that the war was over—to his letter addressed to Joseph Banks:

What vast additions to the conveniences of life might mankind have acquired, if the money spent in wars had been employed in works of public utility![2]

Thirty-five years later Samuel Whelpley took a flyer in "statistics" and lamented the disproportionate expenditures for military purposes:

If the contributions levied on nations for the support of war, or but half the sum, were skillfully disposed of for the aid of the indigent and poor, we would have no poor.[3]

A little better grounded in the use of figures were the writers of the Second Annual Report of the Massachusetts Peace Society, which pointed out that

the annual expense of war to the United States would furnish 108,273,092 copies of quarterly pamphlets, besides extra publications; nearly enough for every family in the world; and the expense of war to Great Britain would supply the same to more than four times the families on the globe. Now we venture to express the belief that such a dispersion of pacific tracts (if practicable) would be found ultimately a more efficacious and permanent security against war, than all the fleets and armies on which nations rely for their safety.

These figures were based on the years during the War of 1812. Taking the year 1815 as a basis for the purchasing power of the money used for war in that twelvemonth compared with its power for the promotion of education, the Society's Committee arrived at the following conclusion (basing education costs on the once-famous and advanced Lancasterian system):

It is reputed that not more than 16 millions can come of age to be educated annually in the world; if, therefore, we allow four years' education to each, 64 millions would constantly require education; consequently three-fifths of the annual war expense to the U. S.; or one-eighth the expense to Great Britain; or one-sixth the expense to France would educate all the children in the world on the Lancasterian plan, at the expense in England.

This by Worcester and his colleagues. Ladd and his fellow-officials of the American Peace Society published a detailed study based on the total expenses of our national government for the year 1833 which, itemized, stood as follows:

For the Civil List	$ 2,717,368
For the Navy	3,926,209
For Pensions	1,555,543
For Internal Improvements	1,282,586
For the Military	3,734,666
For Fortifications	653,000
For the Indians, for land, etc.	1,251,722

Miscellaneous items to make the total...... $16,657,669

Of this expense nearly one-half is for war, and if we include the pensions which are paid to soldiers, more than half must be put down to war. Less than one dollar out of sixteen to improve the country, and produce the positive good for which government should be established. Population of the United States in 1830 was 12,856,407. Of these 2,010,436 were slaves.[4]

I hasten to evidence the normal responsiveness to traditional opportunities by contrasting these figures with a recent report of the Secretary of the Treasury, which indicates that in this age of further enlightenment the cost of war—"past, present and future"—amounts to eighty-two cents out of every dollar of federal disbursement.[5]

Not to stretch out details with too much repetition, it is only necessary to state that through succeeding years the peace movement hammered away manfully at the war-cost argument for peace. They used day in and day out for many years Longfellow's verses, written after he and Charles Sumner had gone through the arsenal at Springfield:

Were half the power that fills the world with terror,
Were half the wealth bestowed on camps and courts
Given to redeem the human mind from error,
There were no need of arsenals or forts.

They were provided with material in 1917 through the assertion by a strong advocate of industrial preparedness, when we had not yet entered the War, that

Three days of the war would build the Panama Canal.
Eight days of the war would rebuild Boston.
The wages of all the workmen in the United States for ten months would run the war but two weeks.

All the money in the savings banks would carry the war only one month.

The cost of the public schools in 1913 would carry the war less than one week.

The cost has exceeded the expenses of the United States for its 128 years as a nation.[*]

Yet what of that? Speedily we were embroiled and the costs sent sharply skyward.

And nearly a decade after the War had ended, a great drive was on for a huge naval expansion in this country. It was opposed by valiant wielders of figures who massed them—not without effect, since this was peace time—in irresistible phalanx:

The Commissioner of Education reports that there are scattered over the United States several hundred colleges and universities supported by endowment. Of these institutions, several hundred in number, only nine have total endowments exceeding $20,000,000. Every cruiser we build represents, therefore, a greater sum than any endowed college or university in the land possesses, with nine exceptions, of which six are in the East. Moreover, the cruisers wear out or become obsolete and must be shortly replaced at equal or greater expense; but a $20,000,000 university does not die; it becomes ever increasingly effective as the years roll on.[7]

A telling argument, even should there be at its very end a possible *non sequitur!*

Telling, but old. And never so telling, despite its logical force, but what our country has gone to war in every generation.

War and Crime Waves

Not yet have we ceased to hear the reverberations from the guns of post-War bandits. There is one factor in the crime wave following the World War, according to a peace worker who speaks like many,

that is easily recognizable and can be eliminated if people are sufficiently desirous of eliminating it. That factor is war.[*]

A Canadian educator declares:

Since the war the Anglo-Saxon race has been overcome with a plague of vulgarity.[9]

Not only the Anglo-Saxons, it appears; for Francesco Nitti, former premier of Italy, also saw the War's moral damage:

The losses in human life and property in the last war, great as they are, are small evils compared to the undermining of morals and the lowering of standards of culture and civilization.[10]

'Twas ever thus. Witness that pair of innovators, David Dodge and Noah Worcester. Said Dodge:

The state of morals, so much depressed by the American Revolution, was only raised by the blessed effusions of God's holy spirit.[11]

And not, at that, till Worcester, speaking as a veteran, had stated:

Let anyone who was old enough to observe the state of morals prior to our Revolution, ask himself, what was the effect of that war on the morals of New England?[12]

What a disturber of D.A.R. traditions is this man! Yet he spoke out of first-hand knowledge:

The depravity, occasioned by war, is not confined to the army. Every species of vice gains ground in a nation during a war. And when a war is brought to a close, seldom, perhaps, does a community return to its former standard of morals.

Does not this sound familiar? Said *The Friend of Peace* in 1816:

It is not to be doubted, that after the war was over a greater number of criminals were condemned at the Old Bailey [London] in two years, than had been in the same length of time during the war.

The Recorder, in that same year, reported a natural-sounding item:

The New-York State prison is overflowing with convicts. The present number is 722, although the prison was calculated for 500.

Noah Worcester could not pass this by. He elaborates—in

thoroughly modern manner—on the implications of such a state of affairs.

The complaint of an increase of crimes, and of convicts, is not confined to New York; it is so general in our country, that it is time to investigate the causes, and, if possible, to apply some remedy.

The natural increase of population may, perhaps, account for some portion of the evil. The influx of foreigners who had been inured to crime during the wars of Europe may account for a still greater portion. But may we stop here? No, verily. What other cause, then, may be assigned? The enormous increase of convicts, complained of, has principally occurred within four years. Now let it be observed that within *five* years, our country has expended one hundred, perhaps one hundred and fifty millions of dollars, in supporting "a school of vice." Is it not probable that this expense, considering the opportunity which the scholars had to learn, would produce some effects? Can such a number of scholars, as were educated in the business of pillage and piracy, robbery and murder under the sanction of public authority, be let loose upon the community without some display of the proficiency they had made?

Once more not to bring in too much detail, it may suffice to say that through the next fourscore years "the old refrain" was sung in the solemn protests of peace spokesmen. In 1903 the Reverend James M. Buckley, one of our leading clergymen, wrote in *The Century Magazine* on "The Present Epidemic of Crime," and after tracing it to the recent war, he went still further back and said:

Among the influences which have powerfully affected the primary causes of crime, and are sources of this present epidemic, is the effect of the Civil War. . . . The evil done by that war to public and private morality was almost irremediable. Its effects were seen upon Congress, upon politics, upon reconstruction, upon business, upon society, and upon the habits of the people.

The proceedings of the Lake Mohonk Conference for 1907 contain a detailed and documented study of war in its contributory relationship to crime, covering many wars of Europe.

Even in the pastimes of the masses war's effect seemed clear.

There are recurrent post-war protests over cock-fighting; but over prize fights far more tears were shed.

A few years away from the War of 1812—a time when prize fights were not far removed from the character of Roman gladiatorial combats—*The Friend of Peace* had said,

Boxing has, we presume, been so far abolished in England, as well as in this country, that it is now confined to the lowest and most worthless class of society.[18]

Worcester died sublimely unaware of what was about to happen. With the Mexican War the "fistic art" began to revive in this country; but in England, following the Crimean War that gave the world's peace group a Florence Nightingale to solace them, British prize fighting emerged from the back rooms of "pubs" and illicit cellars, and took to the open with members of Parliament and even of the Cabinet in attendance. Here was a return to the golden days of slugging not seen since the Prince of Wales served as second to Lord Buckingham in a bare-fist grudge encounter of 1790.

Quite naturally, loud cries rose to heaven. When Tom Sayers of England fought Heenan, the heavier American bruiser, to a draw after many blue-blooded Britons had watched the gory fray for two hours and twenty minutes, the London Peace Society (and, following their lead, by reprints, the American Peace Society) spoke to a certain special audience:

It may, perhaps, serve to awaken salutary reflection in the minds of some of our religious teachers in pulpit and press, who have been stimulating the war spirit and glorifying "muscular Christianity," as to whereunto this thing may grow, when they see the worship of brute force which they have helped to promote, culminating in triumphal ovations given to the champions of the prize ring, such as are rarely accorded either to genius, or virtue, or piety; while these brutal displays themselves, though in flagrant and acknowledged violation of law, are made subjects of formal and elaborate eulogy by Ministers of State in the British Parliament, on grounds and for reasons which would equally justify admiration for pirates and highwaymen; nay, for the very lowest order of brute beasts, who often display in still higher perfection the same qualities for which these pugilistic heroes have won for themselves such distinguished patronage and panegyric.

Once again, a rising tide of protests whittled down the zest of the prize-fight-following gentry. By 1896 one of the American Peace Society's leaders was saying:

Pugilism is now regarded as degrading and hideous, and is left to the taste of the coarsest and most vulgar of men.[14]

But now the times again have changed. Boxing with six-ounce gloves is ladylike in comparison with the good old days when almost anything was allowed. Our present-day heavy hitters earn more in one fight than a college president can accumulate and spend in a lifetime; they cater to "the best people," and receive the ultimate pronunciamentos of eternal fitness by representation in the sports bay of the Cathedral of St. John the Divine.

Let those who will, seek to speed up the swinging pendulum. The fact remains that all the complaints about war and its fruitage of crime, brutality, false values and low standards rolled up in one great heap to hamper Mars, he crushes beneath his iron feet each time he goes upon the rampage, like so many fallen, dried-up leaves of autumn.

"It's the Newspapers!"

Janus, that two-faced Roman deity, threw open the doors of his temple in times of war and kept them closed in peace. Here is an appropriate symbol for the technique of misinformation without which wars would be less easy to get started. The outward face is propaganda; the face not seen from in front is censorship.

All this, we usually are persuaded, is an invention of the modern military mind. Certainly in the World War the industry of warping public opinion reached its quantitative acme. All the nations used it extensively, though in none was it so elaborately organized as in England and the United States. Germany's propaganda in this country was stupid rather than crafty, never clever enough to seem very plausible, and never sufficiently widespread to wield much influence. France's intensive propaganda drive of the later war years is typified by the following excerpt from André Tardieu's *The Truth About the Treaty.*

How often Americans have expressed to me the hope that France would be content with an independent and neutral Alsace-Lorraine! How many expressed surprise when, to the statement of our rights, I added that their obvious justice made a plebiscite useless and unacceptable.

A few months later this state of opinion was entirely changed. I venture to believe that the activities of my co-workers and myself, the fifteen thousand lectures in English where young officers, with all the authority of their war record and their wounds, presented the pitiful situation of the captured provinces, had something to do with this transformation. . . .

Thousands of huge posters reproducing Henner's "Alsacienne," with the text of the Bordeaux protest . . . had carried the meaning and scope of our claim to every state in the Union. Support came from all sides. The battle was won.

How Crewe House worked in the United States is vividly shown by Sir Gilbert Parker, in charge of the British "information factory":

I need hardly say that the scope of my department was very extensive and its activities widely ranged. Among the activities was a weekly report to the British cabinet on the state of American opinion and the constant touch with the permanent correspondents of American newspapers in England. I also frequently arranged for important public men in England to act for us by interviews in American newspapers. . . .

Among other things we supplied 360 newspapers in the smaller states of the United States with an English newspaper which gives a weekly review and comment on the affairs of the war. We established connection with the man in the street through cinema pictures of the army and navy, as well as through interviews, articles, pamphlets, etc., and by letters in reply to individual American critics, which were printed in the chief newspaper of the State in which they lived and were copied in newspapers of other and neighboring states.

We advised and stimulated many people to write articles; we utilized the friendly services and assistance of confidential friends; we had reports from important Americans constantly, and established association, by personal correspondence, with influential and eminent people of every profession in the United States beginning with university and college presidents, professors and scientific men, and running through all the ranges of the population.

We asked our friends and correspondents to arrange for speeches, debates, and lectures by American citizens, but we did not encourage Britishers to go to America and preach the doctrine of entrance into the war. Besides an enormous private correspondence with individuals, we had our documents and literature sent to great numbers of public libraries, Y.M.C.A. societies, universities, colleges, historical societies, clubs, and newspapers.

It is hardly necessary to say that the work was one of extreme difficulty and delicacy.[15]

On our own part, the government organized a Committee on Public Information with George Creel as chairman. According to a record proudly published by Mr. Creel, the Committee utilized "the printed word, the spoken word, the motion picture, the telegraph, the cable, the wireless, the poster, the signboard." [16] One hundred and fifty thousand men and women devoted themselves to specialized activities. Thirty booklets, characterized to hindsight as composed of half truths and "lies by silence," were prepared by prominent historians; of these, 75,000,000 copies were used in the United States and many millions abroad. A corps of 75,000 speakers operating in 5200 communities delivered 755,190 speeches as Four Minute Men. Says a critic:

Translators, advertisers, artists, publicists, movie actors and producers were called in to help. Libraries and reading rooms were flooded with pamphlets and books; movie plots included "Huns" that looked not half as civilized as the Neanderthal man, "Huns" who never saw a church but they set fire to it, who cut the hands off every child they met. "Actual war pictures" were produced immediately outside New York City. Pulpits and lecture platforms were filled by hysterical men and women, victims of this poisonous propaganda, who were "doing their bit" to spread more hatred. All this is called a "record of stainless patriotism and unspotted Americanism." [17]

Too much blame should never be leveled at any body of individuals for war propaganda; they only served a cause, as loyally as they could, in the true spirit of warfare. As Arthur Ponsonby says forcefully, "In war-time, failure to lie is negligence, the doubting of a lie is a misdemeanor, the declaration of the truth a crime." [18]

Meanwhile, in charge of the military censorship section of

the Military Intelligence Division, was Rupert Hughes, author of a life of the First President written to correct the generally false perspective on Washington. Ten years later Mr. Hughes had the frankness to admit a lot:

I could secure the suppression of any newspaper, book, photograph, news item or speech by putting certain machinery in motion. I did my best to prevent anybody from saying a good word for the Germans or a bad word for any of our Allies. I was particularly eager that nobody should say a word against war in general, and that war in particular.[19]

There was ample justification for the statement of a plain-speaking war-made pacifist:

We cannot successfully carry on a modern war if we tell the truth, the whole truth and nothing but the truth. But if we can make ourselves think that the enemy are "boche," "swine," "Huns," "devils," and "baby-killers," we can believe that we are rendering God service by ridding the world of such demons.[20]

Yet all such customs are not modern. Said the *Solemn Review* in 1814:

If anything be done by the army of one nation, which is deemed by the other as contrary to the modern usages in war, how soon do we hear the exclamations of *Goths and Vandals!* Yet, what are Christians at war, better than those barbarous tribes? and what is the war spirit in them, better than the spirit of Goths and Vandals? When the war spirit is excited, it is not always to be circumscribed in its operations, by the refinements of civilization.

David Low Dodge had also complained about the press:

Newspapers must be ushered forth with flaming pieces to rouse, as it is called, the spirit of the countries, so as to impress upon the populace the idea that the approaching war is just and necessary, for all wars must be just and necessary on both sides.[21]

Jonathan Dymond asked a common rhetorical question:

When a war is in contemplation, or when it has begun, what are the endeavors of its promoters? They animate us by every artifice of excitement to hatred and animosity. Pamphlets, Placards, Newspapers, Caricatures—every agent is in requisition to irritate us into malignity. Nay, dreadful as it is, the pulpit resounds with declamations to stimulate our too sluggish resentment, and invite us to slaughter."

Noah Worcester appealed directly to the peace societies that he visioned, before they had been born:

Should peace societies be formed, several points will demand their attention.

In the first place, it will behove them to investigate some mode for effecting a reformation in the manner of conducting news-papers—some mode which shall make it for the interest of editors to exclude from their papers every thing of a vindictive and in-flammatory character; and to give the preference to such things, as are of a pacific, friendly, and uniting tendency.

His admonition has been heeded by the peace societies, and heeded ever since. Short of censorship for peace, in which no-body believes, they have not yet found a better solution than to present the facts in their always struggling journals.

Positively it may be asserted that all their labors to counter-act war propaganda have not diminished it, when a crisis comes, one least iota. As long as we have war at all, the necessity for war lies will be paramount; and until we throttle war, we may expect to see the prostitution of truth continue to thrive, bold and unashamed.

The Plea of Personages

If there is anything conducive to sardonic merriment among the gods who preside over political circles, it must be the spec-tacle of anti-war workers seizing upon each reed of pacific sentiment that springs up in the fields of fame and nailing to it the flag of peace.

Every four years thousands of peace workers go out and vote for a presidential candidate whose faith in peace methods to obtain world peace is about as deep as the skin on a cannon ball. Only on rare occasions they have found their confidence not betrayed.

Always, however, the peace movement has sought the en-dorsement of the mighty. The pacific utterances of the presi-dent in office at a given time have been grasped at and used to win converts to the peace cause; the converts, however, promptly following their national leader whenever he went in a non-pacific direction.

So far has this custom spread that one of our livest peace organizations in 1926 was circulating petitions asking our delegates to a preparatory disarmament conference to place "universal abolition of conscription and complete world disarmament" on the agenda—a most excellent move; but stating beforehand at the top of the petition, "Believing with President Coolidge that 'No nation ever had an army large enough to guarantee it against attack.' " ²² Of course President Coolidge did not believe in universal abolition of conscription or complete world disarmament, if indeed he believed seriously in any disarmament at all. Probably, also, signers in general, persuaded by the prestige of the Presidential lead-off, would vanish from the support of peace projects the very moment the President decided to propose a naval increase—as he later did!

One of the first ambitions of the Massachusetts Peace Society was to gain the endorsement of the President and others politically influential. With Madison, then President, they made little direct headway. No. I of *The Friend* purported to be "A Special Interview between the President of the United States and Omar, an Officer Dismissed for Duelling," and it was tantamount to an "open letter." Followed "Six Letters to the President."

The energetic Worcester addressed himself, with more returns to show for it, to the two living Ex-Presidents, Thomas Jefferson and John Adams. Adams replied on the sixth of February, 1816, to a letter inviting his support:

I have also read, almost all the days of my life, the solemn reasonings, and pathetic declamations of Erasmus, of Fénelon, of St. Pierre, and many others against war, and in favor of peace. My understanding and my heart accorded with them, at first blush. But alas! a longer and more extensive experience has convinced me, that wars are as necessary, and as inevitable, in our system, as Hurricanes, Earthquakes, and Volcanoes.

Our beloved country, Sir, is surrounded by enemies of the most dangerous, because the most powerful and unprincipled character.

Collisions of national interest, of commercial and manufacturing rivalries are multiplying around us. Instead of discouraging a martial spirit, in my opinion it ought to be excited. We have not enough of it to defend us by sea or land. Universal and perpetual peace, appears to me, no more nor less than everlasting passive obedience and non resistance. The human flock would soon be fleeced and butchered by one or a few. I cannot therefore, Sir, be a subscriber or a member of your society.

Without pausing to wonder who, exactly, would butcher the human flock, since Wells' invading Martians were not then invented, it may be remarked that at first the hopeful Worcester fared but little better with the sage of Monticello. Kind, but discreet, the elderly solon of democracy replied:

Age, and its effects both on body and mind, has weaned my attention from public subjects, and left me unequal to the labors of correspondence beyond the limits of my personal concerns. I retire therefore from the question with a sincere wish, that your writings may have effect in lessening this greatest of human evils, and that you may retain life and health to enjoy the contemplation of this happy spectacle; and pray you to be assured of my great respect.

After so courteous a response, however, the peace promoter persistently sent to Jefferson his pamphlets as he got them out, and it was not long before announcement was made in *The Friend of Peace* that Jefferson had consented to be listed as an Honorary Member of the Massachusetts Peace Society.

From the second annual report of the Massachusetts Peace Society, December 25, 1817, we find that

It has been particularly the aim of the Executive Committee to excite the attention of men of intelligence and respectability, whose opinions and exertions would have influence on others. In this attempt they have been successful.

The word "respectable" had a more literal connotation than it does to-day. Even so, the efforts of the peace movement from that time to this to enlist the support of famous personages have indeed been strenuous. If an early peace society could not report a list of members impressive from mere numbers, the next best thing was to assure a skeptical world that all in the peace movement was well, by noting the "respectable gentlemen" who had dignified the cause by their adherence. They have not been content to let the cause win through on its merits, nor have they seen how superior were their own leaders, often, to the more eminent but also more compromising dignitaries to whose stars of destiny they had hitched their frail little go-carts.

Even as recently as 1917, the Yearbook of the Carnegie Endowment for International Peace, blazing with a red heading, "Peace Through Victory," gave as one reason for reprinting the address of William Jay on stipulated arbitration, the

importance to show that believers in international peace are not recruited only from the emotional class [sic] and that they have what seems to be indispensable in a democracy, a respectable ancestry.

A nationally known leader of the peace movement went so far as to say:

The talk of vox populi is often more of delusion than a reality. Let us make enough of the preachers, teachers, editors, and particularly statesmen to see the reasonableness and inevitableness of the new order, and it can be at once established and the great changes made.**

Long before, Lord Acton, hardly accusable of "sour grapes," had wittily remarked to Bishop Creighton that "Nearly all great men are bad men. Power is poison. . . . Imagine a class of such celebrities as More, Bacon, Grotius, Pascal, Cromwell, Bossuet, Montesquieu, Jefferson, Napoleon, Pitt. The result would be an encyclopedia of error."

Be that as it may, the peace movement has always been a greater respecter of persons than the devout could find authority for in Scripture or the non-religious in the experience of everyday observation.

The serious defect of this technique in obtaining popular influence is twofold.

It induces not a thoughtful understanding, but a merely imitative following—just the kind the peace movement can rely on least in peace or war. And it teaches people who are already warmly interested in peace to follow open-mindedly not the leadership of the peace groups, but instead the leadership of those who as a rule are loyal to peace only when the skies are fair. The peace movement ought not to put its trust in princes.

It matters little in the long run—and the winning of peace is certain to be no overnight affair—whether a few or a great many more people are persuaded to a temporary allegiance. It matters incalculably whether there is being built up a body of informed, intelligent, and, above all, independent public opinion free from mob-mindedness either for peace or war, but which can be counted on to the crack of doom because it has thought its way through, even though it has not yet worked its way through, the barriers which lie across the path to peace.

The Appeal to Horror

Looking back at the uproar created by the introduction of each new destructive weapon, one can almost fancy the conclaves of tree dwellers or cave men, shaking shaggy heads over the novelty and unfairness of stone-headed spears in contrast to the comparatively humane clubs hitherto employed in the chase and in clan combat. Well, they probably decided, fighting would soon have to cease now such murderous weapons were invented.

The Gauls no doubt felt something like this when they ruminated on the future of Cæsar's wall-scaling enginery. There were many who felt that powder and ball had signalized the coming end of war. Buckle, in his *History of Civilization in England* (1857), prophesied that the intellect of man would revolt against war and overthrow it, in view of the increasing potency of gunpowder, and the development of political economy and easy locomotion. Victor Hugo expressed the belief that mechanical inventions and scientific research, in their application to the manufacture of war instruments, were reaching a state of perfection where, in a short time, the destruction of life in war would be so terrible that sheer necessity would compel people to abolish warfare. The same prophecy was made with the coming of iron ships. Jan Bliokh, the Polish writer, toward the close of the last century asserted that men could no longer stand the horror of modern war and war, therefore, was doomed. When submarines came in, the cry was lifted up again, and yet again with the arrival of the airplane. It has been raised—though briefly!—regarding poison gas. Even such a man as Dr. Antonio de Bustamente, member of the World Court, was led into the same old cliché. When interviewed after the Pan-American Conference of 1928 he said:

War itself, and science, are doing more to end war than any human agency or diplomatic agency. It is becoming so horrible that people revolt at it.[25]

The *New York Times,* in the tones of a discoverer, editorialized a few months later in like vein:

The conviction grows that the more horrible war can be made to appear, the brighter is the promise that mankind will cease to settle disputes by appeal to arms.

When our delegation went to the first Hague Conference of 1899, they bore instructions not to support any limitation on warlike inventions, on the following ground:

It is doubtful if wars are to be diminished by rendering them less destructive, for it is the plain lesson of history that the periods of peace have been longer protracted as the cost and destructiveness of war have increased.[26]

Mankind ought to have recoiled from war in horror long ago; and yet it has not done so. Even when menaced by overwhelming force and terrible superiority in weapons men seem to have fought, if anything, more readily and bravely.

This is one lesson militarists have never had the wit to learn. Terrorize a foe, has been their view, and he will never dare withstand you. Ruthless destruction has often been considered the most merciful way to get peace—peace the way the ruthless wanted it. Our own General Sheridan, while being fêted in Berlin during the Franco-Prussian War, and when the question was raised whether the French peasants in Bazeilles had been too harshly treated—as some of the German staff thought they had—counseled stern measures to Bismarck. The recorder says :

. . .Abeken considered that Bazeilles was hardly treated, and thought the war ought to be conducted in a more humane manner. Sheridan, to whom MacLean has translated these remarks, is of a different opinion. He considers that in war it is expedient, even from the political point of view, to treat the population with the utmost rigour also. He expressed himself roughly as follows : "The proper strategy consists in the first place in inflicting as telling blows as possible upon the enemy's army, and then in causing the inhabitants so much suffering that they must long for peace, and force their Government to demand it. The people must be left nothing but their eyes to weep with over the war." Somewhat heartless, it seems to me, but perhaps, worthy of consideration.¹⁷

In the courage of people under the rigors of invasion, siege, and all-around devastation militarists never exhibit trust, though they of all people ought to have a higher estimate of human fortitude. *Shrecklichkeit* usually induces resistance rather than surrender. Fear does not end conflict but renders its prolongation all but inevitable.

And that is why it impresses one as strange that the peace movement has so steadily inculcated war-horror through its speeches and printed matter. Many of the earlier peace periodicals, especially, rivaled the worst exhibits of Mme. Tussaud's wax works or the Eden Musée. Rapine, pillage, burning, slaughter, torture—all the horrible aspects of war were thrust home like the red point of a hot poker. As early as 1813, Jacob Catlin wrote on *The Horrors of War*.

Passing years brought no let-up. At the close of the last century two pamphlets sold widely by the peace societies were "A Battle, As It Appeared to An Eye-witness," and "War As It Is." To-day peace periodicals follow the old method, though they are more dignified than their forerunners and less like our daily "tabloids."

Cauterization may be necessary for the wounds of war ; those who do not do the fighting ought to know what war is like lest they move toward it too easily. But the steady recital of war's cruelty as used in articles appearing by the hundreds since 1816, or the spine-shivering accounts of "the next war" so often indulged in by writers and speakers in the peace societies, are likely to assume in their minds the character less of a mere description than of a rehearsal.

The fact is obvious, I contend, that men are not as a rule cowardly; that they will not be deterred from war by the terrors of it so long as they deem it right and necessary.

It would be to dwell in a fool's paradise not to hammer home the *danger* of war and its effect on the future of the race. But to dwell on its horrors as a deterrent is unsound psychologically. And even to point out the danger of war unaccompanying such warnings with a definite hope of war's abolition and a program on which, however far-reaching, people may begin to act at once, is merely to defeat the high ends that peace makers have in view.

All the alarms of impending eruptions do not serve to keep people from building their homes under the shoulders of volcanic mountains. Even the threat of hell fire has served morality but poorly.

You can frighten people into war, but you can't scare them out of it. The effect, especially in a rather effete civilization, is not entirely unlike that achieved by a window made opaque except for one round transparent hole, labeled "Don't look in here." You know, of course, what happens.

Anticipating Norman Angell

"What *The Great Illusion* did," says its justly famous author, "was to show why in numberless relations in the modern world, particularly in international relationships, physical preponderance, military victory, coercion, cannot give those results in political security and economic advantage, which men had always heretofore assumed as a matter of course." [28]

Essentially a sound proposal, it is not as new as people usually think. In 1816 the Reverend Thomas Chalmers of England called for just such a work as Mr. Angell obligingly produced some ninety-four years later. Said he, in laying out tasks to which lovers of peace might turn their hands:

Let another pour the light of modern [sic] speculation into the mysteries of trade, and prove, that not a single war has been undertaken for any of its objects, where the millions and the millions more, which were lavished on the cause, have not all been cheated away from us by the phantom of an imaginary interest.

As far back as 1788 Benjamin Franklin had written to Johannes Ingenhousz, the Dutch physician:

I grieve at the wars Europe is engaged in, and wish they were ended; for I fear even the victors will be losers.

Before this—in 1763—an English tract by Josiah Tucker was circulated in this country, *The Case of Going to War for the Sake of Procuring, Enlarging, or Securing of Trade, considered in a New Light.* "Conquer the whole world," said Bentham in his *Principles of International Law*, "it is impossible you should increase your trade one halfpenny:—it is impossible you should do otherwise than diminish it."

Samuel Whelpley in 1818 ventured to inquire, "Does joy return to the nation whose army is victorious?" In 1832 the peace journals were reprinting Franklin's letter to his sister, written from Philadelphia, September 20, 1783, after a hard day's work in the constitutional convention, in which he said:

I agree with you perfectly in your Disapprobation of War. Abstracted from the Inhumanity of it, I think it wrong in Point of Human Providence, for whatever Advantages one Nation would obtain from another, whether it be Part of their Territory, the Liberty of Commerce with them, free Passage on their Rivers, etc., etc., it would be much cheaper to purchase such Advantages with ready Money, than to pay the Expense of acquiring it by War. . . . It seems to me that if Statesmen had a little more Arithmetic, or were more accustomed to Calculation, Wars would be much less frequent.

Professor Upham also developed the idea, in 1836, and a bit more aptly:

And can there, so far as the national resources and wealth are concerned, be any reasonable doubt as to the injurious and destructive tendency of wars! "England and France (says Bonaparte in one of his Conversations at St. Helena) held in their hands the fate of the world, and particularly that of European civilization.

What injury did we not do to each other! What good might we not have done! Under Pitt's system (he says nothing of his own guilt) we desolated the world, and what has been the result? You imposed on France a tax of fifteen hundred millions of francs and raised it by means of Cossacks. I laid a tax of seven hundred millions (probably meaning pounds sterling) on you and made you raise it with your own hands by your parliament. Even now after the victory you have obtained, *who can tell, whether you may not sooner or later sink under the burden?"* In this last inquiry, by whatever jealousy of spirit it might have been prompted in Napoleon, there is something worthy of the attention of the friends of England. Great Britain, with all the wealth of her cities and the grandeur of her nobles, with all the resources of her commerce, and the unrivalled skill of her manufacturers, finds it difficult to conceal it from the world, that her giant footsteps are treading on the brink of bankruptcy. If she fails, it will be the result of war, of *victorious* war; for war is destructive to the victors, as well as the vanquished.

The trouble is that those who make the wars don't do the paying for them. The destinies of all within a country are not so closely wrapped up as appears to nationalistic vision. Though a nation's masses may suffer ruinously from a war—victors along with vanquished—war breeders in all countries fatten and enjoy prosperity or at least a coveted prestige.

Until freed from nationalism, populations may still be driven out to die and kill in a process guaranteed to wreak calamity on the majority of survivors.

In any event, the peculiar benefits derived by many in the United States during the World War make this country sterile soil indeed for such a doctrine as *The Great Illusion.* This time at any rate, by selling munitions and everything else at a terrific rate before we entered the War, we managed pretty well. There is, however, another side even to that; for by selling bonds to pay for the War instead of instituting a drastic war taxation or a capital levy, the cost of the War was transferred chiefly to the workers of this and succeeding generations. But that the people do not see, and their reaction to war is going to be, of course, not to what it is and does, but to what they think it is and does. To short sight, and in a country which experienced the actual ravages of warfare comparatively little, the financial risks of victorious war have about as great a threat as the possible danger of a rocking chair to a new-made champion flagpole sitter.

The Imbecility of War

There are those who believe the moral, religious and economic appeal against war is of little practical value in affecting public opinion. Such a one is Lord Ponsonby, the British pacifist and statesman, who says in his *Now Is the Time:*

The religious, humanitarian, and economic arguments against war by no means cover the whole ground. I now come to what I will call the rationalist argument, which, to my mind, is by far the strongest, the most useful, but hitherto the least developed.

War may be wrong, but the churches have never unanimously condemned it. War is cruel and barbarous, but people will not on that account ask for its abolition. War is wasteful, but people do not count the costs. The supporters of war, therefore, admit that they are ready to undertake something which can be morally condemned, and which is increasingly cruel and expensive, because by it some specific object can be secured.

I maintain that by far the most tragic thing about war, is not its immorality, nor its cruelty, but its manifest and colossal futility and imbecility. I maintain that war achieves no single object of advantage in the high sense to anyone, nor does it attain any of the supposed aims for which it is waged.

Though William Jay shortly before 1845 wrote on "The Inefficacy of War," there is strikingly scant use of the direct appeal to reason, in the peace movement's history, on such grounds as Lord Ponsonby's. Even this argument, however, appears to contain weaknesses. Though the churches in face of an early conflict would probably show a real gain over their record in the World War, Lord Ponsonby is certainly right in not expecting any "unanimous" condemnation. And as I have just indicated, there seems little chance for the argument of war's barbarity.

But why assume any better luck with so logical a proposition as war's supreme stupidity? That happier result will come only when all argument is reënforced—as Lord Ponsonby also believes—by a strong minority movement among the people to dramatize the issue and rouse the apathetic masses; and which through definite action repudiates war on grounds which are, whatever the outward differences of individual expression, essentially compounded of revolt both against war's ethical atavism and its quintessential folly.

CHAPTER XII
MORE ARGUMENTS OF THE FIGHT FOR PEACE

The logic of one age is not that of another. It is one of the chief useful purposes of a study of the mores to learn to discern in them the operation of traditional error, prevailing dogmas, logical fallacy, delusion, and current false estimates of goods worth striving for.—WILLIAM GRAHAM SUMNER, *Folkways.*

CHAPTER XII

MORE ARGUMENTS OF THE FIGHT FOR PEACE

War and Liberty

WHEN the World War sucked the United States into its bloody whirlpool, cartoonists sprang to crayons and rendered what service they could to the cause of "democracy." None of them, however, drew a certain picture that would have shown the actual situation.

That picture would have revealed an ocean—the Atlantic. Germany on the far side, the United States on this. On our shores a brick building, in process of completion. Label on door: DEMOCRACY. An outraged, highly overwrought Uncle Sam is shying bricks, one after the other across the waves, in an effort to smash a sinister castle. The esteemed Uncle is desperately tearing the bricks out of his own fair structure, to its rapid ruin.

Nor did any artist depict a certain other scene. Uncle Sam, worried by a pool of ink on his floor, kneels anxiously and presses over it a blotter. Legend on puddle: MILITARISM; on blotter, FREEDOM, Result: what might naturally be expected.

In that last great conflict there was an active, intelligent, and courageous organization, the American Civil Liberties Union known then as the Civil Liberties Bureau, an outgrowth of the American Union against Militarism. Since it was seeking to preserve the spirit of free press, free speech, and free assembly embodied, for instance, in the first article of the Bill of Rights, the opening word of its title has nobly justified itself.

Such an organization was needed as never before. Free speech, of course, was rigorously repressed in all of our war periods, but never quite so thoroughly. There was open, unpunished skepticism about the holy wisdom of our War of 1812, and the Reverend Benjamin Bell did not hesitate to utter and publish—and "got away with it"—some bitter animadversions on federal officials. Declaring it to be "impolitic and unnecessary, and consequently murderous," he queried whether the administration leaders waging the War were "fit to hold the reins of government and direct the destinies of the nation," expressing the opinion that "they, who say they are, either betray great ignorance or wickedness or both." "Do they not richly merit the title of the murderers of their subjects? Ought they not like the tyrant Nero to be branded with perpetual infamy, and 'damned to eternal fame'?" He also "obstructed recruiting."

Let me entreat you, my dear hearers, if you have any regard to God and your fellow men—to your own honor, and peace of conscience in a dying hour, and to your future happiness, not to say, or do any thing, in the least, to encourage others to enlist to go, and fight against their fathers and mothers, sisters and brothers, in Canada—on the lake or ocean; for you will not prosper.[1]

One of the richest satires ever published in wartime was *The Wars of the Gulls,* circulated in 1812, "in three chapters":

Chapter I. Shewing how, and why, and with whom the Gulls went to war.
Chapter II. Shewing how the Gulls make the deep to boil like a pot.
Chapter III. Shewing how a certain doughty General of the Gulls goes forth to play the game of HULL-GULL in Upper Canada,
     "And from the pinnacle of glory,
     Falls headlong into purgatory."

Says this "Historical Romance":

It was on a foggy afternoon, such as Virginians are accustomed to counteract with a *mint julep,* and such as cloudy heads find congenial to cogitation; that the Sage of Montpelier, the commander in chief of the armies of the Gulls, retired to his lolling chair to ponder on the destinies of the nation. The declaration of war, by virtue of which the whole nation of Gulls were to pounce *unguibus et rostro* upon the unprotected heads of the *Bulls,* their lawfully appointed enemies, was in his hand. A map of British America was under his feet. . . . The margins and spaces usually blank because unexplored, were copiously filled with the names of their future dignitaries, the favorites of their puissant commander. Here was a viceroy of Labrador, and there was a collector of customs on McKenzie's River. A victorious general was military governor over the fragments of Quebec, while an uncouth looking colonel was plenipo. to the Dog-Ribbed Indians. "Who," said the chief of the Gulls, as he cast one eye over his dependancies, "who can like me put his thumb on a whole continent at once? What potentate so colossal that in bestriding his empire, he can cool one toe upon the north pole, while he warms the other at the southernmost cape in Florida?"

In the Northeast the Mexican War was boldly denounced; Lincoln, though he voted in Congress for war credits, nevertheless spoke forcibly against the War itself.

Kindly as he was by nature, however, he permitted a despotic slaughter of civil rights from 'sixty-one to 'sixty-five; although he hardly secured such immunity to criticism as Woodrow Wilson demanded and ruthlessly enforced.

Though the Universal Peace Union experienced one riot during the Spanish-American War and was expelled from its quarters in Philadelphia's old Independence Hall, its outspoken leaders were not jailed, nor were its publications blackjacked by the Post Office Department; and the American Peace Society's frank comments in *The Advocate of Peace,* if they opened the vials of wrath, found in them nothing more lethal than the soured milk of human kindness.

Active spokesmen for the peace movement have been thoroughly alert to the dangerous effect of war and militarism on democracy and freedom. David Low Dodge, on the inception of the War of 1812, tried to make his countrymen realize the threat to liberty:

If we examine the history of nations we shall find that they have generally lost their liberties in consequence of the spirit and practice of war. . . . Where martial law is proclaimed, liberty is cast down, and despotism raises her horrid ensign in its place and fills the dungeons and scaffolds with her victims.

The Noah of Boston, braving the reefs of militarism on one

224 THE FIGHT FOR PEACE

side and the shoals of fundamentalism on the other, steered his ark as few would then have dared:

In all the writings of Thomas Paine, he never advanced a more just sentiment, than what he affirmed of war,—"It is the art of conquering at home."

William Ladd was also at some pains to make his meaning unmistakable:

It is wonderful that the chief who most frequently breaks over the limits of the constitution, tramples on the laws and infringes on the liberty of his fellow citizens,—if only successful in attacking an enemy, or repelling an invasion—is hailed as the savior of his country, and receives all the honors, which that country can confer;—as though territory were dearer to us than our liberties.

And he added, profoundly:

No country was ever free but once.

Eight years afterwards Leonard Bacon was also saying:

An intelligent nation, jealous for its liberties, will always be jealous of armies and warlike armaments, and therefore will always be opposed to a war policy.[2]

Militarism, the real "enemy within," was seen in its true rôle by Thomas C. Upham, who declared that

War always has been, and so long as it continues to be practiced, always *will* be, the bane of freedom. . . . When do we find prisons filled with persons, guilty of nothing which in the ordinary condition of the community would be considered a crime?

There is no need to enumerate in wearisome redundance the sharp lances of argument leveled at war by the defenders of freedom. Suffice it to indicate with necessary reiteration that this plea, too, has been thus far unavailing and seems likely to possess no added potency in the days that stretch before us.

"Let Rulers Fight It Out"

Resentment, tinctured with irony, has frequently prompted the suggestion that war-makers be allowed to determine the issue themselves on the field of honor. When it comes to finding rulers and statesmen actually in battle, however, every square foot of every sector is a no-man's land. As far as actual personal combat is concerned, every "slacker" in Leavenworth is a "very model of a modern major-general."

There was acid, perhaps, in Dodge's analysis, but who can say it was devoid of justification?

Very few, comparatively, who are instigators of war, actually take the field of battle, and are seldom seen in the front of fire. It is usually those who are rioting on the labors of the poor that fan up the flame of war.

Two blistering lines from an unnamed poet appeared in *The American Advocate of Peace* for December, 1835, regarding that class of citizens which Mr. H. G. Wells, in a later period, described as the "fergawdsakers":

> Secure from actual warfare, we have lov'd
> To swell the war-whoop, passionate for war!

There is a certain warrant for such a feeling. The French Senate, recently, rejected a section of M. Paul Boncour's bill for the mobilization of France's entire population in war time, which would have allowed the conscription of members of Parliament.

Samuel E. Coues, President of the old American Peace Society in the 'eighteen-forties, gave a clever riposte to the taunts of his critics:

I have heard non-resistance ridiculed; but nations require non-resistance with a witness. Rulers declare war at pleasure, and then expect the people, without resistance, inquiry or reflection, to submit, and go forth to kill and be killed. Here is non-resistance with a vengeance!

Elihu Burritt in 1846 sarcastically noted the fact that

Kings, Presidents, Governors, Representatives, never pay nor fight. These vulgar duties are left to the People.

Don Arturo de Marcoartu in 1876 complained strenuously about "the unrestricted power conferred on the heads of nations—even in representative monarchies—to dictate war without expressly consulting, by a 'plebiscitum,' the very people they are sending to death."

Nothing more iniquitous can be imagined than to see the instigators of war in the Press, the Tribune, and the Parliament holding themselves aloof from, and keeping out of the range of, war's missiles, and leaving the unhappy people who yearn for peace to face the cannon's mouth. . . . The power to declare war ought to be again deposited in the hands of the people, to be exercised by means of a plebiscite, and neither the head of the state nor society possess any just right to compel a population to fight who may refuse voluntarily to offer their lives for that purpose. If universal suffrage is at any time justifiable, if a duty of conscience ever imposes it as a duty to listen to the *vox populi*, it is assuredly when the nation is called upon to declare war.*

Dr. McMurdy, of the National Arbitration League, wrote in his 1884 report:

Every proposition for declaring war should be referred to the people. If a majority favor it, let this majority do the fighting, substitutions being forbidden by law.

Belva A. Lockwood prefaced a pamphlet of 1901 with the quotation:

Let those who make the battles be the only ones to fight.

In 1911 Allen S. Will of the *Baltimore Sun* asked of the Third American Peace Congress:

How many of the world's wars have been, as Tennyson says, broad-based upon the people's will? If war is for the benefit of ambitious princes, politicians, agitators and other harpies who usually dominate at a time when organized conflict is impending, it may well be that the decision should be left to them; but if it is for the benefit of the nation—and this is always the guise in which it is presented—is it not just that the judgment of the people should approve the necessity for such a tragic enterprise before they embark on it?

It was Kant who insisted that if war was to be eradicated, the civil constitution in every state should be republican, and war should not be declared except upon a plebiscite of all citizens.

Few decades have since passed, I venture to believe, in which a covert or an openly challenging expression of this complaint against autocracy has not been made. On a recent lecture tour to the United States, General Fritz V. Holm, a Danish lecturer, writer and war correspondent, rattled the old bones anew. He proposed a law (which has been agitated for Denmark) providing that if a nation becomes involved in war the following measures shall be put into effect within ten hours:

A. There shall be enlisted as simple soldiers or simple sailors with rank of privates, in the nation's armed forces on land (although only in the infantry shock troops), or at sea (although only for service on board submarines), or in the air, for the earliest possible participation in actual hostilities under fire against the enemy, the following persons:

1. The Head of the State, if male, whether president or monarch.

2. All male blood relatives of the Head of State having attained the age of sixteen years.

3. All civilian officials, and military, naval and air officers attached to the household of the Head of State.

4. The Prime Minister and other Secretaries of State, as well as all Under and Assistant Secretaries of State, of the Government, except the Secretary of State for Peace, hereinafter mentioned.

5. All representatives elected by the nation for legislative work, viz: all members of Parliamentary or Congressional bodies, of both Lower and Upper Houses, except such members as voted openly against said armed conflict or war.

6. All Bishops and prelates or ecclesiasts of similar rank of the nation's Christian and other churches, whether state churches or no.

The above enlistments as privates are for the duration of the armed conflict or war and are enforced in disregard of the individual's age and/or condition of health, upon which the military officers will pass after enlistment.

Relatives Included

B. There shall be enlisted as simple nurses or servants in the medical auxiliaries of the army, and for service only at the front, as near actual hostilities under fire as dressing stations and/or field hospitals are established, the following persons:

7. The Head of the State, if female.

8. All female blood relatives of the Head of State having attained the age of sixteen years, and all male relatives according to A-2.

9. All female officials attached to the household of the Head of State, and all male functionaries according to A-3.

10. All present wives, all daughters of present marriages, and all sisters, provided said women are entitled to vote at general elections, of the persons mentioned under A-(1-6).

The above enlistments as simple nurses or servants are for the duration of the armed conflict or war, and are enforced in disregard of the individual's age or condition of health, upon which the military medical officers will pass after enlistment.

No Promotions

C. Promotion in rank, even for conspicuous military or medical service, is denied the persons mentioned under A) and B) forever; but their services, if worthy, may be recompensed with available national decorations.

D. The official positions vacated by the enlistments of the persons under A) and B) shall be filled immediately by their pre-elected or pre-appointed deputy successors as follows:

x. The position of Head of State is filled by the Secretary of State for Peace, hereinafter mentioned.

y. The positions of Prime Minister and of other Secretaries of State, including Under and Assistant Secretaries of State, are filled by the successors deputed for that purpose at the preceding general elections, or by previous appointment by the Head of State.

z. The positions of the elected representatives of the nation, except those who voted against the armed conflict or war in question, and who therefore remain in office, are filled by their deputy successors, designated at the preceding general elections.

This is a scheme of charming simplicity, calculated to tickle at once the imagination and one's sense of justice. It is a sort of stern fairness all but reduced to the absurd. The underlying principle has never made much headway, nor will the more elaborate modernization—for at least two major reasons.

First, if wars are to be fought at all, nations fighting them will not and cannot do other than fight as efficiently as possible; and efficiency demands that we select the physically fit young men—the males at least thus far in warfare—and send them out to slaughter and be slaughtered in trivial millions.

Second, because it is a fallacy to assume that war makers are physical cowards. Call them stupid, heap on them every kind of invective you can think of, and there might be truth in different degrees in all your accusations. But if the politicians, military leaders, imperialists and superpatriots who are especially responsible for most of the world's wars could be convinced that the winning of a war rested more on their going into combat instead of other posts behind the lines, the great majority would go as bravely and unquestioningly as that unthinking Light Brigade whose brute-like plasticity and dumb valor Tennyson immortalized.

During the years just before the United States entered the World War and for a time thereafter, the idea of a war referendum was brought forward by one or two progressive Congressmen. The scheme is not new; it was promoted by Continental socialism extensively between 1890 and 1907. The most prominent recent spokesman for it is Alanson B. Houghton, former Ambassador at the Court of St. James. At Harvard University's commencement exercises in 1927 he vigorously presented the case for a popular vote before war. He has since reiterated the proposal several times. Even when running for the Senate in New York State in the 1928 elections, he stated at a political rally:

The power to declare war, it must be remembered, stands on a different plane from all other powers of government. It is the one power which of all others a self-governing people would logically reserve to itself, since it puts in jeopardy their collective lives and property. And yet, strangely enough, it is the one power they do not directly possess.[4]

One man has probably put more solid work on the war referendum project than any other. He is Dr. Thomas Hall Shastid, of Duluth, Minnesota. He has spoken before many audiences; he has drawn together in a small organization a number of others who put strong faith in his plan; he has issued a great many pamphlets of a popular nature, and a book, *Give the People Their Own War Power*.

He has worked out the text of an Amendment to the Constitution embodying his plan, and has published answers to a multitude of common questions raised by critics of the referendum project.

Clearly, delay would be an essential feature of any such referendum; the thirty days required in Dr. Shastid's Amendment would be a practical minimum. Every moment of delay would afford an opportunity for a public discussion of the international issues at stake, whereas at present such discussion as there is must be centered in the question of what the government is going to do, instead of what you are going to do yourself.

On the other hand, a period of delay would be far from a guarantee of peace. It would mean that the forces of peace and the forces of war would settle down to a grim battle of rival propaganda. In such a race for public opinion it is by no means certain that special interests, such as unscrupulous steel and ammunition manufacturers *et al*, would not carry the day by the tremendous resources they could wield.

However, let it be not forgotten that always, in any population, there is a tremendous inertia, or social lag. No mass of individuals reacts favorably at once to an upheaval, or likes to have its habitual procedure uprooted. At present, a war-bent government can profit from this fact by going ahead with its war program, counting on the sluggishness of the masses not to oppose it in time.

Coming before the people with a war proposal, any government would be in a very different position. It would be likely to encounter a strong reluctance. It was not until the boys were actually in camp that the reluctant groups of American parents were won whole-heartedly to our overseas crusade in 1917. One great thing would be accomplished in large measure by the existence of a war referendum: the ever-vast public inertia would be transferred from the credit to the debit side of the war ledger. And the chance of that alone, to say nothing of democratic justice, makes the proposal sound and worthy of effort.

Again, however, we must not overlook the resentment which

has accumulated over war's undemocratic tyranny in the hearts of many a previous generation. While war is at all a threat, it will be a simple thing for governments everywhere to appeal successfully against the adoption of any such scheme. Each will declare it practicable only when all nations jointly put it into practice; and before any such unanimity can be expected, a far more drastic blow must be struck at the whole war system, a blow capable of rousing the attention of the masses as no undramatic referendum project ever can.

Redefining Patriotism

So heavily charged with emotion is the word "patriotism," so utterly irrational is all ordinary discussion of it, that most of those who realize how great a menace it may become even to the nations most effervescently patriotic, seldom venture to criticize the term. They take recourse, rather, in a more academic and less explosive word—the word "nationalism." Thus an internationalist can analyze nationalism and live to tell the story; but woe be to that individual who undertakes in public to scrutinize the idea of patriotism with anything remotely resembling scientific detachment. And yet for all practical purposes, irrespective of meticulous differentiations, nationalism and patriotism are in our day one and the same.[5]

Of nationalism we have outspoken critics, almost every last one of whom accompanies his strictures by loud protestations of his unassailable patriotism.

Others, recognizing that love of country is not without its socially useful manifestations, seek to redefine patriotism. According to this effort, patriotism is conceived of as a love for the highest welfare of your country's people. Thus articles are written on "The Patriotism of Peace." Thus one of the wisest leaders of thought among the Quakers is led to say:

Friends are patriotic and loyal not to the wrong but to the right. They recognize that men of every race and creed are their fellow-men. Love of country does not imply hatred of enemies. The flag is loved not because it excludes, but because it draws to higher and better things.

Thus a conference of pacifist churches in 1928 decided that

What is needed is that patriotism should be given a newer, fuller meaning. Material on the better patriotism is needed and we should try to make it available.

All this appears to my judgment as an untenable position. Let us take an illustration. It is much like saying that all religious people are going to be loyal to the Bible, when the Bible contains numerous flat contradictions. To be loyal to the good in the Bible (that is, what the individual himself considers good) means also, of course, being disloyal to the bad. Fundamentalists and modernists alike have asserted on innumerable occasions their fidelity to Scripture; loyalty to the "right" in the Bible has driven many to the stake—the "right" as the martyrs saw it, and the "right" according to their conscientious persecutors. Loyalty to the Bible has driven many literal pacifists into dungeons, while it impelled Charles Kingsley to write his *Brave Words to Brave Soldiers and Sailors,* in which he said:

The Lord is not only the Prince of Peace; He is the Prince of War too; He is the great Master and the God of Battles, and whosoever fights in a just war against the tyrants and oppressors he is fighting on Christ's side and Christ is fighting on his side; Christ is his keeper and He is his mainstay, and he can be in no better service. Be sure of it; for the Bible tells you so.[6]

This species of patriotic pluralism, as it were, may be an excellent thing in theory—a *laissez faire* go-as-you-please. But in practice it is not workable simply because the *patria* will not let it be worked. When nothing which a government deems of crucial importance is at stake, citizens of a country may be granted a certain liberty of definition; but not in regard to anything of national import. In times of critical values to posterity, when great issues are involved, governments define patriotism and define it with a vengeance.

In terms of international relations, patriotism is the sanction which gives force to that anarchic "individualism" in the family of nations technically called "sovereignty." According to

Edmunds' *Lawless Law of Nations,* the term sovereignty was originated in 1577 by Jean Bodin in his work *De la Republique,* to furnish an "alibi" for the French absolutism which Louis XI had inaugurated in the preceding century. It was defined as "Supreme power over citizens and subjects, unrestrained by the laws." Grotius worked it into the law of nations, to designate the irresponsible and unlimited power of the State not only in national but in international relations. Patriotism: my country, right or wrong. Sovereignty: my country's right *to* wrong.

In international relations, a definite weakening of sovereignty is perhaps the most needed emotional change on the part of the world's peoples. But such a change must wait upon deeper-lying transformations within national frontiers. What is needed there, to speak bluntly, is a weakening of patriotism, a dilution of loyalty to fatherland by love of the larger human family: "Above all nations is humanity."

Not a one-hundred-per-cent, but a "fifty-fifty" patriotism, in short, is the emotional basis for which there is an imperative need. Not a redefining, but a wider distribution, of loyalties. What is required is precisely that which will be deplored and shrieked about by the more volatile superpatriots. Not those who shrink from internationalism in patriotic timidity, but those who have "a passion for the planet" [7]—these are the ones who lead us toward the promised land of world-wide friendship, freed from arbitrary reservations.

It is possible to love your country with undiminished ardor and still love the whole world with a passion for humanity; but only when there exists a community of interests and not a conflict of interests. Is it possible that the strong flame of patriotic devotion is somewhat responsible for the conflicts of interests that exist? I have no doubt about it. Interests may diverge, but they conflict only when they are evaluated by the traditional test of patriotism. Since there is little chance of resolving all the differences in national interest, the obvious need is for an internationalization of emotion, a transference of loyalty to a wider field.

The peace movement at times has had its far-sighted internationalists. In the *Rhode Island American,* in 1818, appeared the following "Lines Addressed to the Rhode Island Peace Society on Their First Anniversary":

> Ye Friends of Man, whom nobler zeal inspires
> Than laurel'd chiefs, or wary statesmen, fires;
> Whose gen'rous aim embraces, unconfin'd,
> Not *friend* and *country,* but entire *Mankind.*

Garrison's *Liberator* bore the famous slogan, "My country is the world; my countrymen are all mankind." William Ladd even grew so bold of utterance soon after his arrival at a radical pacifist view that he put his convictions into print.

> Patriotism as it is generally understood, is in direct opposition to Christianity. One is founded on self-love; the other on the love of God's creatures. Patriotism prefers the good of our country to the good of the whole human race. It approves of injustice to another country, when that injustice promotes the interests of our own. But the man, who would lie, deceive, rob, or murder, for the sake of his country, is no better than he who would commit all these crimes, for his own individual interest. For patriotism, as it is usually practiced is but an extended selfishness, and is as much inferior to philanthropy, as a narrow, clownish spirit, which loves none but its own party, or its own friends and relations, is to the most expanded patriotism. He, who prefers the interest of a part of mankind to the interest of the whole—the interest of his own nation to that of the world in general—though he may come up to the highest mark of patriotism, falls far below the lowest grade of Christianity.[8]

Some of the moderns are also speaking out. Raymond B. Fosdick, for example, in his book *The Old Savage and the New Civilization,* goes straight to the point in dispute:

> What is this thing we call patriotism? Once a sacred flame upon the altar, it has grown into a conflagration of devastating proportions. Once a noble passion that broke down local provincialisms and stretched the mind to broader loyalties, today, with the expansion of international life, its tendency is to narrow rather than widen the sympathies of man. Once the issue was patriotism versus a small parochialism; now the issue is between patriotism and the enlarging fellowship of human life on the planet.

Such forthright speech is rare, however. For so great has

been the emotional pressure, so eager to serve their fellow countrymen unselfishly in other ways than by war have been even the most radical members of the peace movement, that they have been extremely loath to take a position certain to bring upon them all sorts of outraged maledictions.

Not thus deterred, however, have been the military interests, whose patriotism is mistakenly conceived of as unassailable. Between the military leaders of all countries exists in all periods an extraordinary professional camaraderie. After a war, successful generals invariably make world tours, and are received everywhere with great acclaim, sometimes even in the countries of their erstwhile enemies. It is a customary courtesy to permit foreign officers from neutral countries to witness military operations: our officers so observed tactics and strategy in the Crimea and during the Franco-Prussian War. A few nationals of other countries are regularly trained in our government military schools. For instance, permission was granted in 1927 for the matriculation at West Point of two Siamese subjects and two Chinese subjects; and students of other nationalities have studied military tactics under our fraternal hospitality. We send military missions to other countries to assist them to formulate training policies.

Every naval vessel of the United States is supposed to carry the flag of every country in the world, for ceremonial purposes.

In the Old World, the intermarriage of royalty has never seemed a matter of diluted patriotism, excepting as it was a sacrifice to diplomatic pressure.

Immediately the World War was ended, French naval officers justified the German submarine campaign and Lord Fisher in England wrote Von Tirpitz that he did not blame him, for England, could she have done so and were she in a similar position, would have acted precisely the same.

Von Bülow, the German Chancellor, also wrote to the Kaiser, about Roosevelt, Sr., "the President is a great admirer of Your Majesty and would like to rule the world hand in hand with Your Majesty, since he considers himself in a way the American counterpart of Your Majesty," whereupon Wilhelm

II wrote upon the margin, "Very flattering to me!" [9] A libel-
ous misconstruction of Roosevelt's ideas? Very likely; but not
without a certain warrant. For in 1904, according to the records of Von Sternburg, the German Ambassador, President
Roosevelt had said to him, "The only man I understand and
who understands me is the Kaiser." [10]

Prior to the World War, Krupps numbered many nations
among their clients. A dozen years before the War German
contractors built the fortifications in Belgium which later they
had to smash. Cannon made by Armstrong's in England were
captured from the Turks on Gallipoli, one of them finding a
resting place on the green at Bedford Park. On one side of
this gun is an inscription regarding the gallant deed of the
Bedford regiment and on the other side is the inscription,
"Armstrong, Witworth and Company." [11]

The end of the World War did not mean the end of armament rings or the international control of munition manufacture. A union of American firms with British to buy heavily
into central European companies was announced within a few
years after the Armistice, and even the Skoda works of Czechoslovakia, a state-owned plant, have exported war materials to
other countries. It is the inevitable outcome of the munition
business to sell where customers want to buy, and where trade
is sluggish, to drum it up. As A. Fenner Brockway, M.P., has
aptly called it in his little play, it is indeed "The Devil's
Business."

Patriotism is all things to all men. It is not only the last
refuge of scoundrels as Samuel Johnson said, but is frequently
the first.

It is used to make money, as witness the poultry food advertised during the War in red-white-and-blue "literature"; the
use of the colors for store sales and movie extravaganzas; and
such slogans as once shone forth in electric signs: "Be patriotic
—drink ——'s" (beer).

It is used to bulwark economic orthodoxy, as evidenced by
a conservative magazine which stated in 1920 that "you cannot
indeed be a good American, in the sense of being loyal to

American traditions, unless you are proud of the capitalist system." [12]

In time of war its excesses are beyond recording, varying all the way from the committee, in an Ohio town, which forced German fried potatoes off the local menus, or the organization of Unconditional Surrender Clubs, as in Flint, Michigan, to recruiting verse, like the one appended to "Are you a good sport? Enlist in the Navy and go hunting for U-boats":

HUNT THE HUN DUCK
(Sing to the tune of "Hold the Fort")
Shoot the Hun duck,
    Send it skidding,
Down among the whales.
    Hit the Hun duck in its gizzard,
Punch! until it fails.

Or there is General George H. Harries, who still had so much steam up thirteen months after the World War ended as to regret openly, with alarm and sadness at Summit, New Jersey (and, incidentally, in a church), that there was no Allied blunder equal to the signing of the Armistice. [13]

Patriotism, too, has lifted out of a self-centered existence many an individual and moved him to think unselfishly for the first time in his life. It has opened tight purses, and stirred young men to offer themselves for what in all honesty they have accepted as just and necessary conflict.

It has become to many people a *bona fide* religion, with the flag as an ikon and the flash of a bayonet on its way through human ribs as a counterpart of the cross.

All in all, it serves to hold back peace and the dawn of a world society. In the resounding words of H. G. Wells,

We regard our country as something primary and eternal. We must never think of it subordinated nor imagine that its separateness can end.

It is to go on for all time just as it is, only more so. The rest of the world may go to the devil. If patriotism is not all that, then what is patriotism?

Now, I maintain that in this matter you cannot run with the

hare and hunt with the hounds. You cannot be an advocate of organized world peace and a full and complete patriot also. A great number of worthy people are trying to achieve this impossibility.

If we subtract them from the total of those who are "working for world peace," I doubt if any large number of people remain.[14]

Wells' mathematics is probably correct. But if those who remain are small in numbers, they are nevertheless the ones who, in the vanguard, are moving out of old compromises and academic, unsound "redefinitions," toward a day when Man will be Man's earthly first and sacrosanct allegiance.

On what psychological factors does one-hundred-per-cent patriotism fatten? On many, of course. But at the root of them all is one central influence that seems strangely overlooked. It is not so much that excessive patriotism is a cause of war, as it is that war is a major cause of patriotic inflation, always most in evidence after every conflict but lingering for many years. An amusing example of how persistent war's traditions are is the repeated shelving of a bill for the discontinuance of State appropriations to a Virginia military school, as recommended by an educational survey commission of eleven well-known Virginians on the ground that it devotes too much time to military affairs. Reason? In part at least, because the school is a long-revered State institution, since its cadets distinguished themselves in the Civil War and a great general was a member of its faculty.[15] One can sympathetically understand the traditional Virginian; for several years the writer's whole outlook on war and peace was influenced by a pocket-piece, given me by a sweet-spirited old veteran, made of cannon captured in the same sectional strife.

The best way to deflate patriotism from menacing proportions to a useful social force is, above all others, I submit, to abolish war, thus eliminating the invariable hangover of false reverence, "pooled self-esteem," and identification of love of country with veneration for all the manifestations of militarism.

Until war is prevented and kept prevented for a long time,

all the arguments against inflammatory superpatriotism merely dampen the flying sparks; they do not put out the fire that smolders always and periodically breaks out with its devastating flames.

Peace by Prizes

If not an argument precisely, one method of stirring public opinion against war is the peace prize. And such prizes have been offered partly in the hope of discovering an argument that will be persuasively effective.

The practice is by no means new. As far back as 1766 an anonymous donor offered through the French Academy a prize for the best anti-war treatise received. Writers in several countries entered the competition, and at least three important essays were written as a result, while others followed in the years succeeding.

The span of years from Nemo to Bok is sprinkled with more or less generous showers of prize money. In the 'thirties a member of the American Peace Society offered a hundred dollars for the best tract on "the duty of Christians, to do what they can to abolish the custom of war," provided the American Tract Society should adopt the tract as one of their own! Ladd gave to several colleges two hundred dollars, the income from which, twelve dollars, was given for the best annual essays on subjects, given out by the donor, on peace and war. Similar twelve-dollar prizes soon were offered through other institutions, such as Newton Theological Institute and the theological seminaries at Andover and Bangor, principally by the gifts of the Reverend Howard Malcolm.

In 1853 the Reverend Thomas Merrill, a Vice President of the American Peace Society, offered five hundred dollars for the best essay on "The Right Way, or the Gospel Applied to the Intercourse of Individuals and Nations."

In Europe, prizes were also being offered: at Geneva, for the best essay in French on the Means for Establishing a General and Permanent Peace; another at London, of one hundred guineas for the same general theme.

When Charles Sumner made his will, it included a bequest of one thousand dollars to Harvard University for the best essay on methods, other than war, for the settlement of international differences. This fund has not been used to the full and since only one prize of one hundred dollars appears to have been offered each year, it has mounted up to more than eight thousand five hundred dollars.[16]

At the annual meetings of the Universal Peace Union held in their famous grove at Mystic, Connecticut, prizes were offered for peace recitations by children, the chief prize usually consisting of an India proof engraving of Penn's treaty with the Indians; just as Mr. Clement Biddle recently has donated one thousand dollars for similar contests.

Many minor prizes were offered through the nineteen-eighties and 'nineties, such as a ten-dollar prize for arbitration essays at Bowdoin, and one at Maine Wesleyan Seminary.

The American Peace Society in 1893 announced three prizes of one hundred dollars, fifty dollars, and twenty-five dollars, respectively, for the best essays by college students, on one or another aspect of peace.

Other well-known prizes were the Pugsley Prize of one hundred dollars offered through the Mohonk Conferences by Chester D. Pugsley in 1908 and successive years, and the prizes of two hundred dollars and one hundred dollars donated by Mrs. Elmer Black for women students writing on peace or arbitration.

For many years the prizes offered by the Misses Mary and Helen Seabury through the American School Peace League have stimulated thousands of normal and secondary school pupils to write on peace.

Prior to the Church Peace Union's endorsement of our entry into the World War, it offered a prize of one thousand dollars for the best peace essay, which was won by Dr. Washington Gladden's "The Forks of the Road."

One of the most lively experiences with prize contests was that of the American Peace Society in 1829 and the following eleven years. Always interested in a Congress of Nations, the Society at its first annual meeting offered a prize of thirty dollars for the best essay on that subject. No essays were forthcoming. The amount was increased to fifty dollars, but of the four or five essays resulting not one was of any serious value. In 1831, two members of the Society (a Mr. Batchelor and the Society's treasurer, L. D. Dewey in all probability) proffered five hundred dollars for the same purpose. Forty essays were entered in the contest. A distinguished committee of award, composed of Joseph Story, William Wirt and John McLean, were unable to pick a single outstanding essay among five which they deemed worthy, and suggested a division of the prize, whereupon the donors refused to accede. They extended the time another year, raised the prize to one thousand dollars and selected a new committee made up of John Quincy Adams, James Kent (the noted Supreme Court Justice of New York State) and Thomas S. Grimké, the radical pacifist of South Carolina, though on the death of Grimké in the ensuing year Daniel Webster agreed to serve as the third member.

Surely this jury of eminence could have been expected to render a satisfying verdict! And yet they, too, had to deal with substantially the same essays, since only one new one was offered during the entire year; and their conclusion was almost the same as that of their (less) esteemed predecessors. The donors pleaded vainly for a first choice, but the committee was adamant, whereupon the gentlemen who held the money bag again refused to give any prize at all and declared the contest off, leaving everybody disgruntled and some essays of significance and merit buried beneath the wreckage.

For a time even the patient and resourceful Ladd was stumped, and as he put it, the Society was left "in a very awkward predicament." Up and down he went, soliciting subscriptions for a volume containing the five essays that seemed best to his judgment, plus his own composite essay. His faithful labor, and his own pecuniary generosity also, were rewarded if belatedly by the publication—though not until 1840 and only one year before his death—of the large volume of *Prize Essays* which has been referred to in an earlier chapter.

A quarter of a century has passed since the Nobel Peace

Prize provided an opportunity for gambling, should anyone care to do it, more ruled by sheer chance than any race course in the world. Some of its winners have been celebrated for their militarism. There have been deserved awards, such as the honoring of Bertha von Suttner in 1905, Alfred H. Fried in 1911, Premier Branting of Sweden in 1921, and M. Buisson and Herr Quidde in 1927; but while other recipients of the award have been highly estimable figures, few have been more than fair-weather pacifists and some have been notorious apologists for peace-via-war—Roosevelt, Root (a former Secretary of War), Wilson and Dawes, not to mention those of other countries.

Since the World War much attention has been attracted by the Filene peace prizes offered in Europe, the prize of twenty-five thousand dollars offered through the National Education Association by Raphael Herman and won by David Starr Jordan, and preëminently the fifty thousand dollars offered by Edward Bok, won by the late Charles H. Levermore.

As a means of advertising peace in a vague and hazy way to the general public, such prizes have a distinctly practical use. Of undeniable value and influence have been the Seabury prizes, for their effect in vitalizing the interest of countless young people in peace, year after year. A new and somewhat similar prize essay contest has been launched as the Zelah Van Loan World Friendship Award, offering fifteen hundred dollars in prizes to young writers on "Christ and World Friendship."

The fact is interesting and significant that 22,165 plans complying with all conditions were sent in to Mr. Bok's committee of award and that many thousands were submitted which in some way violated the rules.

As a technique of finding practical approaches to peace, however, they amount substantially to zero. That plan is always bound to be accepted which represents the greatest common denominator of the award committee; and the committee is uniformly composed of people influenced by commitments to peace projects as well as by factual knowledge. Quite apart also from any inability of a highly important body of citizens to shape the prize undertakings to realities is the fact that plenty of excellent peace plans have existed and still exist, and that what is lacking is not so much intellectual ideas as emotional drive, willingness to sacrifice rights, courage to run the risks of peace instead of war, and in particular, to guide the development of national policies by altruistic criteria. From her storied abode the angel of peace broods over the earth with questioning eyes; she is not only asking "How?" or "What?" but "When?"

A real boon to humanity would be a plan that is deserving of the highest prize of all, namely world peace. Any such plan for the United States will be obliged to deal less with machinery and organization, however, than with interests and policies. It will have to answer certain problems, of which I venture to suggest the following as samples. It must:

1. Throw into productive employment a vast number of war strategists, navy boosters, and ammunition manufacturers, without losing the vote of American patrioteers.

2. Lift from our taxpayers the burden of spending eighteen per cent of our national budget on current preparedness, and at the same time retain armed forces on land and sea sufficient to cope with any conceivable adversary.

3. Provide for the free international exchange of goods without giving up high protection for American industries.

4. Safeguard our right to penetrate any part of the world for the increase of our prosperity, without being obliged to weaken our one-hundred-per-cent American citizenry by the admission of foreigners—except in such quantities as will also increase our prosperity.

5. Carry on the War settlements with a spirit of benevolent neutrality in the manner relied on hitherto—for example, our fair-minded desire to see Germany pay no more than she can and the Allies collect all that they want and all that we can take.

6. Open to our indignation all such encroachments on the rights of small nations as that of Italy on Corfu, without depriving us of the right to maintain order in the Caribbean.

7. Allow Soviet Russia to take her place among respectable

nations in such a way that her communism, which has prostrated her, cannot possibly make her so strong as to endanger the capitalism of other nations.

8. Work out a *modus operandi* whereby the nations may associate in true democratic fellowship, but which will render large countries like the United States immune to the international idealism of smaller ones.

9. Devise a technique of open diplomacy that will enable diplomats to make international adjustments without the risk of popular unrest.

10. Instill into the youth of the world a hatred of war without depriving them of the benefits of military discipline, target practice, bayonet drill, and the spirit of "for Yale, for Country and for God."

11. Repair the damage done by our entry into the World War and our attitude toward the peace, without forcing us to admit, even to ourselves, that the results of American participation were anything but good.

12. Organize the intellectual classes for a complete repudiation of war in general, yet in no way committing them to an opposition to any—and every—war in particular.

13. Elevate into international ethics the principles of the Sermon on the Mount without embarrassing in any degree the thousands of clergymen who have proved that Christianity and war are compatible.

14. Follow the peace leadership of other nations in such a way as to preserve our supremacy in the struggle against war.

Now *there* are fourteen points! Let me hasten to state with the utmost gravity that I have never sought a peace prize or a job with any foundation, that I have neither ax to grind nor sour grapes to squeeze. I do assert, however, with becoming modesty, that when peace plans more worthy of a prize are offered I may on that day try. For if such schemes are nonproductive in raising impenetrable barriers against the hounds of war, so, certainly, have been all others in the archives of Time, the greatest historian of them all.

Also an argument only indirectly, but nevertheless a recurring focal point of pleas against war, is the suggestion of a Cabinet portfolio for peace. Doubtless the most carefully worked-out proposal of this nature, with a tentative budget outline, is that of Kirby Page, published in 1926. Since then, the same suggestion has cropped up intermittently in Friends' and other journals. Mrs. Carrie Chapman Catt recently said:

> My solution of the disarmament question is to proceed by a movement to build up a peace institution that will be positive not negative. . . . Put the peace institution under the Department of State and develop that Department into an active power for peace.[17]

Dr. David Starr Jordan has spoken to the same end, as have numerous others. Miss Agnes C. Macphail, a member of Canada's House of Commons, introduced a resolution on March 26, 1928 for a Canadian Peace Department, though it met the usual reception faced in most legislative bodies by peace proposals.

But as far back as 1790 Dr. Benjamin Rush put forward an elaborate scheme for a Peace Department. Rush was a figure renowned in the annals of medicine, of war, and of public service generally. He was a signer of the Declaration of Independence. Here is the Rush project in brief:

> Art. 1st. Let a Secretary of the Peace be appointed to preside at this office, who shall be perfectly free from all the present absurd and vulgar European prejudices on the subject of government: Let him be a genuine republican and a sincere Christian, for the principles of republicanism and Christianity are no less friendly to universal and perpetual peace than they are to universal and equal liberty.
> Art. 2nd. Provides for the maintenance of free schools and the principles of the Christian religion, for it belongs to this religion exclusively to teach us, not only to cultivate peace with all men, but to forgive, nay more, to love our enemies.
> Art. 3rd. Provides for the free distribution of the Bible at public expense.
> Art. 4th. Let the following sentence be inscribed, in letters of gold, over the doors of every State and Court house in the United States: "The Son of Man came not into the world to destroy men's lives, but to save them."
> Art. 5th. Provides for the repeal of sanguinary laws.

Art. 6th. To subdue the passion of war, which education, added to human depravity, have made universal, a familiarity with the instruments of death, as all military shows, should be carefully avoided. For which reason, military laws should everywhere be repealed, and military dresses and titles should be laid aside.

What more could be asked by advocates of drastic disarmament? In part Dr. Rush was driving at the same objective as the Women's Peace Union, for example, which succeeded in persuading Senator Lynn J. Frazier to introduce his Amendment to the Constitution, on which two hearings have been held, in 1927 and 1930—a most thorough Amendment designed to put Mars out of business, cremate him, and scatter his ashes to the winds.

Symbolism, too, lured Dr. Rush to elaborate flights of decoration:

Art. 7th. In the last place: let a large room, adjoining the federal hall be appropriated for transacting the business and preserving all the records of this office. Over the door of this room let there be a sign, on which the figure of a lamb, a dove, and an olive branch should be painted, together with the following inscription, in letters of gold: "Peace on Earth—Good Will to Men. Ah, why will men forget that they are brothers?"

One answer to this rather agonized inquiry, perhaps, may repose in the penumbra of the fact that spokesmen for peace have so long either bleated like lambs, cooed like doves, or quivered vernally against the harsh and wintry gales of war.

But there was a gusto about good Dr. Rush. He had a corollary to his first proposal. It is worth inserting, as a bouquet for the galaxy of war promoters whose ministrations are never absent from the land.

In order the more deeply to affect the minds of the citizens of the United States with the blessings of peace, by contrasting them with the evils of war, let the following inscriptions be painted on the sign which is placed over the door of the war offices:—

1. An office for butchering the human species.
2. A widow and orphan making office.
3. A broken bone making office.
4. A wooden leg making office.

5. An office for creating private and public vices.
6. An office for creating public debt.
7. An office for creating speculators, stock jobbers and bankrupts.
8. An office for creating famine.
9. An office for creating political diseases.
10. An office for creating poverty and the destruction of liberty and National happiness.

In the lobby of this office let there be painted representations of all the common military instruments of death; also human skulls, broken bones, unburied and putrefying dead bodies, hospitals crowded with sick and wounded soldiers, villages on fire, mothers in besieged towns, eating the flesh of their children, ships sinking in the ocean, rivers dyed with blood, and extensive plains without tree or fence, or any other object but the ruins of deserted farm houses. Above all this group of woful figures, let the following words be inserted in red characters, to represent human blood:— "NATIONAL GLORY."

Ere the hand of the National Security League, Military Order of the World War, American Defense Society, D.A.R., Better America Federation, Scabbard and Blade, National Civic Federation, Industrial Defense Association, or some other watchdog of the public weal, descends heavily on my shoulder and I am loudly rebuked, let me hasten to remind all and sundry that I never said these words, never thought them, and, being a child of our modern age imbued with restraint of utterance, should never have spoken them had I been their fond inventor. The honors, and in my opinion they are not inconsiderable, should go to Dr. Rush, American citizen, born December 24, 1745, graduate of Princeton, original Signer, and experienced in war as a surgeon to a part of the army in 1776. And so what can be done to put him in his place to-day must be left to our ingenious national salvationists.

A year or two after Dr. Rush brought forward his plan, or so it would appear by circumstantial evidence, Benjamin Banneker, a free Negro, published in his *Almanac* a very similar peace plea. Banneker had won attention by his development, self-taught, into an amateur astronomer and mathematician, a marvelous achievement to people not yet weaned of their notions concerning the Negro's mental inferiority. His project follows that of Rush's point by point; but the wording is somewhat different, and from a literary standpoint far less effective. While it has been suggested in some quarters that Benjamin Banneker may have been America's first pacifist, there is strong internal evidence that he copied the Rush plan and adapted it to suit himself. In outlining to President Jefferson, for example, the ideas to which he was devoted, he was detailed and specific, but nowhere in his letter does he mention peace as laying any serious claim upon him. The early writers on peace, all of them eager to seize upon any accomplishment by Negroes, agree in attributing the plan and the outspokenness with which it was presented, alike to the more eminent Benjamin.

Now and then, in succeeding years, the plan of Dr. Rush's was resurrected by the peace movement, but never wholeheartedly pressed. After the Civil War there were occasional revivals, initiated by individual peace workers. After the Spanish-American War, John Hay, Secretary of State, hospitably entertained a delegation from the Universal Peace Union, which laid special stress on a Department of Peace in their discussion. When the Department of Commerce and Labor was inaugurated in 1903 (separated in 1913) the pleas for a Bureau of Peace in connection with it rose strongly for a brief period. In 1909 and for a short while following, President Taft's Department of State had an under-secretary for peace. The Conference on the Cause and Cure of War, in 1925, called for the restoration of such an official.

At one time, before his appointment to President Wilson's cabinet, William Jennings Bryan expressed himself in favor of such a federal department. Admiral Goodrich, after the War with Spain, suggested a Department of Education and in connection with it a Department of Peace.

In December, 1926, at Atascadera, California, there was organized the American Association for World Peace, with a membership of seventy persons, whose object was "to create a Nation-wide demand that Congress enact a law establishing the office of Secretary of Peace, with portfolio in the Cabinet, and setting aside all funds derived from our Allied war loans to be used under his direction to educate and prepare the world for Peace."

Nevertheless, the idea of a federal peace department has never caught hold of the peace movement's imagination. And why? On the face of it nothing could seem more logical.

Thoughtful analysis, however, relates such a move directly to the state of politics in the United States of America. Any appointee of any government we are likely to get while there exists so uncrystallized a sentiment for the prevention of war, and so little determination to abolish war as a social menace, could merely broadcast, on a larger scale, war-peace ideas and projects of a thoroughly respectable, anæmic character. No real peace scheme involving the necessary sacrifices of traditional values could be anything but anathema to a government in the United States to-day. No leader of such projects could be other than *persona non grata* in the councils of Washington. No peace propaganda or peace education carried out by an official government agency can rise to greater heights than the government itself. And while our government continues to derive its sanction primarily from economic motives that are inimical to peace, peace policies fathered by bureaucrats can never rise to heights; we are lucky if only they do not sink to depths.

All this does not mean that the government is in the hands of wicked marplots, bent on war and not caring for peace. Men are only the instruments by which the trend of conviction (or, often, inertia) in a nation is registered on passing events. The nation and the government alike want peace; but are not ready to make the economic and psychological adjustments—and these are not minor—to insure it.

Furthermore, a Cabinet cannot exist—or, certainly, cannot function smoothly—half slave to war, half free for peace. So long as we retain the War and Navy Departments, the injection of a so-called Peace Department would present a situation of ludicrous incongruity. In fact a recent writer arguing for a Peace Department ends his article:

And one incidental benefit would result as a very welcome by-product of the establishment of this department: it would make peace workers respectable, and remove from peace organizations the stigma of failure in patriotism, and it might even be that the dove of peace would be allowed to appear. in company with the eagle! [18]

Is it conceivable that the Secretaries of War and of the Navy would modify their programs to adapt them to the Peace Department? Then would not the opposite inevitably result?

When the Department of Labor tolerates a Department of Idleness; when the Department of Commerce accepts as friend a Department for the Abolition of Trade; then, and then only, may we expect to see the Secretaries of War and of the Navy fall on the neck of a Secretary of Peace. Short of such a miracle, we may expect to see either an ineffective nonentity in a perfunctory portfolio, or the continuation of peace policies, when there are such, in the hands of the State Department, which does at least have an opportunity to coördinate its work in accord with actual policies, for better or for worse. If an honest-to-goodness Secretary for the Abolition of War ever wormed his way into a Cabinet under anything like present-day conditions, his rival Secretaries would indeed fall on his neck, but not in the precise manner narrated of such incidents in Holy Writ.

Peace through Education

If people were only cultured, well educated in general, peace would be assured. So runs one argument.

If they were let alone by the propaganda of militarism and were educated definitely for peace, war would speedily disappear. So runs another.

The first of these arguments was heard but little in the earlier days when education was the aim, and not the boast, of the American Commonwealth. But increasingly, in the years before the World War, it won adherents in the intellectual world. At the National Arbitration and Peace Congress of 1907, with Andrew Carnegie presiding, Sir Robert Cranston exclaimed:

I do not wish to be a sycophant to you or any other man in this country or in any other country, but I believe the way to obtain peace has been taken by the man who occupies the chair tonight (applause) ; it is to build libraries, endow schools, erect colleges and try to permeate every man and woman with the higher ideals of life, then armaments will fall to pieces.

Seven years elapsed; and then began a battle of the scholars, the pedagogues, and the literati of the world, those in each nation striving to outlie and outhate their counterparts in enemy countries. In the United States, as *The New Republic* proclaimed:

The effective and decisive work on behalf of war has been accomplished by . . . a class which must be comprehensively but loosely described as the "intellectuals."

The American nation is entering this war under the influence of a moral verdict reached after the utmost deliberation by the more thoughtful members of the community. They gradually came to a decision that the attack made by Germany on the international order was sufficiently flagrant and dangerous to justify the country in abandoning its cherished isolation and in using its resources to bring about German defeat. But these thoughtful people were always a small minority. They were able to impose their will upon a reluctant or indifferent majority partly because the increasingly offensive nature of German military and diplomatic policy made plausible opposition to American participation very difficult, but still more because of the overwhelming preponderance of pro-Allies conviction in the intellectual life of the country. If the several important professional groups could have voted separately on the question of war and peace, the list of college professors would probably have yielded the largest majority in favor of war, except perhaps that contained in the Social Register. A fighting anti-German spirit was more general among physicians, lawyers, and clergymen than it was among business men—except those with Wall Street and banking connections.

Finally, it was not less general among writers on magazines and in the newspapers. They popularized what the college professors had been thinking. Owing to this consensus of influences opposition to pro-Allies orthodoxy became intellectually somewhat disreputable, and when a final decision had to be made this factor counted with unprecedented and overwhelming force. College professors headed by a President who had himself been a college professor contributed more effectively to the decision in favor of warfare than did the farmers, the business men, or the politicians.[19]

As the War went on, these same "intellectuals" not only imposed on the public mind all the justifiable resentment against the German cause, but added to it a series of perversions of fact, as witness some of the wrenching of quotations from German scholars out of their context, practiced by scientists under the so-called Creel Bureau. In the name of liberalism they sought to wage war, the apotheosis of autocracy and illiberalism, democratically and with due regard to ideals. At first opposed to conscription, they soon reconciled themselves to it and before long backed it up cheerfully. And what a fanfare of tirade and mouth-frothing was indulged in by the master minds of American education and morality during that period is an open book, available, fortunately, in the public prints for all who can stomach the fetid record.

When the War for democracy and peace was over, the ex-college professor who had sought to win through to high ideals by base and self-defeating methods, still smarting, no more from his personal disability than from his defeats at Paris by the wily Clemenceau and by the secret deceits of his erstwhile allies, was moved to declare, wryly, "I should like to see Germany clean up France and I should like to meet Jusserand and tell him that to his face." [20]

Since those discreditable doings, little has been heard of the idea that education of itself can lead the peoples of the world toward peace. Never could there be a neater or a more tragic instance of the blind leading the blind.

There have been, however, so many discussions of education for peace, so many protests against the militarization of childhood, that it would be a gratuitous waste of effort to recount them here. The literature of the peace movement in all its differing shades of opinion abounds with them. Books have been written on the question, magazines have run articles about it, and educational as well as peace conferences have sometimes run on to great lengths in consideration of its various phases. Everyone cognizant of what is going on in the educational world understands the race between militarization of the youthful mind and the liberating concepts of world brotherhood.

No sooner had the country settled down to business as a constitutional nation, than the public schools became the vehicle for military propaganda. Pupils in New England were given Ignatius Thomson's little wooden-covered book, *The Patriot's Monitor, designed to impress and perpetuate the first principles of the revolution on the minds of youth.* Those principles, as stated, are deservedly inspiring; but the war method and the glorification of national sovereignty are of course taken for granted and efficiently rammed home.

On the other side was Noah Worcester, writing in 1820 that

By information from various parts of the United States, we learn that strong desires have been expressed in favor of the general introduction of school books which may be adapted to imbue the minds of the young with a love of peace and an abhorrence of war. A more reasonable and important desire has seldom been expressed. Should it prevail, and its object be attained, durable benefits will unquestionably result.[21]

Alas, it was not then successful, any more than now. In 1832 the devout Thomas S. Grimké vigorously declaimed:

Peace can never triumph, till education in all its departments, shall teach youth, that those which are called heroic virtues, are expressly prohibited by Christ both in precept and example; that the only warrior, if I may venture the term, whom Christ acknowledges, is the Martyr, laying down property, liberty and life, in his cause; but resolute not to bear arms in defence of them or in vindication of his master's rights. . . . I speak, therefore, the language of a faithful, enlightened friend of the people, when I declare that their highest good is not consulted, unless the *whole scheme* of education be in its elements, practice and influence, decidedly, unchangeably peaceful.[22]

William Ladd, among his first writings and speeches on peace, manifested a passionate interest in education. The Women's International League for Peace and Freedom, campaigning in certain sections against military toys, never felt a deeper resentment than that shown by the Apostle of Peace, as expressed in the course of a passionate address:

The course of education from infancy to manhood at present pursued, tends to inspire the mind with military ardor, and *a love of glory.* Almost as soon as a boy is born, care is taken to give his mind a military turn. The first playthings given him are miniature guns, trumpets, and drums, with pewter soldiers and wooden swords. Ah, fond mother! little do you think, while you dress the forward urchin with the paper cap, and arm him with some mock instruments of death, and delight to see him march round your parlor to a military tune, affecting the manners of a soldier,—little do you think, that you are giving his tender mind a wrong direction, and making impressions which may last forever. . . . It is the duty of every mother, of every father, and of every instructor of youth, to educate children in a manner very different from the prevailing custom.

I greatly fear it would not be quite so simple a matter to turn this trick to-day. In the first place, we have—at least among progressive modern educators—something of a conscience about even our own propaganda when it comes to indoctrinating children. But from the above apostrophe, the most hard-boiled behaviorist and his psychological opposites—if there are any left—would agree on one revealing phrase: "little do you think." And they would agree also that the problem requires educationally a different approach from that of the straight-line moralist Ladd:

A distinguished instructor of youth told me his sons were so taken up with military notions, that he could not reason with them; and he asked me to talk to them. I took the oldest boy, aged about seven years, between my knees, and something like the following conversation ensued:—"Do you love to see the soldiers?" "Yes, I love to see the rub-a-dubs." "Would you like to be one yourself?" "Oh, yes!" "Well, but do you know what these soldiers are for?" "No." "Why, they are learning to kill people. Those bright guns are made to kill people with, and those bright bayonets to stab them with." The boy turned pale; such a thought never before entered his head. "Do you know who crucified our Lord, and drove the spiks through his hands and feet?" The boy was silent. "They were soldiers, and soldiers would burn *your* house, and cut down *your* fruit-trees, and kill your pa, if they were told to." Both the boys were astonished; tears stood in their eyes. "Do you want to be a soldier?" "No." "Do you want to see the rub-a-dubs?" "No."

Neither Ladd's methods nor Grimkés eloquence availed

much if anything at all. Military toys came in for their perennial criticism all through the succeeding years of alternating war and breathing spells. In 1901 the Honorable Andrew J. Palm, of the Pennsylvania State Legislature, was saying vociferously to the Universal Peace Union:

Militarism is encouraged in the home when toy guns are furnished, thus cultivating the feeling which ultimately reaches a point which should cause a nation to blush with shame.

In 1903 there was general agreement when a speaker in a Philadelphia peace conference declared that our real peace work was with the children. Yet those very children were the ones conscripted and shipped overseas in 1917 and '18, and who now, as veterans, are often assiduously engaged in keeping alive in the public schools the tradition of war and faith in war as a method of solving international issues.

There is a common feeling that if the children of the various countries can be taught about each other in a spirit of good will, they will grow up to be less inclined toward any future war. Well and good; too much good will, even if somewhat abstract, can never be built up. Friendly imagination is a resistant to hatred.

But too much may easily be expected from this type of peace education. It is not so simple as put in some magazine verses:

When children's friendships are world wide
New ages will be glorified.
Let child love child, and strife will cease,
Disarm the hearts, for that is peace.

Nor is it true, as a writer has said in *The League of Nations News,* that "International understanding, like marriage, is largely a matter of propinquity." That is to say, even if it were true, understanding alone is not an adequate guarantee of peace. Mere propinquity is no sounder a basis for international peace than for marital bliss. Two of our major wars have been fought with the one people of the world nearest to us in language, blood, and institutions, and another great war even between different sections of our own people.

From abundant examples in present-day bookmaking, I select one child's book as a reminder of our failure to free children from war propaganda to-day. Instead of taking one from some reactionary source, however, I prefer to go to the Institute for Public Service, New York City. Its book bears no less imaginative a name than *Liberty the Giant Killer*. The date is 1919. The theme is World War heroism, for very youthful readers. Here is a portion of the foreword: "Need we say more?" We need to, but not much; merely that the rest of the book spreads the war mythology on thick in all its educational glorification.

There are just as many princesses to love, honor and protect in the world right now as there were in the "once upon a time" days. They are your Mothers, Sisters, Aunts, and Cousins. There are just as many Princes, too. They are Princes of the Everyday world called your Daddies and Brothers, Uncles and Cousins. They are the Princes who sailed three thousand miles across the sea to overcome an enemy that was more dangerous than the giants and dragons, witches and elves of the old fairy stories. For this enemy tried to conquer and rule the whole world, and tried to make men and women, boys and girls give up the freedom they love so dearly.

Now that enemy is beaten, and your Daddies, Brothers, Uncles and Cousins have come home. They will tell you stories more wonderful than any fairy story that was ever told or written. [May one not be pardoned for doubting it, with this example before him?] And if you read Liberty the Giant Killer, you will find other true stories about brave Belgian, French, British, Italian and American soldiers, who fought in the World War for everlasting liberty and everlasting peace.

Somehow the victory seems to have produced not liberty, but a multiplication of despotisms; not peace, but a more widespread militarism, for such good results as came out of the War were largely accidental. And yet, what does that signify? It was not the object that mattered. Had the war been any different, would the war supporters have rallied any less like zealots? It was the fighting that mattered, as it has always mattered, in every war in which this country has participated. And from each one we have emerged with an overwhelming ambition to prepare the children for another.

One example, also, of the process in the public schools—perhaps worse than the average; let us hope it is. Some eighty-eight thousand copies in a single edition of a pamphlet for the twenty-fifth annual program for Patriotic Exercises in Schools, were issued February 12, 1926, Grand Army Flag Day, for use among Rhode Island school children by the State Commissioner of Education. Says Walter E. Ranger, the Commissioner, in a special message opening the booklet:

To the boys and girls of Rhode Island schools:
When Lincoln called patriots forth sixty-four years ago, to save our country from disunion and our republic from ruin, there were some who opposed fighting even to defend the flag of our country and our national life. There were pacifists who would let the nation perish rather than make war; and among them lurked slackers, traitors and enemies of government by the people. . . .
There are some who in the cause of peace fear an excessive nationalism and decry patriotism as a cause of war. All true Americans believe that the prevention of all wars would be the supreme international blessing. But there are those who, hostile to American institutions, seek by pleas for peace to weaken our faith in them. Let us not be deceived by propaganda against national security in the name of peace. We recognize international duty but need to beware of the man who masks an attack on Americanism under a plea for internationalism, or who praises other peoples that he may belittle our nation. Pacific as we are, we may detect the treacherous taint in the solicitation of young children to pledge themselves never to obey their country's call if called to defend her by arms. Loyalty to country forbids such a pledge.

What are some of the things this commissioner would teach? If the things in the rest of the booklet are a reliable guide, here are some of them. There is a quotation from Edward Everett Hale's *The Man Without a Country,* which if followed would have silenced some of our now-worshiped leaders, even Lincoln, and certainly many in the historic peace societies:

If you are ever tempted to say a word or to do a thing that shall put a bar between you and your country, pray God in His mercy to take you that instant home to his own heaven.

He also cites excerpts from Henry Van Dyke's *True Americanism Is This,* one paragraph of which holds up the ideal that

To believe that for the existence and perpetuity of such a state a man should be willing to give his whole service, in property, in labor, and in life.

Which means, being translated, not to give life, but to take it in war. William Ladd and the other pioneers who labored for a better kind of peace education in schools, would hardly relish this tidbit from Mrs. Anthony Wayne Cook, former President General of the estimable D.A.R.:

> We should see that our school boards are not allowing our public school systems to be used for the dissemination of propaganda which, in the guise of so-called peace literature, is in reality dangerous and insidious pacifist dogma.
> As a matter of fact, too much this sort of thing has already been disseminated. It has been cleverly prepared so that it might insidiously stir up unrest and discontent in the minds of both pupils and teachers concerning our time-tested American governmental institutions.

Were it true that pacifists do seek to indoctrinate young minds with peace dogmas, the sin would be more terrible than the D.A.R., with its incessant military propaganda, could ever label it. But peace propaganda of the mildest form is only a pebble in the powder horn; it may cause some interruption in the smooth flow of nationalist war dogma, but that is all.

Henry Van Dyke figures again with his poem, *The Peaceful Warrior,* one stanza of which epigrammatizes:

> A peaceful man must fight
> For that which peace demands,—
> Freedom and faith, honor and right,
> Defend with heart and hands.

All of which leads naturally into a conclusion as true of this peace argument as of the others in this chapter and the one preceding. There is no use in seeking to pry militarism out of the school and the home, so long as wars themselves go on. War is no more a result of militaristic education than such education is the direct outcome of war.

Look over the specific ways in which the child mind is inculcated, unconsciously, with the gospel of the goosestep—the toy weapons; the heroic tales; the revered veterans (and for their valor who can deny them homage?); the unforgotten dead; the memorials in stone, in cannon, in literature, in holidays; the paraphernalia of chauvinistic devotion to country, the salute to the flag, the war songs, the idealized national history. Any such analysis leads straight to the conviction that our protests for a hundred years gone by, and no less in this day but hit the slinking shadow of the unharmed wolf of war.

All True, and Yet——

These skirmishes are not valueless; we must press them without rest. But let us not deceive ourselves. They cannot make our homes safe refuges. They are based on an outworn strategy. They have not served to call out the best fighters to our banner; they have not kept war at bay. It is still marauding, and while it roams the world our pleas and protests are but voices flung to frighten it. They cannot slay it; yet it must be slain.

CHAPTER XIII
WOMEN IN THE FIGHT FOR PEACE

You want to know what was the most awful thing? The disillusionment was the most awful thing—the going off. The war wasn't. The war is what it has to be. Did it surprise you to find out that war is horrible? The only surprising thing was the going off. To find out that the women are horrible—that was the surprising thing. That they can smile and throw roses, that they can give up their men, their children, the boys they have put to bed a thousand times and pulled the covers over a thousand times, and petted and brought up to be men. That was the surprise! That they gave us up—that they sent us—sent us! . . . The women sent us. No general could have made us go if the women hadn't allowed us to be stacked on the trains, if they had screamed out that they would never look at us again if we turned into murderers.
—Wounded lieutenant, in *Men in War,* by ANDREAS LATZKO. (Copyright, Boni and Liveright.)

CHAPTER XIII

WOMEN IN THE FIGHT FOR PEACE

Acid words are these of the Austrian World War veteran, bitter and certainly not wholly fair. But behind them lay centuries filled with feminine acclaim of war heroics.

Deborah, prophetess of Mount Ephraim, is exalted as the instigator of the conquering Barak of early Jewish lore.

It is recorded in a legend of Rome how the Sabine women, rather than see war between their avenging relatives and the Romans who had stolen them for wives, ran out between the armies and successfully averted conflict. But against this not altogether lovely tale must stand the Amazons of Greek legend, with their repute for effectiveness in slaughter.

The lion-hearted, martial Queen Boadicea of first century Britain has been dramatized by several poets and half a dozen playwrights.

Zenobia, queen of ancient Palmyra, led a tremendous military insurrection against the Roman Empire in the third century A.D.

Tacitus, in describing the special qualities of the Teuton barbarians, points out how their own women accompanied them into battle, nursing their wounds and cheering them on; and Justus Lipsius, his editor, added in 1575 the comment that they demanded, in their pride, that their loved ones should not return unwounded.

Among certain primitive tribes the torture of military prisoners has been a regularly assigned function of women, because of their demonstrated capacity for cruelty. Even as late as the French Revolution some of the men Terrorists were appalled and sickened by the ferocity of their women aides.

There are records of women, some of them courtesans,

some from the nobility, who served in early medieval armies— such as Margheritona of the light horse cavalry of the Count de Gaiazzo, and the noble swordswoman Luzia Stanga; these and others are mentioned by the Italian raconteur Bandello. Duels between women were surprisingly numerous, especially in France. The story of Saint Joan is too well known to need more than casual mention. In the eighth century the Duke of Bohemia was compelled to war against large bands of embattled women. Black Agnes, Countess of March, demonstrated warlike prowess in holding off a terrific siege of nineteen weeks against the Castle of Dunbar, led by the Earl of Salisbury in 1338. Mary Anne Talbot, an Englishwoman, in the latter part of the eighteenth century, won fame and a pension for her exploits as a drummer boy in Flanders Fields and for her bloody naval adventures. The Maid of Saragossa, celebrated by Lord Byron in his *Childe Harold,* is famous for her aid in the defense of the Spanish town in 1808. Even as recently as 1851, in France, the cross of the Legion of Honor was bestowed upon a woman—Angélique Duchemin—for three wounds sustained in the course of seven war campaigns. In the World War battalions of women fought at the front for Russia and Austria and perhaps for other countries.

At the very first glance [says Edward Beaumont in his crotchety work, *The Sword and Womankind*] it is found that, dating from the best days of chivalry onwards, with all that was most distinguished among dashing, dainty dames, "great ladies a man sees at arquebus range," as the old Spaniards put it, the Sword had undisputed command of all advantages. Always fond and festive, always at lovemaking in times of leisure, always showing a gallant affectation of reckless gaiety and ease of manner, it represented in the eyes of women yet other telling and seductive qualities besides. It was an indispensable ally in their indulgences, giving a certain flavour of "high life" to their caprices, a surfeit of caresses after battles fought and victories won, presents from overseas and fresh news of the great outside world.

Now this is pretty hard. But it is scarcely sterner than the nettled words of the Reverend David Bogue in 1813:

The influence of the female sex is universally acknowledged and felt. I want that influence to diffuse peace and love over the face of the earth. I scarcely know how to address myself to respectable matrons, who after nursing their sons with the tenderest affection send them away to the work of desolation, and rejoice at their success—when they make women like yourselves widows, and their children fatherless. . . . In which of your works have you come forth as the advocates of humanity and the champions of peace? Tell me, that I may withdraw the censure. You are silent: you blush at this reproach, and well you may: they may justly be the most burning blushes that ever reddened the female cheek.

Both the critics of women on this score, and their defenders, it seems, were given to a highly exaggerated notion of the influence of women in a state of society where they were all but universally considered, as Schopenhaur called them, "number two of the human species."

Noah Worcester paid them a glowing compliment:

Permit me then to express my firm belief, that the abolition of war will be completely in the power of the fair sex, if they can be persuaded to act the part of christians indeed, and to combine their influence for the heavenly purpose. . . . All women professing godliness should take a decided and active part. . . . By thirty years of faithful and united experience on the part of females in Christendom, war might lose all its fascinating charms, and be regarded by the next generation with more abhorrence than the people of the present age look back on the gladiatorial combats of Rome, the papal crusades, or the flames of martyrdom.

The Massachusetts Peace Society's third annual report developed the same fervent theme:

There is still another numerous and respected class of the human family, on whom great reliance may be placed—the CHRISTIAN LADIES. In former ages the influence of the fair sex was abundantly employed for sharpening the swords of ferocious men; and it is but a few centuries since the ladies of England were not ashamed to be seen at the publick tournaments, riding in troops with swords by their sides! But in this age the ladies set a noble example, by encouraging humane and beneficent institutions. A great accession of strength may therefore be expected from them, as soon as they shall have been duly apprised of the extensive influence which they may exert, for saving the lives of men and giving peace to the world.

Not only Worcester, but William Ladd as well, sought to apprise them duly. At Portland in 1824 he spoke directly to the feminine contingent of the Maine Peace Society:

To gain your smiles we rush into the deadly conflict and destroy each other. Oh how melancholy is the fact, that female beauty, softness and delicacy should so often have smiled on scenes of carnage and bloodshed, and rewarded the perpetrators of the blackest crimes with smiles of approbation!

Said the opening broadside of the American Peace Society:

We have one appeal left, which, should all others fail, we are sure will prove successful . . . and that, *ladies,* is addressed to you. . . . Plead for peace, for "who can plead like you?"

Ladd appealed to women to read peace literature, circulate it, assist in forming peace societies, and in 1835 issued his special work on *The Duty of Women to Promote the Cause of Peace*.

N. L. Foster, before the East Haddam (Connecticut) Peace Society (1825), struck the tonic chord when he exhorted:

Ye venerable matrons! Ye mothers in Israel! Ye wives, ye daughters, ye sisters! It is you who control the stronger sex. It is you who sanctify and form man's dearest ties. Your influence is universally felt and acknowledged; you can make man a murderer, or a christian—an angel or a demon.[1]

The process of angelizing was earnestly tried—by some of the women among the handful reached by these pillars of prophecy. Ladd mentions the formation of "female peace societies" with approval, and helped by his presence to organize them, for example one in the Bowdoin Street Church of Boston. The Female Peace Society of Cincinnati was founded in 1820. Others exclusively for women followed, though never were they either numerous or influential. The Hartford (Connecticut) Peace Society in the 'forties had an unusually active female auxiliary.

In keeping with the temper of the period, women's work for peace was not such as to bring them conspicuously before the public eye. The Bowdoin Street society set out to "obtain information on the subject of Peace, to instruct children in the Sabbath school and at home in its principles, and to endeavor to carry out these principles in everyday life." It had required the passage of four years' time in the Massachusetts Peace Society before two women, Mrs. Sarah Blake and Mrs. Sarah Phipps, became the first representatives of their sex formally to join the peace movement. The American Peace Society encouraged ladies' societies in the churches to elect their pastors to life membership, at a cost of twenty dollars, the fee for non-ministers amounting to ten dollars more.

Peace Work—for Men Only

How widespread was the desire for this growing, if still subordinate, public activity of women? Most of the peace society leaders eagerly welcomed it; they were progressive in more ways than merely one. But by no means could all of them reconcile such incursions on their male prerogatives.

In the last years of the decade beginning with 1830 there was a widespread upheaval over self-assertive women pioneers. The Grimké sisters, Sarah and Angelina, whose brother Thomas had been so active an influence for peace until his death in 1834, had swung northward into the midst of the abolition crusade. Garrison and Samuel J. May (May very timidly at first) looked upon them with appreciative esteem. But hardly so the generality. As their audiences more and more came to include men as well as women, opposition to the innovators gathered force. That women were permitted to speak to mixed audiences under holy spires indicated to critics that "the abolitionists were ready to set at naught the order and decorum of the Christian Church." When the sisters spoke to enthusiastic congregations in the Unitarian Church at Hingham from the pulpit of the Reverend Charles Brooks—of whom we shall hear later as a leader in the fight against military training—the "Pauline prejudices" of many were dispelled.

Soon, however, came an attack in the form of an official bull (to use May's word) from the Pastoral Association of Massachusetts on "The Rights of Women." Nevertheless the

New England Anti-Slavery Convention held in Boston in May, 1838, voted (fulfilling the dire fears of the bachelor Whittier) that

> All persons present, or who may be present, at subsequent meetings, whether men or women, who agree with us in sentiment on the subject of slavery, be invited to become members and participate in the proceedings of the Convention.

The vote was five hundred and fifty-seven to four hundred and fifty-one. An irreconcilable minority of eight orthodox ministers resigned at once, and seven others, though remaining, filed a protest. Judge William Jay also left the Society, saying:

> Married women without their husbands were associated with men in the Executive Committee—a committee to which is confided the management of the society, and whose meetings have hitherto been and will probably continue to be, both frequent and private.

How slender a reed seemed marital loyalty in those regulated years! There were further committee complications. A committee of three, one of them a woman, was authorized to prepare a memorial for all the ecclesiastical associations of New England. It was received with boorish resentment generally, while the Rhode Island Congregational Association, even with the consent of clergymen who had been keen for abolition—under masculine auspices—unitedly voted

> to turn the illegitimate product from the house, and obliterate from the records all traces of its entrance.[2]

Over in London, two years later, an anti-slavery convention was also to bar women from its sessions, in obedience to "the plain teaching of the word of God."

So much for the character of the opposition to women in public life. It was no different when they desired to labor actively for peace. In Garrison's *Liberator* for December 15, 1837, the abolitionist leader announced that no longer could he be content with the emancipation of slaves alone. "Next to the overthrow of slavery," he declared editorially, "the cause of PEACE will command our attention." The rest of the editorial is an exposition of non-resistance. Significantly, too, the utterance ended with these words:

As our object is *universal* emancipation, to redeem woman as well as man from a servile to an equal condition,—we shall go for the RIGHTS OF WOMEN to their utmost extent.

Abolitionists, criticized widely for possessing only one idea, now had to endure still more condemnation for being all-around radicals and innovators. They recognized, however, the close connection between ends and means, and when a peace group met in Boston in May, under the chairmanship of William Ladd, and called a peace convention for the following September, they eagerly made plans to take part, seeing a chance to test the feminist issue in its relation to the peace movement along with their pacifist position.

The maneuvering of radicals and conservatives alike to swing this convention in their respective directions justifiably amuses the student of early tactics, and will be discussed later in some relevant detail. Not the last of the moot questions was the place of women in the meetings.

Women gamely attended, not knowing what their reception was to be. Garrison drove straight into the thick of the matter by suggesting immediately on the opening of the first session that slips of paper be passed around, for the registration of members, each individual to "sign his or her name." Garrison wrote about it to his wife:

There was a smile on the countenances of many abolitionist friends, while others in the Convention looked very grave. Several of the clergy were present, but no one rose to object. Of course, women became members, and were thus entitled to speak and vote. A business committee was then appointed, upon which Abby Kelley and a Miss [Susan] Sisson were placed. Mrs. [Maria] Chapman was added to another committee. In the course of the forenoon, Reverend Mr. Beckwith [George C., of the American Peace Society] was called to order by Abby K. Endurance now passed its bounds on the part of the women-contemners, and accordingly several persons (clergymen and laymen) requested their names to be erased from the roll of the Convention, because women were to be allowed to participate in the proceedings! They were gratified in their request.[*]

The *Liberator* lists seven of these angry dissenters; but the printed report of the proceedings shows a total of fourteen, among them several who had been strongly hopeful of women's influence in the eradication of war! Ladd was not among them; on another occasion he expressed the view (though it sounds resigned!), "Shut the gate in the face of woman and she will jump over the pickets. Open it wide and she will not be assuming."

The movement for women's emancipation was scarcely launched by the year of 1838. Susan B. Anthony was only eighteen years of age; Lucy Stone but twenty; Margaret Fuller twenty-eight; and Elizabeth Cady Stanton twenty-three, ten years younger than the first women's rights convention held in her home soon after the end of the Mexican War.

Though in that conflict Mexican women followed their men to the battlefields, where their ministrations to the wounded of both sides inspired Whittier's lines on "The Angels of Buena Vista," something of the fire of Revolutionary days seemed lacking in the reaction of women in the United States toward the piratical struggle across the arid southwestern border— though in their attitude toward the War there was nothing unique. They supported that War as they had the wars of earlier years. The capture of Tampico on November 14, 1846, was made possible largely through Mrs. Ann Chase, wife of the United States Consul, who supplied the invaders with plans of the city and other information.

As in most wars our own Revolutionary conflict drew into the fighting ranks a few combative women. Sarah Hull, wife of Major William Hull, went with him to camp and engaged in the famous Battle of Saratoga. In South Carolina, Grace and Rachel Martin put on their husbands' clothes, and in this convenient assumption of masculine prowess waylaid and took captive two British officers. At Fort Washington, Margaret Corbin fought shoulder to shoulder with her husband; when he was killed, she took over his labors in the artillery till she received a wound, for which she later won Congressional praise. At Monmouth a gunner's wife did likewise, and for her act was awarded a commission. Hannah Weston at Machias, Maine, gathered powder, ball and foodstuffs for the town's male defenders, and thereby won a local immortality and twelve yards of "Camlet" cloth, the last of which was paid for by a grateful State. Deborah Sampson, who did not hesitate to aid in killing but was overcome with shame at being caught in male attire and at "man's work," served three years and twice was wounded. Every schoolgirl has heard of the exploits of Molly Pitcher.

As always, however, the vast majority of womankind aided in more conventional ways. In some localities—for example two counties in South Carolina—it became quite the fashion for young women to join in a pledge "not to receive the addresses of any suitors" who had not enlisted in the army.

In Philadelphia alone, in 1780, women gave up jewels and other valuables until a sum upwards of seventy-five hundred dollars was gathered to aid the "rebel" cause; more than twenty-two hundred shirts were made by them in the winter of that year. Long after the Revolution, when work on the Bunker Hill monument had twice ceased and a period from 1823 to 1840 had elapsed without the memorial shaft's completion, it was a group of women who supplied the funds and energy to finish it—the funds being earned by knitting needles and crochet hooks.

The abundant support of the war by women won them a tribute from the ever-gallant General Washington:

The army ought not to regret its sacrifices or its sufferings, when they meet with so flattering a reward, as in the sympathy of your sex; nor can it fear that its interests will be neglected, when espoused by advocates as powerful as they are amiable.[4]

Elizabeth F. Ellet, in her book *The Women of the Revolution*, credits John Adams with a letter to his wife, in which he said:

I believe the two Howes have not very great women for wives. If they had, we should suffer more from their exertions than we do. This is our good fortune. A smart wife would have put Howe in possession of Philadelphia a long time ago.

The story of women in the War of 1812 is substantially the same as in the Revolution; though the later conflict happily produced a great many fewer Daughters.

Women and the Civil War

Mary A. Livermore, famous as feminist, Civil War worker, and who later joined in the labors of the peace societies and came to see much in socialism, published in 1887 a book about the Rebellion as she saw it. In that revealing work she says:

> The great uprising among men, who ignored party and politics, and forgot sect and trade, in the fervor of their quickened love of country, was paralleled by a similar uprising among women.[5]

Said a popular verse of the time:

> Just take your gun and go,
> For Ruth can drive the oxen, John,
> And I can use the hoe.

Thomas Buchanan Read urged Northern women on to loyal sacrifice:

> The wife who girds her husband's sword,
> 'Mid little ones who weep or wonder,
> And bravely speaks the cheering word,
> What though her heart be rent asunder,
> Doomed nightly in her dreams to hear
> The bolts of death around him rattle,
> Hath shed as sacred blood as e'er
> Was poured upon the field of battle.

A poet of the South did likewise, admonishing women to lay aside their bright gowns and gewgaws, and

> Come with your souls in your faces—
> To meet the stern needs of the hour. . . .
> E'en if you drop down unheeded
> What matter? God's ways are the best;
> You've poured out your life where 'twas needed,
> And He will take care of the rest.

They came, indeed, in 1861 just as they did in 1917. It was neither helmets nor sweaters that they sent to the troops, sometimes in embarrassing profusion, but the useless "havelocks," a headdress named in honor of the British General famed for his imperialist exploits in India. Delicacies were showered down, too often with a heartbreaking lack of facilities to transport them.

In North and South at one and the same time, women's fingers were busied with everything from letter-writing to tobacco bags. Those who recall the home life of early World War days, or of previous wars for that matter, will understand how these tobacco bags "were supposed to serve the same purpose as scalps in another kind of warfare. They marked, at least, the long roll of pleasant words and kindly glances, if not of incipient flirtations."

No less than their sisters of the North for one cause were the Southern women ready to sacrifice themselves for another. An appreciative Confederate veteran summed it up when he declared, after the War, that

they were joined to the Southern cause to love, honor, and obey—for richer or for poorer, for better or for worse, and until death them should part!

In a single word, the Southern women, old and young, gentle and simple, had but one thought, and that was to aid and encourage, in every conceivable way, the soldiers of the South.*

Not only in the sewing circles at home but at the front women were found in plenty. Mrs. Livermore states, of the Northern women, that

The number of women who actually bore arms and served in the ranks during the war was greater than is supposed. Sometimes they followed the army as nurses, and divided their services between the battlefield and hospital.

There were Annie Etheridge, of Michigan, who fought in many battles all through the War; Bridget Devens, or "Michigan Bridget," who fought by the side of her husband till the War ended, and then enlisted with him in the regular army; Mrs. Kady Brownell, who served as color-bearer to the Fifth

Rhode Island Infantry, and earned fame as a skilled sharp-shooter and swordswoman; Georgianna Peterman, drummer in the Seventh Wisconsin; and Madame Turchin, who not only nursed her husband when he was taken ill, but took his place at the head of his regiment—the Nineteenth Illinois. Mrs. Livermore quotes an unsubstantiated estimate of the number of women actually engaged in fighting for the North as nearly four hundred. Frank Moore, in his *Women of the War* (1866), tells the story of many more Civil War heroines whose exploits were varied, but equally colorful and demonstrative of women's ability to serve the state in the ancient masculine manner.

Yet it was through the Sanitary Commission, founded by Antoinette Brown Blackwell, that women showed their vigor-ous war support most generally, both in gifts from those at home and in active service with the armies. It was in such labor that Clara Barton revealed the great capacity for organiz-ing relief work, and acquired the experience, which enabled her so successfully to found the American Red Cross in 1881 and serve as its active president until, in 1904, she retired at the age of eighty-three.

The work done by such women in the Civil War was recog-nized as "exerting a greater moral force on the nation than the army that carried loaded muskets." Of these women President Lincoln said, at a meeting in Washington:

I am not accustomed to use the language of eulogy. I have never studied the art of paying compliments to women. But I must say that if all that has been said by orators and poets since the crea-tion of the world in praise of women, was applied to the women of America, it would not do them justice for their conduct during the war.[7]

And once more women had stood by; stood by with loyalty to the North or to the South, and, North and South alike, with loyalty to war.

Tidewaters of the Suffrage Struggle

By 1866 enough noise had been made by the advocates of equal rights to flush with disapproval many a manly cheek.

Men of peace, especially what might have been called at the period late men of peace—for there were few who held out under the beating of the Civil War's deep waves of feeling —were hardly different from other men in their attitude toward the women's movement. One sterling exception was Alfred H. Love, leader, in that year of 1866, of the Universal Peace Union, whose call for organization had contained this explicit assurance of drastic universality:

We invite to these meetings all persons, irrespective of Sex, Color, Race or Faith.

This, be it noted, antedated by three years the formation of the National and American Women's Suffrage Associations.

"Having manhood, and womanhood," said the Universal Peace Union in one of its earliest resolutions, "we agree with the wise man of Athens, who settled the disputes of his distracted age by the principle, 'Equality causes no war.'" It was further

Resolved, that the keen moral sense of woman, her power and influence, are needed in the great reconstruction, that with the ballot in her hand, peace principles must prevail in our government.

Out of its thirty-eight officials, the organization allotted nine places to women, an extraordinary batting average for those days or even days, as we shall see, considerably later. One of the Vice Presidents was Lucretia Mott, who recalled stitching, years ago, the articles of Noah Worcester to her almanac for special reading, and who could not fail to link with her other ideals of freedom the banishment of warfare. Another active sympathizer was Lucy Stone, who attended meetings of the U.P.U. and, as was natural, demanded the voting privilege for women as an essential step if they were to register effectively their influence for peace; and if latter-day events have thus far failed to bear her out, indubitably the opportunity to meet with men on a plane of equality signified a gain for the cause of equal rights and added a new zest to meetings in the past appallingly uncolorful.

No one, reading the proceedings of these conferences, could

doubt that it was not easy to remain an advocate of passive peace before such women as Lucy Stone, Cora Daniels, Josephine Griffing, and others who had learned a technique of bloodless but unrelenting battle. With what sublime courage (or was it strategy, a subtle reliance on feminine appeal?) must have moved the U.P.U. when it appointed, in 1868, a finance committee consisting of three women and not one man to exercise wisdom, restraint, and "experienced guidance"! Alfred Love's loyalty to the woman suffrage movement was rewarded, in 1884, by a tender of the Vice Presidential nomination of the Equal Rights Party, which polled for its Presidential candidate, Belva A. Lockwood (running alone), some twenty-five hundred votes!

A new impetus toward peace was given the women's movement by Mrs. Julia Ward Howe at the time of the Franco-Prussian War. Long disliking Louis Napoleon and his rule, but filled with admiration of the French people and their works of art, Mrs. Howe was deeply moved at the suffering caused by the War and the defeat of the French, a calamity brought upon them, to her view, by an unworthy government. In her *Reminiscences* she says:

As I was revolving these matters in my mind, while the war was still in progress, I was visited by a sudden feeling of the cruel and unnecessary character of the contest. It seemed to me a return to barbarism, the issue having been one which might easily have been settled without bloodshed. The question forced itself upon me, "Why do not the mothers of mankind interfere in these matters, to prevent the waste of that human life of which they alone bear and know the cost?

Anyone blessed with sufficient perspective might have answered Mrs. Howe's inquiry. He could have told her frankly that women, like men, when a conflict is not remote, insist on seeing it as necessary. It seemed as necessary to French and German women that they should support the War of 1870 as it had to Mrs. Howe that she must aid in the Holy War of 1861. That this had never occurred to her is evident by her next sentence: "I had never thought of this before."

But if she was late in catching her vision, she delayed not at all in going into action. "The august dignity of motherhood and its terrible responsibilities now appeared to me in a new aspect, and I could think of no better way of expressing my sense of these than that of sending forth an appeal to womanhood throughout the world, which I then and there composed."

Dated September, 1870, and translated into French, Spanish, German, Italian and Swedish, the peace appeal was sent out all over the globe. It read:

APPEAL TO WOMANHOOD THROUGHOUT THE WORLD

Again, in the sight of the Christian world, have the skill and power of two great nations exhausted themselves in mutual murder. Again have the sacred questions of international justice been committed to the fatal mediation of military weapons. In this day of progress, in this century of light, the ambition of rulers has been allowed to barter the dear interests of domestic life for the bloody exchanges of the battlefield. Thus men have done. Thus men will do. But women need no longer be made a party to proceedings which fill the globe with grief and horror. Despite the assumptions of physical force, the mother has a sacred and commanding word to say to the sons who owe their life to her suffering. That word should now be heard, and answered as never before.

Arise, then, Christian women of this day! Arise, all women who have hearts, whether your baptism be that of water or of tears! Say firmly: "We will not have great questions decided by irrelevant agencies. Our husbands shall not come to us, reeking with carnage, for caresses and applause. Our sons shall not be taken from us to unlearn all that we have been able to teach them of charity, mercy, and patience. We, women of one country, will be too tender of those of another country, to allow our sons to be trained to injure theirs." From the bosom of the devastated earth a voice goes up with our own. It says: "Disarm, disarm! The sword of murder is not the balance of justice." Blood does not wipe out dishonor, nor violence indicate possession. As men have often forsaken the plough and the anvil at the summons of war, let women now leave all that may be left of home for a great and earnest day of counsel.

Let them meet first, as women, to bewail and commemorate the dead. Let them then solemnly take counsel with each other as to the means whereby the great human family can live in peace, man as the brother of man, each bearing after his own kind the sacred impress, not of Cæsar, but of God.

In the name of womanhood and of humanity, I earnestly ask that a general congress of women, without limit of nationality, may be appointed and held at some place deemed most convenient, and at the earliest period consistent with its objects, to promote the alliance of the different nationalities, the amicable settlement of international questions, the great and general interests of peace.[8]

On the call of Mrs. Howe, William Cullen Bryant, and Mary F. Davis, a meeting "for the purpose of considering and arranging the steps necessary to be taken for calling a World's Congress of Women in behalf of International Peace," was held in New York in December, 1870. Addresses were made by Lucretia Mott, Octavius Frothingham, and Alfred H. Love. At a later meeting in New York Bryant launched the stern interrogation:

When a battle is fought, women come and bind up the wounds of those whose bodies are torn by cannon balls and grape shot; they tend them in hospitals; they watch night and day by the bedside of those who are delirious with pain; they smooth the pillows of the dying. Shall they be limited to this? Are they to make no effort to *prevent* the evil which they so tenderly seek to mitigate?[9]

They were not, as it happened; they were to act for a while longer just as they had always acted and still act, when war is on. Though Mrs. Howe declared that "our husbands shall not come to us, reeking with carnage, for caresses and applause," they came, and got both, in 1898, their women's doubts assuaged by the appealing strains of "Just Before the Battle, Mother," and "Just Break the News to Mother." They came again, in 1917.

Even Mrs. Howe's campaign was not to be successful. Another meeting in Tremont Temple, Boston, was followed, in the spring of 1871, by the organization of the American Branch of the Women's International Peace Association under the presidency of Mrs. Howe. So controversial was the matter that five meetings were required to consummate the organization. Although *The Advocate of Peace,* descrying in the face of the churches' failure a new Galahad, declared that "women can prevent war if they will"; though Elihu Burritt let his linguistic accomplishments lead him into remarking that "the daughters of those who were last at the cross and first at the sepulchre of the Prince of Peace; the daughters by spirit-birth of those women who washed the thorn-prints from his lacerated brow, are coming to the rescue of his great inheritance and kingdom on earth"; in spite of all this there were more who saw in this effort of women only fanaticism, sentimentality, or even a menace to public sobriety. Some objected especially to Mrs. Howe's characterization of the movement as Christian; to them it had about it for such an appellation all too faint a smell of powder to seem natural.

In 1872 the aroused peace crusader went to England in the hope of arranging there the longed-for congress of women for peace. Anti-feminist prejudice was strong, however; and when she attended a Paris Peace Congress and asked permission to present her project, she was told "with some embarrassment" that she might address the officers of the society after the meetings had adjourned. Her mission a failure, Mrs. Howe was obliged to return and do the next best thing: arrange a "mothers' day" for peace to be celebrated simultaneously by women all around the world, acting in their home localities.

Some success she had; yet the pamphlet she edited afterwards, containing reports of these meetings, shows what obstacles, both among men and with her own sex also, were in her path. The great Women's Peace Festival of June 2, 1873, produced after all nothing more immediately tangible than meetings, none too well attended and still dominated by men peace leaders, in Boston, New Bedford, Nantucket, New Haven, Ledyard (Connecticut), New York, Brooklyn, Poughkeepsie, Orange (New Jersey), Philadelphia, Wilmington, Chicago, St. Louis, London, Manchester, Geneva, Rome, and Constantinople.

If the world-wide demonstrations were something of a fizzle, because the time was not yet ripe, they served a useful purpose none the less. The American Peace Society was stirred

up so much that for the first time in its career of forty-three
years it elected women to office: Mrs. Howe and the widowed
Mrs. George C. Beckwith. New determination was given to
those already won to a general desire for more peace effort,
and some felt their devotion greatly deepened. Among these
was Julia Ward Howe herself, who wrote in her diary as her
project unfolded:

I confess that I value more those processes of thought which
explain history than those which arraign it. I would not therefore
in my advocacy of peace strip one laurel leaf from the graves so
dear and tender in our recollection. Our brave men did and dared
the best which the time allowed. The sorrow for their loss was
none the less brought upon us by those who believed in the military method.

Until her death four years before the War that would have
crowned her life with unendurable thorns, Julia Ward Howe
struggled—one almost uses without a qualification the patronizing old word manfully!—to speed the end of the war system.

Lucretia Mott, Julia Ward Howe, and Belva A. Lockwood:
these were the forerunners of the later women leaders whose
work for peace will always, let us hope, be gratefully remembered. All these were subject to the peculiarities of their times
and possessed of traits not uncommon to those who must buf-
fet the bulwarks of entrenched traditionalism. But their labor
counted, if not heavily at once; and as Mrs. Howe at one time
said (and might have said of radicals in general), "The special faults of women are those incidental to a class that has
never been allowed to work out its ideal."

Mrs. Lockwood became one of the earliest officers of the
Universal Peace Union. She founded the National Arbitration
Association at Washington later on, and served for many years
on the Commission of the International Peace Bureau.

Women came into the international peace congresses only as
visitors until 1889, when they were given the status of official
members. In the United States, women had to contend during the last half of the century against very much the same
curious mixture of appeal and denial that characterized large

sections of the peace movement in the earlier half. In the 'eighties such movements as the National Arbitration League urged women to use all their power to abolish war. In 1887 the National and the World's W.C.T.U. formed at Nashville educational Peace Departments under the direction of Hannah J. Bailey. In the following year, at Washington, was founded the International Council of Women, which in the next two decades grew until it included seven million members the world around; though actually very conservative in its peace interests, the organization did something to promote the idea of world organization. It stood for "the removal of prejudice, national and racial, and the education of children, youth, and the general public in a proper estimate of what the different nations have successfully contributed to the world's wealth and joy."

The League of Women for Universal Disarmament asked for too much to attract many to its meaningful program; the Women's Universal Alliance for Peace secured the signatures of five million women to a statement disapproving war.

The idea that women of themselves, men's opposition notwithstanding, could by some potent exclusive force drive war from the earth as Saint Patrick de-reptiled Erin, hung on into the twentieth century. That prophet of the flaming penpoint, Olive Schreiner, in her *Woman and Labour* predicted that

> The day when the woman takes her place beside the man in the governance of the affairs of her race, will also be that day that heralds the death of war as a means of arranging human differences.

In her valuable book, *Between War and Peace*, Florence Brewer Boeckel quotes the Swedish feminist, Ellen Key, as saying, in *War, Peace and the Future*,

> The characteristics that are now scornfully called feminine . . . were in the springtime of Christianity active in the suppression of violence. If these assets are again to hold violence at bay, it will be only through the power of women to make them living again, living not only in the souls of men but in the growth and intergrowth of the communities.

And likewise a quotation is selected from an address before the Conference on the Cause and Cure of War, by Dr. Beatrice Hinkle:

War is the product of the irrational (that is to say, unrational) impulses of men toward self-assertion and power; reason is not yet strong enough to control such impulses; they can be controlled only by other and stronger irrational impulses; the impulses of women are toward creation and preservation of life; and because they have been less suppressed and modified than those of men, they are stronger and will be able to overcome them if given full play.

Even the conservative Justice David J. Brewer years ago grew lyrical and spoke, though "not as champion or prophet of female suffrage," of woman and the fact that

Her patriotism is as certain and as strong as that of her brother, and whenever the need comes, although she may not shoulder the musket or draw the sword, she does all that is possible to ameliorate the hardships of war. . . . But while all this is true, you need no assurance that her voice is and always will be potent for peace.[10]

Now it is a cheap and gratuitous indoor sport to contradict the dead; and yet he would be a rarely disciplined realist who could refrain from pointing out that "while all this is true," woman's or any other voice for peace will be voice only. Sounder far on this point was the frank statement of woman's position made by a woman, Mrs. Ellen M. Henrotin, to the National Arbitration and Peace Congress of 1907:

During the Civil War the women on both sides, instead of restraining, urged on the men; in the Austrian-Prussian and Franco-Prussian wars, the same phenomenon was observed—as it was also in the South African and Russian-Japanese wars—perhaps slightly less in the Spanish-American War. When all the considerations are taken into account which should operate to influence women in favor of peace and arbitration, the attitude towards war which she has taken in the past is difficult to comprehend.[11]

Up to the very brink of the World War in which women were to prove indisputably their adaptability to the war machines, they were patronized and assigned a very minor rôle in the peace movement; the only exceptions being those women of outstanding force of character and intellectual vigor who could not be denied, and of course the consistent welcome shown to women by the more radical peace bodies, including the Friends.

In its entire existence, for example, the American Peace Society from 1828 to 1928 had 691 members of its Executive Committee, Directors, Vice Presidents, and Honorary Councillors, of which only 28 were women—barely more than 4 per cent. In 1914 the American Peace Society had 107 officers, of whom only 12 or 11 per cent were women.

Among the 210 registered members of the American Conference on International Arbitration held at Washington in 1896, not one was a woman. When the Peace Department of the Women's Christian Temperance Union was established in 1887, so poverty-stricken for strong justifications were the leaders who announced the project to the world that the best thing they could find to print was William Ladd's appeal to women, written three-quarters of a century before! The Year Book of the New York Peace Society for as late a year as 1910 reveals that of its 788 individual members 359 or 43 per cent were women; but only three or approximately ⅜ of 1 per cent held any office. Let the Lucy Stone League of to-day add to its chamber of horrors the historical note that the 1915 Lake Mohonk Conference was still prefacing its published lists of guests with the laconic comment: "The asterisk following the name of a gentleman indicates that he was accompanied by his wife." If anyone still wonders at the formation of separate peace organizations composed of women and women-led, here is grist for the mill wheels of his thought.

In his addresses around this country on Women and the Cause of Peace, Baron d'Estournelles de Constant in 1911 paid tribute to the pacific influence of woman. As usual, however, with the bulk of peace speakers, he made his reservations, befitting in his case a patriotic Frenchman:

The doctrine of republican France is to defend its own if necessary, but not to attack. This is the national sentiment, which our women fully share with our men. On this point their accord is definite and complete.

Their accord, of course, was exactly like that of women in Germany, Austria, Belgium, England, Russia, Italy, and everywhere else in the combatant countries of the war of 1914. Including, let us not forget, the United States of America. Before any discussion of that conflict it is right to consider a reasonable question certain to be asked. Is there no difference between wars? Are all wars to be treated with equal condemnation? The answer, of course, is No. But it is equally reasonable to insist that if women are ever to function effectively in war prevention, they must recognize that the differences between the ethical motivation of some wars and certain others is infinitely less than immediate war propaganda makes them seem. They will have to contribute, sooner or later, more substantially than they have as yet, to that clamor of anti-war sentiment which, at critical junctures, clogs the war god's chariot wheels.

With the exception of a brave minority of the faithfully defiant, women in the United States took nothing more advanced than the official government position. They proudly wore the military leash; they turned on "slackers" and generously gave their loved ones to the shambles—all from a motive the nobility of which I should be last to deny. There were women, just as there were men, who fought the war policy to the last ditch, and who thereafter used their immunity from combat to solace the persecuted and abused ones among the conscientious objectors and political prisoners. But seekers for a vital difference of behavior between the male and female sexes would need more than a powerful microscope; he would require the lenses of imagination.

The story of those days is still surcharged with passion, and there is no need to comment further on it. The central facts are needed, nevertheless, to round out the volume of war stories of our womanhood, and cannot be omitted. Suffice it to write in the record a few significant congratulatory utterances. Said Senator George E. Chamberlain, Chairman of the Committee on Military Affairs:

The women of America up to this day have been more active, have rendered a greater service, and have more carefully fitted themselves for hardship and future effort than ever before in the history of our country. And I say this without disparaging the splendid work that has been done by our mothers, wives and sisters in every prior war.[12]

Said Josephus Daniels, Secretary of the Navy:

American women have always been ready to answer the call of service and have cheerfully undergone the untold sacrifices and burdens which war places upon them so much more heavily than upon men. . . . Unless our women feel the greatness of the moral issues involved in this contest, and unless they have raised their boys to fight, if necessary, for the things for which we stand, the war can not be won.[13]

In words not without an admixture of irony when seen in the perspective of this historic study, Newton D. Baker, Secretary of War, addressed himself to women thus:

I think there is a significance in the fact that the department of the Government especially charged with the making of war should appeal to the women for the success of such an undertaking. One does not ordinarily associate the making of war with the activities of women. Ordinarily, I think one's mental picture of women in a country at war portrays them as the principal sufferers. And so I think there is a certain significance, perhaps an indication of the extent to which our civilization has gone, when a Secretary of War says to the women that the success of the United States in the making of this war is just as much in the hands of the women as it is in the hands of the soldiers of our army.[14]

The great conflict was won, not by the Allies but by War. Everybody else lost. The fighting stage came to an end, though for many years to come the War will still be fought in economics, politics, and social conditions; for no modern war can stop when the armistice is called. The cessation of battle ushered in a few real changes in the work of women for world peace.

To the names of Lucretia Mott, Julia Ward Howe, and Belva A. Lockwood history will add the names of later women peace leaders whose lives have counted nobly: Anna Garlin Spencer, Lucia Ames Mead, of course Jane Addams, and many another less well known than her life service warrants; just as, abroad, not soon forgotten will be the work for peace of Bertha von Suttner in Austria, whose book *Lay Down Your Arms* for many years served as an *Uncle Tom's Cabin* for the peace movement; Ellen Robinson, England's great peace orator; and Senora O. C. Angela de Costa, of Argentina, largely responsible for the erection, on a high Andean borderline peak, of the famous peace statue, "The Christ of the Andes." Our American trio still work with vigor for the cause they have never lost sight of.

Since the War of 1917-18

The peace work of women since the War has been greatly multiplied, fostered too, no doubt, by the inevitable post-War disillusionment. It is chiefly of two kinds, the first, though of great educational value, following very much the objectives of the pre-War groups; and the second exhibiting a far more thoroughgoing character and a prophetic daring very different from the movements of twenty years ago.

At the more moderate end of the spectrum is the Conference on the Cause and Cure of War, which meets every year in Washington. It was founded in 1925 by Carrie Chapman Catt, veteran of the woman suffrage struggle, who, if she is not more careful, will make ample amends to posterity for her acceptance in 1917 of a post of leadership in the Women's Committee of the Council of National Defense (and Aggression). In this Conference are joined eleven large women's organizations totaling not far from six million members. They are the American Association of University Women, the Council of Women for Home Missions, the Federation of Women's Boards of Foreign Missions of North America, the General Federation of Women's Clubs, the National Board of the Young Women's Christian Associations, the National Council of Jewish Women, the National Federation of Business and Professional Women's Clubs, the National League of Women Voters, the National Woman's Christian Temperance Union, the National Women's Conference of the American Ethical Union, and the National Women's Trade Union League.

Official action, perforce, must be limited to fairly conservative points of view to which agreement may be secured from so large and diverse a body. The Conference has endorsed the World Court, arbitration, progressive unilateral disarmament, the Kellogg multilateral treaties renouncing aggressive war, etc., but carefully eschews any connection with uncompromising pacifism beyond a tolerant fairness. Its discussions are very much more realistic in tone than those of the larger peace gatherings prior to 1914, and its educational work is of high value. Each of the groups comprising the Conference carries on, by itself, educational activity for international good will.

It is not necessary, and in view of the rapid growth of peace groups would not be wise, to attempt a covering list of all work done by women since the War. Of the more prophetic movements, three stand out significantly. One is the Women's International League for Peace and Freedom, counting well above half a hundred thousand members organized in national sections in twenty-five countries and with corresponding societies in at least eighteen more. The League was founded in 1915, by fifteen hundred women meeting at The Hague, electing Jane Addams as its President. Except during the rest of the War years, it has held annual international conferences. It is alert, aware of sub-surface problems, and contains within its ranks some of the ablest women of the world. Its position on war affords an interesting contrast even to the most thoroughgoing women's peace societies of pre-War vintage:

It aims at uniting women in all countries who are opposed to every kind of war, exploitation and oppression, and who work for universal disarmament and for the solution of conflicts by the recognition of human solidarity, by conciliation and arbitration, and by the establishment of social, political and economic justice for all, without discrimination of sex, race, class or creed.

Another of the thoroughly pacifist societies of women is the Women's Peace Society, founded in 1919 by the late Fanny Garrison Villard, non-resistant daughter of the abolitionist, whose faith in the halfway peace organizations, like that of many other peoples all over the world, was shattered by the war-time spectacles of spineless opportunism. Says the official purpose:

The underlying principle of this Society is a belief in the sacredness of human life under all circumstances.

Its immediate program is International Co-operation, Complete and Universal Disarmament, and Free Trade.

Centering its attack on the institution of war, another pacifist society of women which has sprung up since the World War is the Women's Peace Union of the Western Hemisphere. If ever an equally drastic anti-war declaration has been circulated in the history of the United States, I have yet to learn of it. The affirmation made by members asserts:

I affirm it is my intention never to aid in or sanction war, offensive or defensive, international or civil, in any way, whether by making or handling munitions, subscribing to war loans, using my labor for the purpose of setting others free for war service, helping by money or work any relief organization which supports or condones war.

If not large in numbers, this organization has won a unique place of interest for its special efforts toward the outlawry of war by constitutional amendment. As far back as 1866 the Rhode Island Radical Peace Society circulated petitions to Congress to "dispense with war under all circumstances," the petition receiving many hundreds of signatures. In 1867 a committee appointed by the Universal Peace Society (later Universal Peace Union) appealed fruitlessly to the New York State Constitutional Convention to amend the constitution so as to "remove the causes of war and at the same time abolish all provisions for war itself, by not legalizing that which is inhuman, unjust, and unchristian."

In 1901 the conference of the Universal Peace Union at Washington adopted a set of "convictions." Among them were a series of steps toward peace education, to "open the way for an amendment to the Constitution of the United States, that will take out all the war clauses thereof."

All of these semi-gestures contained the germ idea, nationally or by state applied, of that outlawry of war which has preempted the use of the phrase in behalf of international joint delegalization. They were, obviously, very differently conceived. In them, however, is a nearer relationship to the startling introduction into the Senate by Senator Lynn J. Frazier, in 1926, of S. J. Res. 100, re-introduced as S. J. 45, a resolution providing that the Constitution be so amended that

Section 1. War for any purpose shall be illegal, and neither the United States nor any State, Territory, association, or person subject to its jurisdiction shall prepare for, declare, engage in, or carry on war or other armed conflict, expedition, invasion, or undertaking within or without the United States, nor shall any funds be raised, appropriated, or expended for such purpose.

Section 2. All provisions of the Constitution and of the article in addition thereto and amendment thereof which are in conflict with or inconsistent with this article are hereby rendered null and void and of no effect.

Section 3. The Congress shall have power to enact appropriate legislation to give effect to this article.[18]

How fantastic this amendment may seem to nearsight, no one is more aware, in all probability, than its sponsors themselves. It is, I contend, of genuine significance. It supplies real "teeth" to the Pact of Paris and serves as the focal point for a campaign of great educational value while public sentiment is being wooed for so drastic and unevasive a proposal.

It is evident, I think, that there is among women, as among men, a new, aggressive, uncompromising spirit that aims far out beyond the most legitimate forms of time-serving.

However, let no one be deceived. Counting liberally all the women of the United States who openly take the pacifist stand, they are numerically only an oasis in a desert of apathy, fair-weather pacifism, and mob-minded conformity. They are if anything a shade more venturesome than men in occupying their outposts, and they hold their positions with magnificent fidelity. But they are obliged to stand and scan the barren wastes in vain for any great caravans of their sex set out to join them in their far-flung endeavors.

At the second session of the Women's Patriotic Conference on National Defense, a meeting which endorsed, in early 1928, all the militaristic implications of "adequate" preparedness and whose primary aim seemed to be to offset the work of women pacifists, there were present four hundred delegates from thirty-four national "patriotic" organizations of women. General Pershing may be pardoned for exclaiming, in 1926, "I am not disquieted by reports of women's organizations advocating pacifism." Certainly none of the various proponents of military training in colleges who have sought popular girls with pretty faces to serve as honorary officers—possibly the acme of incentive to romantic young janissaries—have had to search with fatiguing diligence. From grandmother to granddaughter the gauntlet of chivalry is handed on. They may not be exactly the same as men in their reaction to war, but they are his sisters under the skin.

Still the hoary old legend of women's special aptitudes refuses to die. It lives in respect to numerous social relationships entirely apart from women's special biological differentiations. It lives, and becomes periodically vocal, to-day just as of old. The superstition that women would vote markedly different from men has been already slain, it seems, by the experience of the few short years since the Nineteenth Amendment became a fact. That its counterpart in the realm of international conflict persists after the lessons of our national wars, is due perhaps less to a truly high regard for the potentialities of womankind than a lingering of that chivalry which accorded superior virtues (along with inferior status) to women for so many centuries.

"We need women in the government," said Ezra Heywood, a pacifist of the turbulent post-War days of 1866, "for their spirit is above war." Their spirit, as she who reads the facts will plainly see, is no more above war than the spirit of men. The contribution of women to the abolition of war is certain to be large; it may fall short of that by men, or it may actually transcend man-directed pacific activities. Increasingly, I predict, the so-called differences between the sexes will fade out of the picture and the achievement of a planetary peace will be the work, not of national or racial or sex groups in any particular sense, but of a coöperating human race.

The hope that the feminine half of humanity will effect a *coup de théâtre* and banish the hated villain of the piece is just another romantic "dream of fair women."

CHAPTER XIV
THE MILITARY JUGGERNAUT

In what light we are viewed by superior beings may be gathered from a piece of late West India news, which possibly has not reached you. A young Angel of distinction, being sent down to this world on some important business, for the first time, had an old courier spirit assigned him as his guide; they arrived over the seas of Martinico, in the middle of the long day of obstinate fights between the fleets of Rodney and De Grasse. When through the clouds of smoke he saw the fire of the guns, the decks covered with mangled limbs, and bodies dead or dying; the ships sinking, burning, or blown high into the air; and the quantity of pain, misery and destruction the crews yet alive were thus with so much eagerness dealing round to one another; he turned angrily to his guide and said—"You blundering blockhead! you undertook to conduct me to the earth, and you have brought me into hell!" "No, Sir," says the guide, "I have made no mistake: this is really the earth and these are men. Devils never treat one another in this cruel manner; they have more sense, and more of what men vainly call humanity."—BENJAMIN FRANKLIN, to Dr. Joseph Priestley.

CHAPTER XIV

THE MILITARY JUGGERNAUT

THE weapons of peace have developed somewhat in the last one hundred years, though basically peace methods are the same. The weapons of war have undergone in the same period an amazing transformation, steadily acquiring new adaptability and deadliness.

From the time when gunpowder was first introduced into warfare in the sixteenth century, weapons using it developed with comparative slowness for three hundred years. When the Pilgrims landed and depended primarily on arms in persuading the native Indians to "have faith in Massachusetts," such weapons as they had were superior to those of the red man, but even at that, in modern language, they were "not so good." Attacked by thirty or forty Indians bent on driving them out, and yelling something described as "Woach, woach, ha ha hach woach!" by an old-time chronicle, the colonists should have wondered, though of course they didn't, if the "ha ha" were not directed at their arms. "Most of their pieces," however, "go off; the rest call for a firebrand to light their matches, and one of Standish's men, seizing a log from the fire and clapping it on his shoulder, runs to those on the shore, who are now able to get off their guns." [1] Often indeed these clumsy pieces "by the moisture of rain were out of order." For a long time whales disported themselves hard by the Mayflower, and made marks for those who would disport themselves as sharpshooters. One day when a whale drew unusually near, a colonist attempted to add to the store of oil. But alas! "his musket flew in pieces, both stock and barrel; yet thanks be to God, neither he, nor any man else was hurt with it, though many were thereabout."

293

The fiery Captain Miles himself was a little better fixed, for he possessed a "snaphence"—a gun with a flintlock; and with this masterpiece of destruction he was able in another encounter to shoot an Indian chief in the shoulder just in the nick of time. Yet even this success cannot be attributed either to Standish or his snaphence; for in the words of another ancient writer, his shot was "directed by the provident hand of the most high God."

By the time that Colonial troops were arrayed at Bunker Hill, had they anything much more effective to rely on? Not if you can trust the official *Regulations for the Order and Discipline of the Troops of the United States,* as adopted four years later in 1779. It took exactly six hundred and ninety-three words of the instructions to tell how a soldier should load and discharge one of the firelocks of that day, in language whose quaintness is accentuated by the sharp contrast between the movements used then and those set forth, say, in one hundred and ninety-four crisp words of *The Plattsburg Manual.* The latter rightly says, "the modern rifle is one of the most perfect pieces of scientific machinery in the world."

Says the same respected authority, "The cave man knocked over his foe with a rude club. The operation is greatly refined to-day." Without pausing to challenge such a concept of refinement, one must admit at once the truth of what is meant.

But most of this development has taken place within the last one hundred years, the same period which covers the origin and rise of peace societies. Perhaps the greatest speeding-up of weapon evolution began with the invention of the needle-gun, by Johann Nicholas von Dreyse, who for this splendid contribution to cultural progress was made a nobleman in 1864, at which time his gun after several modifications had been in use by Prussian armies for over twenty years.

In those unhurrying times, nations were not so quick to follow the deadly inventions of each other. Colonel R. Delafield, U.S.A., Major of the Corps of Engineers, carried out the orders of Jefferson Davis when the later Confederate leader was Secretary of War under President Pierce, and served as a

THE MILITARY JUGGERNAUT 295

member of a "Military Commission to the Theater of War in Europe," meaning of course the war in the Crimea. In his report to our government he said:

It is a remarkable fact that notwithstanding a knowledge of breech-loading small arms for at least two centuries, and that every museum of arms in Europe has numerous specimens, no satisfactory weapon for war purposes has yet been invented. . . . Prussia alone, of all the continental powers, has adopted such a system for infantry, using therefor the needle-gun; and although in use in her army for many years past, and well known in all its details, no other nation has been willing to follow her example. Celerity and rapidity of fire are the main points aimed at by the many inventors and advocates of this modification of the musket. We know that with the present weapons hundreds of rounds of ammunition are fired without producing any effect, and probably not one shot in a thousand rounds issued to the soldier ever does execution.[2]

The case of the torpedo affords an interesting example of the once laggard way in which military inventions were carried to perfection. As far back as 1585, it is said, an Italian engineer named Gianibelli partly destroyed a bridge at Antwerp by small boat-loads of powder set off from the action of clockwork. It was not until 1730 that Desaguliers, a Frenchman, started the development of underwater rocket-type torpedoes.[3]

Modern artillery had its inception in 1855 with the invention of the breech-loading rifle by the Englishman, Armstrong, who was knighted in 1859 for his "public services" and in 1887 elevated to the peerage.

Cartoonists in the opening days of the Civil War made merry over the long range runs being gradually worked out. One of them, "Cham" (Amédée de Noé, of France), suggested that the word of command in drill would possibly be "Attention! Spyglass! Fire!" And this actually seemed a joke to people unaware of how things were to change.

Think momentarily of the forty-two centimeter guns and sixty-mile range Big Berthas of the World War; think of the more recent tinkering with death rays and death concussions; think of the increase from thirty usable poison gases at the end of the World War in comparison to more than a hundred now; think of huge four-thousand-pound demolition bombs, ten times the size of any available in 1918! And then for an enlightening contrast think back to the puny thirty-two pounders of the Rebellion, howitzers firing a projectile that contained within itself a pound and a half of powder and was expelled by a pound of the same simple, old-fashioned explosive! '

The development of weapons, whether artillery, sidearms, rifle or whatnot, has been stupendous. There has been no discovery of modern science left unexploited by the military, no device left unexplored for its lethal possibilities. There is nothing but a grimly laughable resemblance between the weapons of combat used a hundred years ago and the up-to-date instruments of death.

The Mobilization of Armament

The "impossibility" of war—meaning its utter incapability of settling any question—was the thesis offered to a skeptical world by the Russian Pole, Jan Bliokh (or Jean Bloch) in the last years of the nineteenth century. An economist and banker, not a peace "worker" at all in the usual sense, Bliokh brought against war a new type of criticism. Of a scientific mind, "keen as a sportsman on the trail of facts," Bliokh in his 6-volume work on *The Warfare of the Future, from the Technical, Political, and Economic Points of View* analyzed the steady mechanization of war and prophesied that increasingly would large-scale conflicts result either in a long-drawn-out stalemate or a pseudo-victory costing far more than any value gained. In 1902, shortly after his death, his "Museum of War and Peace" at Lucerne was functioning to show graphically by various exhibits the general basis of his theory.

In the development of defense, especially through long-range artillery, smokeless powder, and improvements in fortifications and entrenchment, he saw technical factors which to his mind were then assuming a steady trend toward protracted trench warfare. Battle, he concluded, became less and less significant as compared to economic organization—a view taken now by most students of the factors involved in modern warfare.

Bliokh was in England for a time giving some lectures applying his ideas to the Boer War while it was going on. While there he offered a table to show the enormous probable daily costs of a future general European War. His figures struck many as fantastic, just as prophecies to-day by the critics of war regarding the destructive capacity of future warfare are often hailed as unduly sensational. How ultra-conservative were his estimates is shown by the following comparison between his prophecy and the daily cost of the World War to the same five belligerents:

	Bliok's Estimate (1901)	Daily Cost of World War (1914-1918)
Germany	$5,100,000	$25,737,179
Austria	2,600,000	13,219,846
Italy	2,560,000	7,957,691
France	5,100,000	16,546,655
Russia	5,600,000	14,483,301

These figures are not offered to argue the costliness of war. They depict strikingly how warfare has grown to titanic dimensions within a short period, and they warn against an undervaluation of war's consequences should the war method be longer tolerated.

Bliokh foresaw a tremendous advance in the technical equipment of battling fleets and armies. In this field too his vision seemed to not a few projected into the realm of dreams. It is undeniable that time has shown some of Bliokh's detailed fears (thus far, that is) unrealized. But his "dreams" of war technique seem now naïve for their inadequacy. The development of fighting machinery has already reached the point where only a madman could think we have gone beyond the initial stages of a progress in mutual destruction which, if permitted to continue, will bring such desolation to this planet as it has not known since the legendary odyssey of Noah.

In whatever room of Mars' well-financed mansion you may choose to look, you will find horrors stored up, as Bluebeard's wife found in the one room of the now-tame medieval castle. On the surface of the sea float modern cruisers with a speed of thirty-five to thirty-eight nautical miles an hour—a once undreamed-of rate of progress. Such a cruiser's eight-inch guns are now as potent as the twelve-inch guns of just a scant few years ago. Under the water the submarine, called by Rear-Admiral Sims "the most wonderful agent of warfare ever invented," [5] has already progressed from the seventy-four-ton *Holland* of 1900 to the three-thousand-ton VS type of the United States Navy. Professor Oswald Flamm, designer of the renowned *Deutschland,* declares that "development is natural; there is no cessation; every year brings new developments." [6]

Across the breast of Mother Earth crawl death-spitting tanks that dwarf the mighty venomed reptiles of the last great holocaust, rendering in a dozen years the picturesque squadrons of cavalry all but archaic. The range of guns has been more than doubled if not trebled since the Armistice.

Great fleets of man-conceived mosquitoes becloud the air, capable of loosing upon their helpless creators the malarial pestilence of poison gas or the stinging bite of bombs. General M. M. Patrick, formerly chief of the U. S. Army Air Service, has said that twelve bombing airplanes of 1928, in a single air raid, could drop as many tons of bombs as the Germans used on London in the entire World War. [7]

By 1925 planes had succeeded in carrying a load of 13,228 pounds. [8] By the end of 1927 the total number of military airplanes in the world nearly reached 11,000, thrice the number for 1923. If the *New York Times* announces in March, 1928, that in the country leading in military aviation "New French Plane Carries Six Guns—Secretly Built Bleriot Makes 130 Miles an Hour at 18,000 Feet Altitude—Huge Machine Is Called Greatest Fight Craft," it also announces our own checkmate in April next, "Six-Gun Attack Planes to Figure in Mock War—New Machines Will Get First Try-Out in Large Scale Operations at Langley Field." Under the "five-year act" passed by Congress in 1927, the United States Army alone will have

1800 first-class airplanes by 1932. Already, as a writer in the *Times* declared, this program in not much more than two years has "made the United States Army Air Service one that will bear comparison with that of any similar force in the world." And yet an Associated Press dispatch of August 20, 1929, quoted Representative W. Frank James of Michigan, chairman of the House Military Affairs Committee, as declaring that the five-year program was even then obsolete. "Where five millions were authorized before," he said, "fifty millions are needed now."

The Medical Corps makes great progress in treatment of the sick and wounded. Sanitary gains are constantly made, such as the discovery of succinchlorimide, a water-purifying chemical. But of what use are these if there is one per cent of truth in the sensational statement by the British Tory, Winston Churchill, that "A study of diseases—of pestilences methodically prepared and deliberately launched upon man and beast—is certainly being pursued in the laboratories of more than one great country"?

More than $3,500,000,000 is spent annually by all the nations of the world in war preparations or so-called "national defense." This vast sum amounts to about two dollars per head, or ten dollars per family, of the entire human race.

In this continuous contest the United States holds its end up proudly, as we shall see. Not only are we mobilizing armament; we are mobilizing the strategy of its use. Following is an Associated Press dispatch from Washington dated February 17, 1927:

War planning is a job that keeps a small group of close mouthed, specially selected officers in the War Department in a state of industry approaching that of perpetual motion.

The plans for offensive and defensive military operations against every possible enemy are in their keeping. They fill huge steel safes and are checked carefully against every international controversy in order that they may be in readiness for instant application in case of a national emergency.

As Secretary Kellogg and his aides, at the far end of the same corridor that borders on the war plans' offices, strive to adjust a controversy by diplomacy, the army experts overhaul their papers relating to the military situation existing at the time between the United States and the other nation involved.

The job of keeping the war plans up to date in the light of ever changing international issues is one that calls for continuous effort. They have to be revised also to give the correct employment to new arms as their superiority over the older weapons is disclosed.

The war planners are constantly in touch with State Department officials, military attachés in foreign capitals and numerous other governmental agencies. It is no secret that the plans in their keeping provide in detail for setting the military machine in motion with a full destructive force against any enemy at the earliest possible moment after hostilities have been declared.

For a major or minor emergency they tell not only how many men will be needed by the army but how they are to be transported, equipped, trained if necessary, and supplied with the many essentials a modern army needs for field service.

The State Department usually refers new treaties to the war planners before they are given final approval and sent to the Senate for ratification, and sometimes even before they are formally drafted.

It is doubtful whether this state of affairs is quite as neatly atrocious as the exigencies of newspaper interest require; but that such a situation approximately exists can hardly be denied.

"War planners" is an unfair term, and the strategists would be justified in protesting its use. They do not, of course, sit like movieland monsters deliberately dragging nations into war. It is not they but their point of view which gives the phrase a certain support. For their arts and crafts are not the kind that erect a house of peace but the charnel house of hate and conflict.

The mobilization of armament has been making gains in its mowing down of human targets. Dr. Thomas Dick, the religious and astronomical philosopher of old Dundee, estimated in 1846 that war had previously destroyed 14,000,000,000 of human beings, making 2,333,333 every year, 6,481 every day, and four and a half every minute—doubtless resting too much confidence in the preëvolutionary dates at that time ascribed to Genesis! Edmund Burke earlier tried to prove that the figure was about 30,000,000,000. The Massachusetts Peace Society, after an "investigation," counted the number killed in all wars as 3,346,000,000. Said Elihu Burritt, also something of a mathematical stuntster, "The blood of the 14,000,-000,000 of human beings that have perished by war would fill a circular lake 17 miles in circumference, 10 feet deep; in which all the navies of the world might float." Allowing for the zeal which produced such figures, it may be seen that there is more poesy than fact in the lines of a modern poet:

> As many men as whose torn flesh is drowned
> In battle-blood on any battle-ground,
> That ground serenely can assimilate.[10]

Laying Genesis aside as beyond the bounds of certified public accountancy, it is possible to quote Colonel Leonard P. Ayres, who has computed the direct losses by war between 1793 and 1914 as six million.[11] This affords a basis of comparison; and at once the mind leaps to the fact that in the four years of the World War alone ten million were killed directly in combat.[12]

Here, too, I am not arguing war's destructive horror. These figures add a certain further weight to the contention that the race is rapidly learning more efficient means of self-eradication. The accompanying map and chart show what has been happening to "civilization."

The Mobilization of Industry

In his book on Industrial Preparedness, published in 1916, C. E. Knoeppel printed an introduction by General Leonard Wood. Said the General:

Preparedness for modern war means not only the training and organizing of men, but the most thorough and complete organization of the industrial resources of the nation.

Such a statement in such a time had something of freshness about it. To-day it would be as original to say that ears of corn could not be grown without stalks.

One of the military lessons of the war was the support of armies in the field by the mobilization of home industry. The

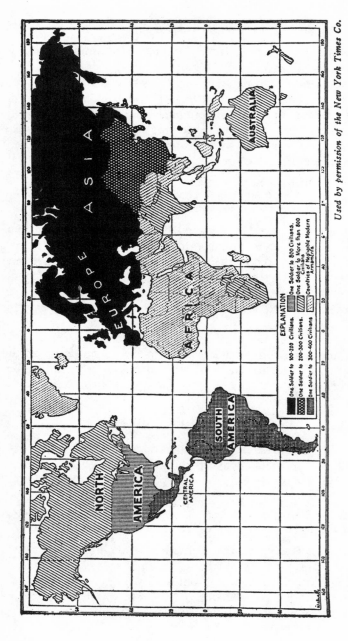

THE ARMED WORLD OF TO-DAY, SHOWING THE PROPORTION OF STANDING ARMIES TO CIVILIAN POPULATION, THE FORCES TOTALING 5,500,000

EXPLANATION

One Soldier to 100-200 Civilians.
One Soldier to 200-300 Civilians.
One Soldier to 300-400 Civilians.
One Soldier to 800 Civilians.
One Soldier to More than 800 Civilians.
Countries of Negligible Modern Armaments.

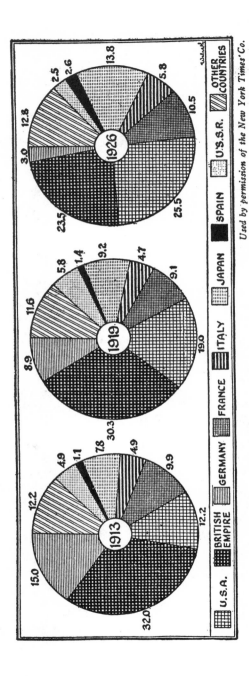

Used by permission of the New York Times' Co.

DISTRIBUTION OF THE WORLD'S TOTAL NAVAL TONNAGE AMONG THE NATIONS (IN PERCENTAGES) BEFORE, DURING, AND SINCE THE WORLD WAR, UP TO THE LONDON NAVAL CONFERENCE OF 1930

lesson has not been forgotten. From the end of the War to now the War Department has zealously worked to regiment the industrial life of our country, and since 1922 with a definite plan. Judge Elbert H. Gary and Charles M. Schwab, two kings of the steel industry, journeyed to West Point for the Advisory Board of the New York Ordnance District, in 1924, and while there Judge Gary said to the officers and associates of the Board:

If industry will lend its co-operation and formulate war plans within its own organization, the requirements of the field armies can be met soon enough to prevent defeat by any enemy or combination of enemies that might attack.[13]

Plans for national defense have been made by manufacturing plants, said Mr. Gary.

Man power can be mobilized and trained now, with the plans formulated by the Advisory Committee, made up of industrialists, in eight months for 3,500,000 men.

On November 24, 1925, Secretary of War Dwight F. Davis addressed Philadelphia's Union League. Press reports of the Secretary's address indicate very adequately what is afoot:

So great has been the progress of the War Department's previously undisclosed programme for preparing to convert peacetime industries to the requirements of war, that, if the United States were to be drawn into a conflict today, the nation would be equipped to place 4,000,000 men in action *anywhere on the face of the globe* [italics mine]. . . .

In the Philadelphia area alone, in its preparedness-inspired programme of industrial conversion for war-time purposes, Secretary Davis revealed that the Baldwin Locomotive Works here have agreed to concentrate its vast equipment on the production of heavy artillery, literally on a moment's notice.

Identical arrangements have been clinched with the J. G. Brill Company, which produces trolley cars and motor bus bodies in great quantities, to turn to the manufacture of mobile field artillery. The Atwater Kent Company, whose facilities are now given over to the production of radio instruments, will convert its machinery and personnel to the manufacture of time fuses and instruments necessary to the proper control of artillery fire.

Secretary Davis went on to say that the War Department contemplated the mobilization of not only men but of all industry as well.[14]

In pursuance of this policy, during the year ending in June, 1927, one hundred and four officers were devoting their full time to "procurement planning."[15] Some thirty-nine were doing likewise with part time while forty-three reserve officers in the various branches were engaged in part-time work on the same sort of jobs. In comparison to the one thousand five hundred and seventy-seven reserve officers working for "the mobilization of man power" this forty-three is small, and the War Department—granted its point of view—is justified in feeling the balance disproportionate. The Army Industrial College, established to train officers for industrial preparedness duties and also to act as something of a normal school in its field, is still small but growing; and if American militarism proceeds unchecked it will inevitably assume large proportions.

This intensified industrial readiness for war is being pushed farther and farther to the limits of efficiency-achievement. The program was expected to be worked out by 1930. No one can blame the War Department for doing this particular thing; it is carrying out as well as it can the commands which it feels have been laid upon it.

The effect may well be imagined of this preparedness doctrine infiltrating into the minds of hundreds of thousands employed in American industries, and also the imitative thoughts it is certain to generate in the minds of peoples that suffered while we profited industrially from the World War, nations that are justly jealous of our present industrial supremacy.

The excuse for putting through such a program is the old one of "peace" and "protection." It is probably true that the psychological effect on the rest of the world is less inflammatory than more obvious forms of preparedness. But on the other hand, our post-War position of being "flush" with this world's goods accentuates a hostility already great enough in the parts of this world whose goods we do not yet possess.

Peace and protection? If continually being on guard against attack is peace, we are in much the calm and comfort of a man wearing a bullet-proof vest. The armadillo is marvelously protected; but who wants to be an armadillo?

The Mobilization of Science

"If it be true that the sciences are noble in proportion as they are useful," exclaimed the author of *Holbrook's Military Tactics* in 1826, "what advantage may not the science of war be said to possess above almost every other."

Are we as far away from such an attitude as a century of marvelous advancement in science ought to make us? If not, what is the reason? It is, I think, partly that science on the one hand and the war system on the other are equally rooted in our economic development. But also there is the fact that men of science, notwithstanding their many services to human welfare—and there is no less selfish professional group in the world—have freely given their aid to the war machine. The "internationalism of science" has succumbed in every crisis to nationalistic considerations. In war and the peace that consists so largely in preparation for war, science is the pliant tool of the military.

Pasteur, during the Franco-Prussian War, returned his diploma of an honorary degree to the University of Bonn, saying, "The sight of that parchment is odious to me." In another place he declared, "Every one of my future works will bear on its title page the words 'Hatred to Prussia. Revenge! Revenge!'" And as Benjamin Harrow points out in his book *The Romance of the Atom*, the great, humane Frenchman set out, by way of a personal revenge, to make French beer better than German!

"If peace continues for any length of time," says Harrow, "the French and German scientists will get together just as they did after the Franco-Prussian War." But what of that? "If war comes again, the scientists will part again, and again call one another names, just as they did during the Franco-Prussian War and during the Great War."

Mr. Harrow offers a suggestion which goes to the roots of the scientist's view of his social responsibility, the generally accepted dictum of the scientific world that the man of science is a cold, precise, machine-like creature, whose only function is to deal with pure science, not with the uses to which his discoveries may be put. Mr. Harrow wonders if there is not a higher rôle:

Admitting the view expressed by Soddy that scientific men stand for something higher in the world than anything which has as yet found expression and representation in governments, particularly in their international relations, the very first task which confronts scientists is to continue to think scientifically after they have left their laboratory. Robinson in his *Mind in the Making* and in *The Humanizing of Knowledge* appeals for the scientific spirit among the masses at large. My contention is that the scientific spirit must first be engendered among the scientists themselves, for them then to spread the gospel. They must be taught to regard the scientific method as one applicable to a universal outlook on life and not merely to a chemical reaction. It follows from this that once such a view has become firmly entrenched, the fundamental difference in method between scientist on the one hand, and non-scientist (including industrialist, diplomat and politician) on the other, will become apparent. It will no longer be possible for the type of men who at present control the destinies of the world to misuse the glorious inventions and discoveries of science.

There is a story, perhaps legendary, in the old *Brewster's Encyclopedia,* about the horror with which Sir Isaac Newton greeted the announcement by Professor Gregory of Oxford that the latter's father had completed the model of an invention for making artillery more destructive.

Sir Isaac was much displeased with it, saying, that if it tended as much to the preservation of mankind as to their destruction, the inventor would have deserved a great reward; but as it was contrived solely for destruction, and would soon be known to the enemy, he rather deserved to be punished and urged the Professor very strongly to destroy it, and if possible to suppress the invention.

True it is that scientists are not to blame if the hand of fate has placed a heavy percentage of their products in a dual relationship, holding power both of good and evil. Can they not, however, throw the weight of their great influence unhesitatingly against the perversion of the good to race-suicidal ends?

Some scientists, like Professor Soddy of Nobel Prize fame

in chemistry, have outspokenly ranged themselves on the side of peace. But how many others have done so? Professor W. A. Noyes of the University of Illinois, feeling a somewhat similar impulse to do what he could to use science for the building of good will, spent a sabbatical year in Europe working toward the reconciliation of French and German scientists. As Harrow reports, nevertheless:

A record of these conversations merely strengthens the conviction that in politics the majority of scientists think like the masses at large.[16]

French and German scientists are possessed of no essential differences from scientists of other nationalities. In June of 1928, our Assistant Secretary of War Charles Burton Robbins told the graduating class at West Point that "Science and warfare now go hand in hand."[17]

Robert Hall, famous preacher of more than a century ago, spoke of war as "liquid fire and distilled damnation." Words would fail him to-day were he to see the prophetic character of his figure of speech. Liquid fire is only one small drop in the great flood of distilled damnation being prepared with an almost religious devotion for the immolation of humanity.

The deadliness of gases has doubtless sometimes been exaggerated. Wild tales have been told of poison gases so powerful that where they had once been liberated vegetation would never grow again. The loose talk, all the same, has not been confined to pacifists. The soothing-sayers have contributed their share, usually basing their contentions regarding the harmlessness of toxic gases on the experience of the World War.

You might as well predict the development of steamships by the experiences of Noah. It is arrant nonsense for a responsible member of our Chemical Warfare Service to say, as he said in 1927:

Alarmists have repeatedly mistaken the effect of new inventions. The ability to wage gas warfare is a blessing—not a curse—and will make for the future security, peace, and happiness of the world.[18]

It is also nonsense for an officer of the American Institute of Chemical Engineers to state, as he did in 1927:

Undoubtedly international conflicts of the future will be fought out with gas, and other chemicals, but they will be far more humane, less bloody, and more painless than if shot and shell were used exclusively.[19]

I naturally hold no brief for shot and shell. But how seriously such romantic imaginings are taken by those charged with the tasks of handling men who are gassed in warfare may be gathered from a booklet published by the United States government, written by Commander E. W. Brown of the Medical Corps and published in 1928. It is entitled *Chemical Warfare and the Naval Medical Officer.* In pointing out "the requirements which a chemical compound must satisfy to be adapted to chemical warfare use," Commander Brown sets down as his opening point:

(1) It must first of all be highly toxic. This indicates that it must reach such a concentration when projected in the field as to be either lethal or at least casualty producing. The gas must also be one which, while fatal in high concentrations, will cause more or less serious injury in concentrations far below that necessary to kill.

"What," asks Commander Brown, "would be the ideal gas for a naval attack?" He answers:

It is generally conceded that a powerful vesicant acting instantly would answer the requirements.

Among the responsibilities which the *Handbook for the War Department General Staff* (1924) charges upon the Chemical Warfare Service is "the formulation and development of the tactical doctrine of chemical warfare, *both offensive and defensive.*"

How humane and how pleasant are the effects of some of the moderate gases, some of the "persistent gases," in the case of which "the area around the point of burst of the shell will be contaminated and will remain a hazard for periods which may sometimes last for weeks"?

There is blue stage asphyxia.

This term was applied in the World War to the stage of lung edema when cyanosis was well developed, but prior to the signs of failing circulation. As the edema develops in the lungs, the breathing becomes more rapid and panting and of a characteristic shallow type. The ears, lips, and, progressively, the entire face assumes a cyanotic, bluish-red tint which may deepen to the intense violet of advanced cyanosis, and there may be visible distension of the superficial veins of the face, neck, or chest. There are copious frothy sputum, frequent cough, with respirations of 40 to 48 per minute, elevated temperature, and a full, strong pulse in the neighborhood of 100. This condition is most frequently seen on the second day after gassing.

There is also gray stage asphyxia.

This term was applied to the stage of circulatory collapse. The patient may recover from blue stage asphyxia or he may pass into the gray stage as the result of a dilated and failing heart. The color becomes an ashen gray, the expression anxious and staring, and respiratory difficulty is shown by the strained effect of the muscles around the nostrils. There is intense oxygen want. The breathing is markedly hurried and shallow and a rapid running pulse of 130 or over develops. The prognosis is distinctly bad in this stage and the outcome is usually determined within 72 hours of the time the victim was gassed. Apparent recovery from gray stage asphyxia may be succeeded by a severe or even fatal bronchopneumonia.

Just as in a previous section I cited figures not to argue the cost of war in life or treasure, but to demonstrate the advances made in killing-proficiency, so I argue here to the same end. There is in gas warfare, science's latest purveyor to the maw of Mars, the same old race between attack and protection. The gas mask used in the Navy in early 1928 had gone through some thirty-three distinct changes. Gases themselves, leaving out the mythical or unknown gases knowledge of which is confined to laboratories, had progressed in killing power:

The comparative toxicity of the lung irritants and vesicants by inhalation is compared in the following table for 30-minute periods of exposure:

Ounces per
1,000 cubic feet

Chlorine	3.0
Chlorpicrin	.8
Phosgene	.3
Mustard	.07
Lewisite	.05

Every government in the world knows of cacodyl isocyanide, a gas so terrorful that hardened chemists and military men have a bad job convincing themselves that any government would ever use it. And the possibilities of toxic gases are only in their infancy.

The airplane is the trusted messenger of death, counted on to hover over cities of well-nigh defenseless, ant-like humans like the avenging angel. Everything from lethal liquids to cremating phosphorous may be rained down on fighting lines or the crowds back home huddled like rats in a sewer. The humans will die either in or out of the house.

There is continually conflicting evidence on the effectiveness of anti-aircraft gunfire. It is highly questionable if its recent development has outstripped that of offensive military aviation. In 1924 Brigadier-General P. R. C. Groves, Chief of Staff of the British Royal Flying Corps during the War, was responsible for the statement that

early in the late conflict the British Ministry of Munitions estimated that in order to score a direct hit upon an aëroplane flying at 5,000 feet and capable of a speed of 100 miles an hour, no less than 162,000 guns would have to fire simultaneously. The experience of the War [which needs checking against every new development] bore out that estimate. There is a difference of opinion as to the number of aëroplanes brought down by anti-aircraft fire over Great Britain in the course of the recent conflict, but the total can be placed fairly safely at under six. . . . In the future war . . . the only effective defense against aircraft attack will be the aerial counter-offensive, and the only effective safeguard against aerial aggression will be the threat of reprisals in kind.[20]

The other side of the argument was well put by J. M. Scammell, former head of the Political Science Department of the

312   THE FIGHT FOR PEACE

University of California in a recent address at that institution.
Says Dr. Scammell:

As a matter of fact, it would be virtually impossible for enough
airplanes to break through the anti-aircraft guns of a city to do
any great damage. During the World War the Germans fired
150,000 mustard gas shells into an area about as large as London,
with a total of only fifty deaths.[21]

There is no standing still. Already in at least four countries
experiments are going forward to work out a type of plane
with silent engine, with the noise of propellers minimized by
using many small blades instead of two large ones, and rendered semi-invisible by peculiar greenish paints.

I had rather, on this matter, trust the military men and
technicians. It is worthy of note that when the Brussels Conference for the Protection of Civilians against gas warfare met
in January, 1928, and went thoroughly into every phase of the
question, these twenty-five experts gathered under the auspices
of the International Red Cross, found themselves nonplussed.
Said a special *New York Times dispatch,* agreeing with those
in other papers:

Although the delegates were disinclined to discuss the conference proceedings on the ground that they did not wish to arouse
civilians needlessly regarding the horrors of gas warfare, it was
learned that most of the protective measures thus far advanced
were considered impracticable.[22]

General von Deimling of Germany, in March, 1930, issued a
public protest over the expenditure of funds for protection of
the civil population against poison gas service, quoting Professor
Haber, director of Germany's poison gas service during the
War to the effect that protection is utterly impracticable. No
mask, he said, can stop the so-called "blue cross" gas, which is
so fine that it cannot be strained out. "Science," said General
von Deimling, "can invent a new gas almost every day which
will always be one step ahead of the best protective devices."

While commercial airplanes cannot always be converted easily into day-time bombing planes, General Groves in a report

THE MILITARY JUGGERNAUT 313

prepared for the League of Nations in July, 1930, stated that without difficulty they can be used as night-bombers.

Winston Churchill's alarm about germ warfare, previously mentioned, is needless, in the opinion of a League of Nations sub-committee reporting in 1924. Microbes were too difficult to spread, most medical experts consulted were agreed, and were too easily combated. Yet in 1925 Dr. J. Maly, a Czecho-slovakian subject resident in Paris, is reported to have offered a project for the use of pathogenic germs in warfare to the United States War Department. The War Department is stated to have replied, "This Department is of the opinion that from the practical viewpoint pathogenic organisms could not be used effectively for military purposes and is therefore not interested in investigations of this character at the present time." [22]

The time may come soon, notwithstanding present impracticability, when the development from obsidian knife to porphyry mace to bows and arrows to rifles to machine guns to lewisite, may take the logical next step.

We have gone rather far as it is. Machiavelli, in his *History of Florence,* asserts that "at the battle of Anghieri in 1440 in the midst of so complete a rout, in a battle so obstinate that it lasted four hours, only a single man was killed, who again met his death not by the enemy's fire or by any honorable blow, but by a fall from his horse and being trodden underfoot by others." Not remotely typical, perhaps, for in many an early war slaughter was enormous. But interesting and not without a certain significance.

There can be no gentle art of combat such as this, in our more educated age. Mr. Churchill is not, I believe, speaking too sensationally when he says:

Mankind has never been in this position before. Without having improved appreciably in virtue or enjoying wiser guidance, it has got into its hands for the first time the tools by which it can unfailingly accomplish its own extermination. [24]

Amazingly enough, the Pollyannas are still among us. In the deadly possibilities of the airplane, many seem to see the ultimate terror that will make war so horrible that men will surely create peace. Even Mr. Harrow, speaking of future wars, is moved to romanticism:

Even here science will render service of a constructive kind, though in an indirect way; for it will so magnify injustice, by inventing any number of death-dealing instruments, that the situation will become too intolerable to be borne, and man will then destroy the roots of the evil.

In this he agrees with Dr. W. Lee Lewis, pacific inventor of lewisite, who recently said:

Science does make war less adventuresome, less romantic and more deadly. It is, therefore, fundamentally an ally of peace.[25]

Chancellor McCracken of New York University said to the Fourth Mohonk Conference of 1898—sixteen years before the supremely catastrophic World War:

Military invention also may well be looked to as a powerful factor in aid of peace. When military invention perfects the flying machine, to which my former associate, Dr. Langley of the Smithsonian, is devoting his time, ability and energy, so that it is able to drop explosives of untold power upon any ship, then it seems to me the nations will receive a very strong impulse to the learning of war no more.[26]

Go back further! Thomas C. Upham in 1836 hailed, as an aid to peace, "the great progress which has been made in the various departments of science and the arts."

We know what has also come, not so beneficently, from science; and it is disquieting to find so level headed a writer as Commander J. M. Kenworthy, of the British Labor Party, hoping in 1927 that the airplane (which the booklet on chemical warfare and the naval medical officer speak of as "the method of outstanding promise")

by making it certain that at any rate amongst the European nations all would be endangered in another war, may rouse the peoples of Europe to the depth of the abyss towards which they are heading."

It is not so simple as all this. With the mobilization of armament, industry, and science, fear on the part of peoples means nothing else than more of the things of which they are afraid. We often speak of war as if it were "brute force." It is not brute force. It is man force, highly scientific, organized and civilized and refined to the very garrote point of destructiveness and cruelty.

That is war to-day; war in which, as William G. Shepherd has vividly said, the family won't kiss father good-by; father had better kiss them good-by.**

The Mobilization of Government

"The first king," said Voltaire, "was a successful soldier." Not only the first, but most of the rest. Militarism and government have been as inseparable as a pair of tweezers.

Still flushed with the hope of revolutionary democracy, many in the early United States saw here a future freer from militarism than was the case in the war-ridden countries of the Old World. Thanks in part to the lingering force of that youthful prospect, but doubtless more to the natural security of this country's geographical isolation, for many years there was, in some degree, fulfillment; for unlike the closely packed-in nations of Europe, we have not had need, even from the military point of view, of European peace-time universal military service. Indeed, to escape such a hated burden, many thousands of Europeans have flocked to our shores.

Not yet have the modern means of international communication destroyed all of our military security. It has been lessened, and will be lessened steadily. Along with the gradual change, but more than keeping pace, has grown the military mobilization of our government.

"Here, thank God," said the third report of the American Peace Society in 1831, "the arts of peace are substituted for the arts of war."

In a little less than a century, however, government lists of official public documents carried on their back covers this significant sentence about our Federal functions: "The arts of war, as well as those of peace, are actively cultivated."

The extent to which the government has been mobilized for military ends may be seen in different directions. One is in the relation of the military to the civil. A hundred years ago the *General Regulations for the Army* contained an article as follows:

SUBORDINATION TO THE CIVIL AUTHORITIES

1559. Respect and obedience to the civil authorities of the land, is the duty of all citizens, and more particularly of those who are armed in the public service.

When discontent over the corruption of General Grant's administration was mounting, all elements of the population did not share the peace movement's willingness to tolerate such a state of affairs merely because Grant favored the cause of arbitration. The Labor Reformers met at Columbus, Ohio, in February, 1872, where delegates from seventeen states held a nominating convention and adopted a rebellious platform. One plank declared:

14. That we demand the subjection of the military to the civil authorities, and the confinement of its operations to national purposes alone.

Already the use of Federal troops against strikers had become a thorn in labor's flesh, goading it on to reprisals which broke out five years later in our bloodiest year of capital-labor conflict, with actual battle raging in Baltimore, Pittsburgh, Reading, St. Louis, and Chicago.

The request of the Labor Reformers was not granted. A government which had been so thoroughly alarmed in 1877 that four warships were converted into immediate fighting service, and which had already decided in the basic economic contest as to which side its bread was buttered on, could never yield regarding the use of Federal soldiers. Likewise State governments and their militia.

In 1881 the article regarding subordination to civil authorities was officially stricken from the army regulations and has never been put back.

To-day, since the World War, State and Federal forces have

been amalgamated, in all essential respects, in one great military body. On the briefest notice from Washington the National Guard units are made a part of the Federal army. Dating from 1915, the same is true of the Coast Guard. Continually Federal troops go into the States to handle any important disturbance. The intent of the Constitution in this regard is obviously distorted, as that elastic document is stretched in numerous other directions to satisfy official dispositions.

Since 1900 our estimates of available military man power have increased from about 11,000,000 to 18,500,000 (1927), an increase of 66 per cent. Our population, meantime, has increased from about 76,000,000 to approximately 117,000,000 (1927), or only 54 per cent. This figure brings our percentage of possible warriors up to 19.6, highest by far of all nations. If it be argued that the development of machines and the penetration of women into industry has made it possible for more men to absent themselves from productive processes, it is equally true that the same factors operate to increase the military efficiency of the human unit.

The military mobilization of government is further evidenced by the ways in which it spends its money, especially in time of peace.

"Since Washington's day," said Lucia Ames Mead in 1927, "our population has increased 28 times, our area three times, and our expenditures for war 650 times."

Here is a comparison. Savel Zimand, writing in the *New York Times* for April 19, 1925, figured that "Since 1872 the military budget of the United States has increased 2,413 per cent; of France, 1,085 per cent; and of Great Britain, 794 per cent."

All such figures have about them one element of unfairness, in that they do not consider the higher relative cost of war materials and labor in this country and also as time goes on. Nevertheless, they are still appalling when all due allowances are made.

Also, other yardsticks show as vividly the militarization of our government. A table issued November 5, 1921 by the

318   THE FIGHT FOR PEACE

World Peace Foundation, using Treasury Department reports, revealed that from 1789 to 1920 inclusive, that is, the years of our government since the adoption of the Constitution, total Federal disbursements have amounted to $66,728,209,409, of which the war expenditures of all kinds reach $52,607,489,927, or actually 78½ per cent!

It is debatable that war expenses are a less accurate index of militarization than the cost of peace-time preparedness. Here is light on that. Leaving out all the abnormal war and post-war years, the following table shows what we have been spending on the army and navy.

Year	Spent On Navy	Spent On Army	Total	Population	Per Person
1820	$ 4,387,990	2,630,392	7,018,382	9,638,453	$0.73
1840	6,113,897	7,095,267	13,209,164	17,069,453	0.77
1860	11,514,650	16,472,203	27,986,853	31,443,321	0.89
1880	13,536,985	38,116,916	51,653,901	50,155,783	1.03
1895	28,797,796	51,804,579	80,602,375	69,471,145	1.15
1905	117,550,308	122,175,074	239,725,382	83,983,421	2.85
1915	141,835,654	172,973,092	314,808,746	98,841,443	3.15
1927	318,909,096	360,808,777	679,717,873	118,628,000	5.73

NOTE: In the above table the population figures for 1895, 1905 and 1915 are only approximate, arrived at by halving the total of the censuses taken five years before and five years later in each instance; the figure for 1927 is the estimate of the Census Bureau. Figures on expenditures up to 1922 include money spent on rivers and harbors but not for the Panama Canal or for civil expenses at Washington; beginning with 1923 figures used by War and Navy Departments include all expenditures except for the Panama Canal.

Again, it is necessary to concede allowances for the rise of prices which makes the purchasing power represented by these figures a bit less striking than the table as it stands. Dun's Index Number, or the wholesale price index in the United States since 1861, shows a rise between 1880 and 1927, from 108.655 dollars to 185.598, indicating that necessary deductions for price increases do not jolt the one fact brought out, namely, a tremendous proportionate increase in expenditure on arms, amounting per person, between 1880 and 1927, when stated in "real" figures, to substantially 300 per cent.

The salary budget for officials of the State Department amounts to $155,800; the Department of Agriculture $178,300;

the Department of Labor $85,100. We have two departments for defense-aggression: the salary roll for War Department officials totals $186,300 and that of the Navy Department $129,200. Thus the last two come up to $315,500, almost twice the amount for the State and Agriculture Departments, and nearly four times that of Labor. It is a duty of the Finance Division of the War Department to watch with care Congress and its appropriation moods:

The Chief of Finance has also been designated by the Secretary of War as Budget Officer for the War Department, and as such prepares all estimates of appropriations required by the War Department, transmits them to the Director of the Bureau of the Budget, and presents to him all questions in reference to pending appropriations and legislation which may affect the financial policy of the administration."

Zeal for increased appropriations is not confined to any one department. But there is a difference. Our country can better run the risk of being agriculturized than of being militarized. The annual reports of no peace societies are printed at the expense of all the taxpayers, while the government performs this service for such organizations, for example, as the American Legion, the Boy Scouts, and the Sons of Union Veterans of the Civil War, as well as the D. A. R.; however, copies used by these organizations themselves have to be purchased. All this is not intentionally or even indirectly reprehensible. But it is in line with the whole trend of the century, which has turned our official ambition to be refreshingly different from other military countries into an earnest desire to follow them or lead.

Arms, industry, science, and government—these are the Four Horsemen which ride into a fearsome dawn. They do not ride alone. Behind them march eager ranks of factless, propagandized, mob-stirred millions, goose-stepping to a doom they do not see. They do not know it, but they, too, are mobilized.

CHAPTER XV
THE FIGHT FOR WAR

For what can war but endless war still breed?—JOHN MILTON, On the Lord General Fairfax at the Siege of Colchester.

CHAPTER XV

THE FIGHT FOR WAR

WITH the individual, and to a degree with peoples, war has become less popular. Its objectives, with the change to impersonal combat, have grown more abstract and remote. Left to themselves the peoples of uncivilized countries would probably keep from large-scale conflict; only less probably the more developed populations. With the evolution of public sentiment —which after all must not be overestimated—need has arisen for new methods of control. How else might be perpetuated this religion of war, deemed quite as necessary to salvation by its devotees as the scourge to the faithful apologists for flagellation? The inquiring mind, the generous heart, the very bodies of its victims, even, this modern Moloch bends to its bloody, inexorable rites.

The Drive for Man Power

The past century or so, as we have seen, has brought a vast development of weapons for use upon an enemy. The greatest weapon of all is not devised for enemies more than for home populations; it works against the greatest foe of war in every country—the people who might decline to fight. That weapon is conscription.

Its rise, in modern form, was rapid. The eleventh edition of the *Encyclopedia Britannica* gravely laid down the dictum that conscription "forms even at the present day the chief guarantee for peace, stability, and economic development upon the Continent of Europe." [1] It appears a bad guess, in retrospect, considering that the World War to demonstrate the Continent's stability began less than four years after! It was hardly the first time, either, that such a demonstration had been made.

Feudalism was accompanied by a general obligation to military service, but even under the feudal system there was nothing approximating modern conscription. It remained for national patriotism to produce this comparatively new invention of the war makers. At the time of the Thirty Years War, Sweden began to raise troops under the so-called Indelta system, by which levies were laid on each district according to its population—a form of conscription "preached in every pulpit in Sweden."

But the use of modern conscription dates from 1793, with the French *levée en masse,* which made it more desirable for the reluctant Frenchman to face the enemy in battle than to confront his own civil tribunals.

Even the *levée en masse* was inadequate in the face of a growing recalcitrance, and in 1798 the famous bill proposed by General Jourdan was put through and conscription for general military service was sprung upon the people of France. It was then possible for Napoleon to snap his fingers at the hated Metternich and declaim, "I can now afford to expend thirty thousand men a month."

Thus in round numbers conscription, like the peace societies, has only recently celebrated its centennial—well in time, however, for the great war of 1914. From 1870 on, practically every European power, with the exception of Great Britain, had settled down to a policy of compulsory army service for shorter or longer terms.

Though men were forced into the service in certain localities during the Revolution and the War of 1812, the United States was slow to take up the European system, even in time of war. In the War of 1812, an attempt was made to conscript the militia of the States into the Federal army; but the law did not get through.

The pioneers of peace were vigorously outspoken on the question. Noah Worcester in 1818 made his opposition plain:

The British impressments and French conscriptions have appeared horrible to the freemen of our country; but similar things on a smaller scale and under a milder name, have been practiced among ourselves. What we have experienced in having men *draughted* and *compelled,* contrary to their inclinations, to join an army, may be regarded as but the beginning of sorrow, unless we abandon the custom of war and adopt a more just, benevolent and honourable mode of adjusting our difficulties.

. . . As a people we should forgive but never forget the step which was seriously proposed for conscription towards the close of the late war with Great Britain. The plan was indeed rejected at that time by Congress; but it may hereafter be adopted.

It was, thereafter, but never completely, sweepingly, ruthlessly, until exactly a hundred years from that protest in *The Friend of Peace.* As true in that later day as earlier, were these other words of Worcester:

And what better is the condition of those who are the victims of conscription for having their lot cast in the United States—in a land of boasted liberty and equal rights? If a man must be a conscript and deprived of personal liberty, without any crime on his own part, why may he not as well be the conscript of one despotism as another? Military conscription is military despotism, by whatever name a government may be called which assumes the power.

A dozen years away from the War of 1812 the twelfth annual report of the Massachusetts Peace Society pointedly referred to the supposed cause of that catastrophe:

Conscription or seduction for recruiting an army, is as really a violation of the laws of Heaven, and of the rights of men, as manning a fleet by impressment.

The post-war appeals for militarization were subsiding in force, and—not seeing far into the future—Joshua P. Blanchard at the thirteenth annual convention of the same society expressed his gratitude:

We have reason to be thankful, that the age when war could be imposed by ambitious rulers on their reluctant subjects, is passing away.

By the combination of short-term enlistments and bounties

326 THE FIGHT FOR PEACE

in the Revolutionary War, almost 400,000 enlistments were recorded, of which many were duplications; but by 1781 the troops which in 1776 had numbered 89,000 had diminished to hardly 29,000. In his Morristown headquarters General George Washington during 1777 complained bitterly about the "almost incredible" number of desertions, and forbade any furloughs even for his officers.

Out of 528,000 men in the War of 1812, says Colonel P. S. Bond, 465,000 were enlisted for periods of twelve months or less, 400,000 for six months or less, and 150,000 for less than one month.

In the War with Mexico enlistments were abundant, though the hardest fighting of that imperialist raid was done by regular army troops early in the conflict. Short-term enlistments and the bounty were again made use of, but not to such excess. In calling for the volunteers, Congress and President Polk used the words "for twelve months or for the war," a tactical error according to our authority, "thus giving to the men the option of taking their discharges at the end of twelve months if they desired, which they invariably did."

After experiencing difficulty with the voluntary enlistment of fighting forces, the Confederacy in 1862 organized a draft to secure adequate cannon fodder. The North, which had employed chaotically one plan of enlistment after another, with occasionally the bounty, both State and Federal, followed suit in 1863. This, so far as the Union goes, was the first legalization of conscription. The law was acutely unpopular. Draft riots occurred in New York City, Portsmouth (New Hampshire), Boston, and Holmes County (Ohio). Pro-slavery hoodlums and alley gangsters led most of the rioting, which in New York resulted in a loss of life estimated at nearly a thousand by the city police. Behind them, notwithstanding, was a strong public resentment, deep and widespread.

Dr. Ella Lonn, in her study of *Desertion During the Civil War,* after the most careful checking of figures, places the number of actual desertions from the Confederate forces at about

100,000, and those from the Union armies at approximately twice that number. In regard to the Southern situation, she says, "By 1865 desertions were no longer counted by the score, but by the hundred; whole companies, garrisons, and even regiments decamped at a time." It was no different with the troops of the North. On both sides, a regular set of signals were evolved by which soldiers could pass into enemy lines without being harmed.

It is not generally realized that the Civil War draft netted less than 50,000 men and about $10,518,000 under the "three hundred dollar clause" allowing the purchase of exemptions. Of those drafted, 20 per cent failed to report; 30 per cent of those who did report were exempted on account of physical disability; another 30 per cent were granted exemption for various other reasons. Of the remaining 40 per cent about half paid their $300; about two-thirds of the rest hired substitutes; and only the other third went to camp. By Colonel Bond the number actually rendered available through the draft is estimated to be only 36,000. The law was adopted in the first place fully as much to convert the status of the enlisted troops to a "duration-of-the-war" commitment.[2]

The Spanish-American War lasted but 109 days. The United States used 50,000 regular troops and 223,000 volunteers.

Conscription—prettified as "selective service"—became securely fastened upon this peace-crusading country in 1917. Far better than England's our Draft Act worked; for John Bull's broke down sadly in Erin and Australia.

In the defeated countries, conscription was tabooed by the conquerors; some of the victors fastened it upon their people still more securely. Even in countries like Great Britain and the United States, opposed by long tradition to peace-time universal service, conscription as a war policy was written on the books of the war colleges with indelible ink. Should a war soon come, it would find the land of the free and the home of the brave ready with the draft machinery, and no time would be lost in hurling at the foe khaki ranks of conscripts, many of them too young ever to have had a chance to vote on any-

thing, much less on the war itself. "Theirs not to reason why;
theirs but to—kill—and die."

In France, where at the Palais Royal, Paris, an early writer
in *The Calumet* saw "amazons" who were "dressed *en militaire*,
with boots, spurs, and sabre," and where he prayed that "the
day might be far distant when such strange sights shall be seen
in this country"—in France of 1927, M. Boncour's bill passed
the Chamber of Deputies providing for the most drastic conscription, in war time, of every important industry, of all labor,
of all persons "without distinction of age or sex." Under its
terms the whole country could be mobilized overnight, all civil
rights abrogated. Not only in time of actual invasion or attack,
be it noted, but in the event of "preparations of an aggressive
character." Happily the bill was snagged in the Senate; but
of the European turn of mind since the War, it is indeed a
vivid suggestion.

Here at home the American Legion, stirred by the great
profits piled up by business interests (which were not taxed
heavily, as in most of the warring countries) and by high
wages (often mythical) received by labor while the conscripts
were getting along on comparatively small spending money,
sponsored a draft of money and men. Such a universal draft
law, prepared for "the next war," would ostensibly "take the
profits out of war," and aid peace by depriving war makers of
gain.

President Harding endorsed the scheme. Its tangible legislative form was the Capper-Johnson bill. Under this measure
it would be possible to draft men into industrial or military
servitude; but as far as the drafting of funds is concerned the
bill was evasive and ineffective. On the other hand, in respect
to the human factor, it made the President a virtual dictator
over the lives of millions, and under circumstances inadequately
defined. The bill provided

That in case of war [any kind of war] *or when the President
shall judge the same to be imminent* [italics mine] he is authorized
and it shall be his duty when, in his opinion, such emergency
requires it

(a) To determine and proclaim the material resources, industrial organizations and services over which government control is necessary to the successful termination of such emergency, and such control shall be exercised by him through agencies then existing or which he may create for such purposes;

(b) To take such steps as may be necessary to stabilize prices of services and of all commodities declared to be essential, whether such services and commodities are required by the Government or by the civilian population.

It will be seen at once that this is no genuine "conscription of wealth," such as a direct levy upon income or means. Furthermore the President—or rather the absolute monarch who would then control us—would find it easier to conscript youths, for which there is precedent, than to make the wealthy pay for the war—for which there is no precedent at all.

Under such elusive language, it will readily be seen that our next war President would have a power hitherto unimagined by any despot. Nero, Cæsar—how mortified they must be in their trans-Styxian retreat! Here is one trick they missed. And some have foolishly declaimed, in song and story, the eternal banishment of slavery from our soil in 1865!

The Capper-Johnson bill, successively introduced in Congress, has never passed. Perhaps it never will. Whether it becomes a law or not, it has served to show how far good people may go toward mobilizing the masses, and all in the sacred name of peace. So benign a person as the late Bishop Brent, Vice-Chairman of the Federal Council of Churches Commission on International Justice and Goodwill, once gave this plan his backing.[3] It is supported by the Legion and numerous "patriotic" societies. The American Federation of Labor, on the contrary, stated in its outline of planks for consideration of the parties in the 1928 campaign:

The American Federation of Labor has declared its opposition to compulsory service and compulsory labor under any form or any guise whatever. For this reason, it is opposed to industrial conscription at any time and it is opposed to conscription for army and navy service except in case of a defensive war where citizens are called upon to take arms in defense of the Nation, its territory or its sovereignty.[4]

The Republican Party platform adopted at Kansas City in 1928 declared for this monstrous enslavement in general terms.

How truly the Capper-Johnson measure provided for genuine conscription of wealth is indicated by some frank testimony before the House Military Affairs Committee on May 21, 1928, by Colonel Edward E. Spafford, then National Commander of the American Legion. Representative James inquired, "How are you going to draft capital under your bill?" Said Colonel Spafford, "You cannot draft capital; you know that, sir." When Congressman Garrett wanted to know why, Colonel Spafford responded, "The Constitution of the United States says that you cannot take a man's property without just compensation. . . . To draft capital and take a man's property would be making us into a United States of Soviet America instead of the United States of America." "You cannot take his property, but you can take his life?" asked Representative Speaks, a little later; whereupon came the reply from Colonel Spafford, "Yes, sir; I think everybody recognizes that."

Only a few months after the signing of the Pact of Paris, Representative James, by request of the War Department, introduced a bill (H. R. 2897) providing for the most stringent war-time conscription, in which there is absolutely no mention of conscripting wealth or regulating prices or any attempt to curb a thing beyond the freedom of the citizen from war service.

President Hoover in 1930 signed an act providing for a commission to study the problem of conscription with a view to working out a plan which would be efficient and ready at hand for the "next war" whenever the administration in office at the time decides on hostilities.

Irrespective of this particular measure's fate, certain is it that war-time conscription, long hated and considered profoundly un-American, is to-day an integral, a central part of our mobilization machinery. Here, too, we have been making "progress."

The Drive for Youth

"I pledge a Legion to my flag and to the Republicans, for

which it stands; one nation, with invisible liberty and justice for all." The boy who is reported to have brought home this version of the flag salute could easily be forgiven; for he was doubtless very small.

The capture of the learning process for the inculcation of a military patriotism is reasonably complete. The indoctrination commences early. Innocent words, with a ring of nobility to them, when taken of themselves; but as actually taught and applied to the ways in which the flag is supposed to symbolize our loyalty, it is a rare youngster who does not acquire a standardized form of national fealty definitely associated with warfare. If there is not a standardization about it, if there is not back of its use an accumulation of militarist fervor, why then must it be so serious a matter? Serious it is.

For example take the State of New York. Section 712 of the Education Law makes it the duty of the Commissioner of Education to prepare for the use of the public schools of the State a program providing for salute to the flag and for instruction in its correct use and display. Assuming that the pupils are required to salute the flag in accordance with these regulations, a failure on the part of a pupil to comply would be deemed misconduct. If persisted in, the pupil may, if over sixteen years old, be expelled; or, if within the age of compulsory attendance, may be suspended, with the consent of the Board of Education, for a period of not more than one week. If he still refuses to comply with the regulations, he may be committed to an institution for the detention of incorrigibles.

If this is not conscription of thought, you may name it yourself.

"During the course of a year the War Department guides, for varied periods, the lives of over 400,000 young Americans enrolled in the Regular Army, the National Guard, the Reserve Officers' Training Corps and the Citizens' Military Training Camps." This from the 1926 Report of the Secretary of War.

In 1928, high schools in twenty cities gave R.O.T.C. courses which were compulsory. Military training was compulsory in eighty-six colleges and universities. In 1929, 13,134 students were taking the advanced course of the Reserve Officers' Training Corps in college, while 73,352 young men in 125 colleges were taking the basic courses. The work of the Junior R.O.T.C. in 103 cities netted 43,472 secondary and high school boys. (See a speech by Hon. Ross A. Collins in the House of Representatives, January 10, 1930.)

To what purpose are these courses given? No better summary has come to my eye than that given by Major William W. Edwards, in *The Infantry Journal* for October, 1922:

The Defense Act has two distinct functions. The first is so obvious as to need no comment, that of training officers and men for the reserve forces; its second function, while not less important, is less apparent, and therefore sometimes overlooked entirely, that of training the popular public mind to the necessity and needs of defense. The Junior R.O.T.C. fulfills the first mission indirectly, and for the second, I believe, there is no greater or better agency at our command. The high school boy in his Sophomore year is in his most plastic and enthusiastic stage.

And with what ideals are these youths being inspired? Good ones, some of them: cleanliness, robust physique, physical courage, orderliness, coöperation. But they are also being militarized. Can anybody deny the truth of it with regard to the youths who heard an R.O.T.C. instructor at Camp Kearney hold forth? Here he goes, in a talk on Military Psychology:

This is a period of truce. The Great Wars of the world have not been fought . . . watch Asia. . . . Think of the hundreds of thousands of pacifists who work night and day to help our most deadly foreign enemies! . . . If you find a man who is opposed to Universal Military Training for all loyal citizens—watch that man! . . . Gentlemen, I envy you. You are to become military leaders. . . . There will be wars until the end of time. Everlasting peace is for the grave—not for life. The wish for everlasting peace is born of fear and ignorance. It is a sure sign of weakness and a declining civilization. . . . The World cannot be made larger. There are few "new worlds" on this planet. The strong will survive. The weak must perish! Steel your arms and draft your bodies for the greatest war that the world has ever seen!

Here is the R.O.T.C. Manual, Infantry, 2nd year advanced, Vol. IV, 7th edition, August, 1925, page 207:

We live in a world governed by Divine laws which we can neither alter nor evade. And in this world of ours force is the ultimate power.

Ditto, page 384:

During the course of a great war every government, whatever its previous form, should become a despotism.

Again, page 255:

An armistice should never be granted at the instance of a defeated foe. It is a confession of weakness, of inability to clinch the victory.

Once more, page 208:

The mainsprings of human action are self-preservation and self-interest, in a word *selfishness*—the "touch of nature which makes the whole world kin."

A student publication in an R.O.T.C. college printed in 1925 certain extracts from Moss and Lang's *Manual of Military Training* (1923 edition), a textbook with a circulation of some three hundred and twenty thousand. Those excerpts showed how crude was the philosophy underlying much of this training. They are distinctly more robust, you might say, than anything in such a work, for instance, as the *Manual of Bayonet Exercise Prepared for the Use of the Army of the United States,* by General McClellan, issued in 1862. In the face of protest and unfavorable publicity, some of the harsher sentiments and instructions have been deleted and bayonet drill given up in the R.O.T.C. It is revealing to note the quotations picked out by the rebellious undergraduates:

The object of all military training is to win battles.
The principles of sportsmanship and consideration for your opponent have no place in the practical application of this work.
To finish an opponent who hangs on, or attempts to pull you to the ground, always try to break his hold by driving the knee or foot to his crotch and gouging his eyes with your thumbs.
This inherent desire to fight and kill must be carefully watched for and encouraged by the instructor.
America needs invincible infantry.

In my opinion the deletion was unwarranted. War cannot be made gallant or ladylike. If our youths are to learn the lovely art, why not learn it with some semblance of reality?

As far as numbers go, the situation in the United States might be much worse. Defenders of the system often point out, justly, that the youths affected are but a small percentage. How honest an argument this is may be seen from the fact that they are doing their level best to reach ever-increasing numbers, their ambition suffering a curb only from a lack of further financial appropriations.

What the proponents of youth-preparedness really want may be inferred from the *R.O.T.C. Manual for Infantry,* 2nd year advanced, Vol. IV, 7th edition, 1925. Some may want more, some less. In a recent edition a part of the program as set forth is eliminated, but in other books used by the R.O.T.C. the *beau idéal* remains the same:

What constitutes a proper military policy for the U. S.?

(1) A Regular Army of about 300,000 enlisted men and 20,000 officers.

(2) A national guard under complete Federal control, numbering from 400,000 to 500,000 officers and men.

(3) An organized reserve of 500,000 to 1,000,000 officers and men.

(4) An unorganized reserve to consist of:

(a) An officers' reserve corps, to include an unlimited number of individuals qualified as officers, to be drawn from the Reserve Officers' Training Corps and other available sources;

(b) An enlisted reserve. . . . (etc.)

(5) The Reserve Officers' Training Corps in schools and colleges.

(6) Universal military training for young men in time of peace. . . . (etc.)

In a *fifteen-year period,* according to the Committee on Militarism in Education in 1927:

federal expenditures on military training in civil schools have increased from $725,168 to $10,696,504, a fifteen-fold increase; the number of institutions giving such training, from 57 to 223, a fourfold increase; the army personnel detailed to conduct the training, from 85 to 1809, an eighteen-fold increase; the number of students enrolled, from 29,979 to 119,914 (including voluntary) a four-fold increase.*

Professor William Bradley Otis, not a pacifist, testifying before the House Military Affairs Committee said, in 1926:

Never before, gentlemen, in American history has the freedom of our higher educational institutions been thus threatened by an Army bureaucracy.

It is quite true that some boys, if they do not like the drill, can change their high schools or colleges at will; but they represent only a very small percentage. Most students are helpless about it as far as high schools are involved, and most colleges are selected for definite reasons which are not readily subject to change.

Compulsory military training may not be government conscription, though it is certainly government-fostered. But it is always, invariably, conscription-of-youth-by-Elder-Statesmen which seeks to fasten upon successive generations the same inept military ideals which have ruined the hopes of so many generations in past years.

How the elders fit on the armor by persuasion instead of out-and-out conscription is shown by certain interesting figures.

One figure is 39,676. This is the number of boys who, in the summer of 1927, took the courses of the Citizens' Military Training Camps. The number for 1928 and 1929 was a bit lower. What did they learn? As in the case of the R.O.T.C., some things of value; but none which they could not have learned as well or better in civilian camps. They learned some other things.

Some of the other things were learned from instructors who were following out the teaching suggested by a new *Manual of Citizenship Training*—a normal-school text, in a way—put out in 1927. These other things are not concerned with the handling of firearms or explosives; they deal with the building up of hair-trigger minds.

"I will take any man who is not an absolute idiot and teach him the trade of a soldier in three months." This from John

Philip Sousa, testifying more enthusiastically than deliberately on behalf of a bill favoring commissions for army bandmasters.*

The military instructors know better than that. They understand that military matters are technical matters, that cannot be mastered in three months or six or a year. But ideas! One lecture may start a train of thought which, tying in with the whole system of deliberate and unconscious military propaganda by which youth is surrounded, may turn out a "right-minded" citizen with little further assistance.

What is "right-minded"? Let the *Manual of Citizenship Training* work on you a bit. The numerals are mine, an aid to later comment.

(1) . . . the philosophy of government, as set up under our constitution, finds its key-note in individualism as opposed to collectivism—that misguided philosophy of government which makes the state paramount in its demands over the inalienable rights of its individual citizens.

(2) The American is the personification of independence. He asks no favors of government or men.

(3) What are the principles of democracy? Demagogism, license, impulse, agitation, discontent, anarchy, chaos and socialism.

(4) How can we best provide for the peace and security of our nation? By being prepared, showing that we are at all times ready for war.7

In these random examples of the principles on which good citizenship is supposed to rest, (1) is of course intended as a swipe against government ownership. The connection between this subject and military training is obscure, unless it be that if all brands and degrees of socialism are avoided, there may be more need for military preparation—a view which I will hardly attempt to refute. To adhere completely to individualism, however, would involve the government's giving up the Post Office Department, all control of roads and waterways and collective activities too numerous to mention. It would be destructive of morale, I should think, to teach what is obviously true if (1) is correct: namely, that the government is continually breaking the constitution.

If (2) is to be taught, clearly all the C.M.T.C. boys must go home to work against tariffs, which surely are favors from government; not to mention military appropriations for schools.

If (3) may be relied on, every young man who fought for the sacred cause of democracy in 1918 was promoting that combustive combination of irreconcilable concomitants against which the C.M.T.C. authorities would sound a solemn warning —look back and count those awful conditions.

And if (4) is the basis of good citizenship and true Americanism, we are late in arriving at this wisdom. Germany was prepared in 1914; German youth learned how secure preparedness made them. The same is true of Belgium, which had put through one year previously a huge preparedness program. France, Russia, Italy, Britain—all were prepared, though of course in varying degree. An examination of the war losses in men killed reveals the curious fact that fatalities occurred most heavily in Russia, Germany, and France—the very countries best prepared of all.

But such facts do not matter to the blithe assurance of the War Department. The flame is beauteous to the heady moth; your true military zealot never heeds such admonitions as that by Shakespeare's Duke of Norfolk:

> Heat not a furnace for your foe so hot
> That it do singe yourself.

The plastic mind of youth—that is the great objective. And if thought can't all be conscript, then let us reach it all by other means. Such is the plan, deliberate with some, traditional and hardly conscious with others. However motivated, the efforts produce results which ought to be more and more gratifying to the military nabobs.

Where military training is on a voluntary basis, constant federal attention is required. In a letter to the writer answering an inquiry, a naval officer stated:

It is with satisfaction that we establish a connection with any institution of education, whereby the young people of the coming generation may be reached with data and information concerning any adjunct so important to their country as the Navy.

Probably so. But the navy should be jealous. The army establishes many a connection, and keeps its hold over the students, by argument, patriotic appeal, or if need be, bribery.

A heavy percentage of American college boys are impecunious. Even those from wealthy homes are not always pampered and kept flush with funds. A strong appeal is made to the poorer undergraduate by the free uniform, which saves him expense in clothing bills. Often the student is provided with an "overcoat suitable for wear with both uniform and civilian clothing."

The New Mexico State College *Round-Up,* a student journal, made this plain:

Advanced R.O.T.C. pays. Whether you juniors believe in military training or not, if you are in need of money you had better take the course. The compensation is nine dollars a month. Besides this, a thirty-six-dollar uniform is given to the advanced student. . . . Some claim that the summer camp is a disadvantage. True they get only seventy cents a day, with board, room and clothing; but most of them make considerable from the transportation appropriation, which is five cents a mile.

The University of Arkansas catalogue declares:

The total money value of uniform received, commutation of subsistence, rations in kind at Camp, pay at Camp, and transportation to and from Camp for each man who completes the four year course, is about $400.00.

And this not for work outside the course of study, but work for which scholastic credit is granted.

At Yale and other colleges where presumably youth is somewhat more gilded, tailor-made officers' outfits are provided, and the military department maintains for artillery students a stable of polo ponies.

The Department of the Interior in 1927, listed one hundred and thirty-two private military schools in the United States. The ideal on which these schools base their character training is of course the military standard, the war standard, the preparedness doctrine. Only in seven of these is aid directly given (1927) by the government.

Schools where the military work is all paid for by the government total two hundred and twenty-eight; fifty more are government-aided.

The government sends rifle coaches to assist the National Rifle Association of America in its marksmanship contests at Camp Perry.

For this national meet the expert shots of the army, navy and Marine Corps, the National Guard from every State in the Union and the best marksmen of the various R.O.T.C. units were selected. Usually about 5,000 men in all are in attendance at the national matches. Of this number, about one-half are regulars. about one-quarter National Guardsmen, and the rest civilians.

To encourage knowledge of military arms throughout the nation and to teach civilians how to shoot, the man in civil life is as much desired at Perry as the best shot in uniform. This includes not only the best marksmen of civilian gun clubs, but the ambitious youngster who has never touched a piece in all his life but is eager to learn how to fire. . . . Regular army officers are detailed all along the firing line as coaches and instructors, lending their skilled aid to any civilian in need. . . . During six weeks in the late summer of 1927 five regiments of regulars were at Perry aiding the civilians in every way.*

Similarly, the United States Revolver Association, which adopted a resolution in 1924 contending that "the training of the citizens of the nation in the use of arms is a patriotic and desirable object," and which adds realism to this "manly form of recreation" by using as targets a silhouette of the human figure, not only spreads what is basically the military view, but labors faithfully to kill legislation calculated "to hamper or prevent the possession and proper use of pistols and other firearms by reputable citizens, for purposes of protection and defense as well as for practice and target shooting." *

The arms manufacturers are active now as they have been in the past. The old Navy League is still on the job though it works less conspicuously than it did during the Navy drive of 1916, when Congressional investigators found that its officials were largely representatives of the big steel, mining and powder interests—including Cleveland H. Dodge, David Low Dodge's great-grandson, who was a life member!

When the President is given the millionth gun made by a

large firearms factory, it need be taken as no sinister gesture. But when the arms companies invade the precincts of childhood, there is reason for concern.

How these companies may go about building a demand for their goods was suggested by a leading editorial in the Winston-Salem (N.C.) *Journal* for November 29, 1926:

Investigation by Jonathan Daniels, the *Journal's* Washington correspondent, shows conclusively that the movement to establish rifle target-shooting "clubs" in the Winston-Salem High School and other public schools of America was originated by the big arms and munitions manufacturers of this country.

Their object is to create a demand for guns. Their purpose is to instill into the hearts of the youth a desire to shoot.

The Winchester Arms Company alone spent $500,000 in promotion of this insidious and effective propaganda to turn the minds of American schoolboys away from books to rifles. . . .

So far as the *Journal* has been able to learn, the arms manufacturers have made their first assault in North Carolina on the Winston-Salem High School. But other schools are not immune. They should be on the alert. Indeed, isn't it time the State Department of Education was taking a hand to prevent our public-school system from being prostituted to the ideals of Prussianism?

In 1918, a war year, the same newspaper reveals, the Winchester Arms Company organized a chain rifle corps among youth, which recently became the National Junior Rifle Corps, which has grown from five thousand to one hundred and fifty thousand members. Rifles were given away to boys and girls in summer camps of the Y.M. and Y.W.C.A., to scout troops, etc., etc. and medals were given—up to 1920, eight thousand of them.

In 1925, the Winchester people withdrew all control and turned the enterprise over to the National Rifle Association of America. The investment of five hundred thousand dollars, according to a spokesman, did not bring that amount of increased sales, "but it got good will." [10]

A like inculcation of the military ideal is not absent in the Boy Scout movement. The annual reports of this organization state that

As an organization the scout movement is not military in thought, form or spirit, although it does instill in boys the military virtues, such as honor, loyalty, obedience and patriotism. The uniform, the patrol, the troop, and the drill are not for military tactics; they are for the unity, the harmony, and the rhythm of spirit that boys learn in scouting.

And follows an appreciation of "the wonderful record of scout nation-wide civic war service. . . ."

Also follows, later, a statement that

One of the things in which the Boy Scouts of America has been particularly fortunate has been in the cooperation of the various service clubs and of the American Legion. An elaborate plan of cooperation with the American Legion has been worked out, in which the Legion is concentrating on giving out-of-door leadership. Every Legion post has been urged by the American Legion officials to promote a Boy Scout troop.[11]

I make no sweeping condemnation of the peace record of the American Legion. It represents only a minority of ex-service men, and its official point of view has often gone farther than many of its posts toward perpetuation of the militarist philosophy. Certain posts without official rebuke, however, have furnished a permanent memorial to the startling fact that those who ought to learn most from war often acquire no basic understanding whatsoever.

I behold no deep and dark conspiracy against which to exhort. Nevertheless, here are some fair inquiries. Where is the peace society at all consistent in its anti-war record, whose cooperation has been sought, and whose advice followed, by Boy Scout officials? In what peace parade have Boy Scouts ever marched in numbers as they march continually in military and Memorial Day parades? What instructions in the arts of peace are being provided for the education of the Scouts? The Scout jamboree in England was a step toward world friendship; but infinitely more than this is called for.

The Scout officials are sincere, I am convinced, in their effort to keep the Scouts, as they think, "not military in thought, form or spirit," but they are careful to do nothing likely to alienate the support of military organizations. Certainly in local situations the Scout troops are often subject to direct military influence. A newspaper, for example, prints a photograph of a group of Boy Scouts beside the tomb of the unknown soldier, at a ceremony honoring the only member of their troop who was killed in the World War. Caption: "In Memory of Those Who Preceded Them in Defense of Their Country." [12] Another newspaper prints a photograph of a cup award being made to a Boy Scout troop by an army lieutenant.[13] *Military and Naval America* contains a chapter on the Boy Scouts, and lists the Scouts as a "semi-military organization," along with the National Rifle Association, cadet corps, et cetera, which are "instilling a love of country and the flag and a willingness to fight for them if need be."

The Handbook for Scoutmasters states, "Scout drill is founded on the infantry drill of the United States Army." By an act of Congress the Scouts are permitted to wear "uniforms similar to those worn by the United States army, navy and marine corps." [14]

The annual report of the Boy Scouts is a government document, printed, though not distributed, at public cost, by an act of 1915, a year when the preparedness drive was at its height. In some places Boy Scout troops have taken part in sham battles, and in countless localities have been reviewed by military officers. Permission for army officers to act as scoutmasters was granted, upon receipt of a request from Boy Scout headquarters.

There can be no juggling of this issue. No man, or boy, can serve two masters. He that is not for peace, is against it. Most, it must be confessed, still stand with one foot in the puddle, and one foot in the edge's mud. Let them stand forth and declare themselves in words of crystal clarity! The issue may well be the life or death of the boys now growing up all over the world.

The struggle against conscription of the learning process, against the militarism of youth, has gone on for a century. Just as the arguments we have previously examined were di-

rected against war recurrently, so the defensive contest against
this militarist menace has fluctuated up and down the battle-line
of the years. Never have the "advocates of peace" napped on
this question but what they have been called from their mo-
mentary bivouac.

After the Revolutionary War, there was a clamor for more
military training. Benjamin Rush met the pleas of military
leaders with these words:

> I know the early use of a gun is recommended in our country
> to teach young men the use of firearms, and thereby to prepare
> them for war and battle. But should we inspire our youth, by such
> exercises, with hostile ideas toward their fellow creatures? Let us
> rather instill into their minds sentiments of universal benevolence
> to men of all nations and colors.

After the War of 1812, the clamor grew apace. Noah
Worcester met it by quoting Herman Boerhaave, the famous
Dutch physician, who had said, regarding poisons:

> To teach the arts of cruelty is equivalent to committing them.

But the military system grew. William Ladd called it "but
one head of the Hydra, war" and cheerfully thought that

> This evil can, and probably will, ere long, be abolished. . . .

The *Letters of Lillian Ching,* which I have quoted, comment
sardonically on the fact that in "this Christian land" "throughout the country the young men spend several days in each year
to learn to fight. . . ."

William Jay in 1842 protested that

> The enrolled militia of the United States is 1,503,592. This
> vast multitude are called from their homes several days each year
> for the purpose of inspection and drilling.

Often it was with wooden guns that the lads strode round
the fresh-mown meadows. It was always with the odor of
liquid refreshments a spur to action; and a large part of the
ardor stirred against the musters was due to the "drunkenness,
profanity, and Sabbath-breaking" they induced.

As time went on and the war fever abated, many states

THE FIGHT FOR PEACE

failed to enforce the militia laws. Where they were not definitely abolished they often fell into neglect. Thus in 1845 George C. Beckwith was saying:

Most of the standing armies of Europe are in a course of reduction, and our own States are gradually ceasing to require military drills. Everywhere the art of war is falling into disuse. . . .[16]

It didn't fall far. For in another year, the forces which had long been gathering to precipitate the Mexican War had finally had their way.

Again history, Time's eternal parrot, repeats itself. After that war, the jingoes were more active, military training was demanded, and the war-peace feud fought over. The Reverend Charles Brooks, in whose Unitarian pulpit years before the Misses Grimké found an open-minded welcome, led an active prototype of our modern Committee on Militarism in Education. Appearing at Albany in 1851 he argued strenuously and with great ability for a bill to eliminate the militia. Though not directly successful, the efforts of this committee to some extent checkmated the rise of a new military-training movement.

Again this one head of the Hydra seemed scheduled for decapitation. But again there came a war. And again there came in its wake a flood of military fervor commensurate with the Civil War's great bloodshed. President Sears of Brown University labored before the Social Science Association and also before a Congressional committee on behalf of legislation providing for compulsory military training in colleges.

Against this move the then young Universal Peace Union spoke sternly, rapping Dr. Sears over the knuckles in sharp language. They

felt it their duty to expose this by the following motion: "That we view with apprehension and sorrow this effort by professed christians, to introduce into professedly christian colleges, the art of *man wounding*, and *man killing*, as a scientific and commendable study for youth, and we regard such teaching not only as *anti-Christ*, but as positively immoral and wicked.

This slightly anti-climactic rebuke was followed by a verbal sigh:

What a strange inconsistency in Dr. Sears—education on one hand for life and happiness, and on the other military spirit for misery and death.

Everywhere, despite all effort, military drill crept into the schools. Boys' brigades spread not only from school to school but from church to church. A score of years; again the nation's temperature dropped; and down at Vanderbilt University "Marse Henry" Watterson of Louisville, one of a doughty line of old-time editors, "denounced the practice of carrying and using weapons."

In Boston, after a hot campaign on both sides, the school committee voted not to put muskets in the city schools for drill, and pledged themselves to keep the spirit of war out of education. While the boys' brigades were persisting and called forth suggestions of substitutes in the form of fire brigades, life-saving corps, mechanics' bands, et cetera; and while President Harrison wrote a letter to the *Century Magazine* approving military drill in the schools—still, things were on the upgrade. A bill introduced into the State Legislature of Pennsylvania, in 1895, providing for military training in the public schools, was successfully opposed by the Universal Peace Union.

Then, once more, came a war. And that war, small as it was by itself, gave us suddenly extensive overseas possessions. Talk arose of naval bases; "Manifest Destiny," hitherto a phrase of pre-Emancipation days meaning the extension of slave power, now took on a significance not yet worked out to its final chapter; and for all these new developments, as well as to satisfy a war lust aroused by the yellow press, our naval appropriations skyrocketed and of course once more the cries were loud for military training.

Now the struggle commenced anew. The Peace Department of the W.C.T.U. printed circulars on "Military Drill," "The Boys' Brigade," "Military Drill in Schools," and "Why Peace

Societies Are Opposed to Military Drill." A short time and the Socialists, never relishing the military so often used against the workers, bitterly castigated our growing militarism. Conservative labor found itself in no better case. Young mill men and mechanics in industrial towns played athletic games in armories and marched around happily, one Company E chanting a parody which reflected the peace sentiment still strong in many homes:

> My mother told *me*
> That she would buy *me*
> A rubber doll*ee*
> If I'd be good.
> But when I *told* her
> I loved a *sold*ier,
> She wouldn't *buy* me
> A rubber doll—*É!*

And on the morrow, that Company "E" was entrained to hold back strikers protesting gamely a wage-cut flesh and blood could not tolerate. All over the country, in those years of labor war and of capitalist penetration to Cuba, Porto Rico, Panama, the Philippines, the same scenes were repeated. And always in the background there swung, now this way now that, the battle for the boyhood of the nation.

Then came a flank attack. History textbooks, always a source of justifiable concern to the peace movement, took on an even louder tone of arrogance. Josiah W. Leeds wrote a booklet, sold by the American Peace Society, entitled forthrightly, *Against the Teaching of War in History Textbooks.* An inquiry was conducted by a special committee of the Society; a detailed and devastating report was the result: *The Teaching of History in the Public-Schools, with Reference to War and Peace.* This in the good year 1906 or 3 R.T.P. (Roosevelt's "Taking" of Panama). Big Bill Thompson of Chicago and Commissioner David Hirschfield of New York had not then awakened to the nation's danger from good-will histories, but their forerunners stalked the land.

Yet gains were once more made, and there was a shred at

least of reason for the optimism that prevailed. And then took place another little conflict about the year 1914. Perhaps that will help to explain the latest large-scale moves to make the goose-step oust the one-step, dating chiefly from the post-war National Defense Act of 1920.

The most obvious corrective thus obtained from historical understanding is to my mind the suggestion that we have the cart before the horse.

In short, military preparedness, especially its folk-aspect in military training, is far less a cause of war, than war is a cause of all military preparedness.

If there is any truth in this, does it therefore follow that the major attack should be directed against war itself, rather than one of its manifestations? I think it does. War is the enemy; and our most murderous weapons of truth, vision, courage, and organized opposition should chiefly be aimed at the heart of the monster war, not at its horrible forked tail.

It does *not* follow, though, that the peace forces can pay no heed to military training. The perpetuation of war is inherent in that practice, whether voluntary or compulsory. Both species must be fought against with vigor. In many ways voluntary military training has its roots deeper in the popular state of mind and will be the harder to hold back. Compulsory military training, for specific reasons, is more immediately menacing. It is worth recalling that in the World War the countries where conscription and compulsory military training were not strong were the only countries where conscientious objection flourished. This is one great value of the fight against compulsory military training.

Again, if young men can be conscripted in time of peace, it will be easier to conscript them and whole populations in the event of another war.

The struggle must be carried on. But it will always be a defensive campaign, fundamentally, until war, bound and held impotent by other factors, chiefly, remains so long with untried muscles that its sinews atrophy and wither.

For the lesson of history, at least the history of our United States, is this: the greatest cause of war is *war*.

The Drive for the People

"Those who admit that the College of Propaganda at Rome once carried the light of the Gospel to the heathen," writes Harold D. Lasswell, an expert investigator of propaganda, "say that the modern publicity department scatters darkness among the civilized." [16]

Such a publicity department is maintained by the army and navy. For instance:

PRESS RELATIONS SECTION

This section is the central coordinating agency of the War Department with regard to publicity. Through the press it attempts to inform the public what the Army is for, what it is trying to do, and of its problems. It publishes a weekly press review and maintains a clipping service. It plans for war-time censorship, propaganda, the handling of war correspondents, and for a visitors' bureau. [17]

"Penalties of Pacifism," "Preparedness and Peace," "Adequate Provision for National Defense"—these are some titles sent to the newspaper-reading public. Reports of speeches by officers fairly flood the press; everything is written up, from the admonitions about pacifism to great bombing demonstrations. No longer do our military solons confine themselves to matters of tactics; they are out to guide the public policy of the United States, foreign and domestic.

Forced to back up by public criticism, they have rallied to their support such bodies as the army and navy service associations, the Reserve Officers' Association, the Military Intelligence Association, the Military Training Camps Association, the American Legion, the Military Order of the World War, the Military Order of the Loyal Legion, and a host of similar groups; including the Navy League, the National Security League, the American Defense Society, the Better America Federation, the Daughters of the American Revolution, the National Civic Federation, and so on. All of these stand ready both to appeal for heavy preparedness and to denounce the opposition.

These agencies appear to work coöperatively. Their united capacity is of course tremendous. They can make it impossible for anyone who reads at all to pass a day without the perusal of one form of propaganda or another. Until exposed by Senator Walsh of Montana in the Senate Chamber on February 27, 1928, it had been possible for some of these propagandists to use the government frank for the free mailing of attacks on pacifists.[18]

The "perils of pacifism" have been decried from rostrums widely separated in space and time by different officers employing identical standardized sentences and paragraphs. Though exploded again and again as groundless myths, such a responsible figure as General Pershing, for whom I have always felt great respect, is able to write for the absorption of American housewives the same old innuendoes:

. . . now we are engaged in another conflict—penetrating and insidious, led by so-called pacifists, demagogues and others who would undermine the foundations of free government. They employ even more dangerous weapons than shot and shell. Through unwholesome propaganda they would lure us into the strange and uncharted sea of internationalism and communism. They would destroy all that we cherish and substitute in its place something of hideous mien.[19]

These wild accusations, couched in generalities, are only the offensive of a campaign to hold this country's nose to the grindstone of the war method. On what stupendous illogic it rests is shown by the same article in two contradictory passages:

In the World War America gave freely of herself to humanity. We may feel content with the part we played. It was indeed a world-saving work.
. . . But even now ten years after the greatest of all wars we see in the world the same conditions that have ever led to conflict.

These military spokesmen credit the public with no more discrimination than O. Henry's New Yorkers who "only know this and that and pass to and fro and think ever and anon."

Counting on the crushing superiority of their propaganda machine and the credulity of the people, the military agencies lose no chances. It was conceded in a House debate of 1926 that 5000 more commissioned officers were in service than were needed for the command of troops, with a reserve of 90,000 officers, 40,000 of whom were admitted to be incapable of active war service. For what purpose do they exist as officers? To be seeded among the people; to reach you and help you to a viewpoint the authorities want you to hold.

The universities often help. Yale announced in 1926 a scholarship which carries free tuition and is open to competition to young men attending the citizens' training camps at Plattsburg and Camp Devens.

The motion pictures help. Every person who sees news reels knows that of the eight scenes usually shown two are often, and on some circuits always, devoted to army and navy activities; but not every person knows the extent of the collaboration which so arranges matters.

Pathé News Reels in a single month listed the following titles: British Navy Gobs; Japanese Sea Scouts Train on Government Warships; Boys 6 to 14 Receive Actual Experience in Navy Routine Under Direction of Trained Officers; Non-Rigid Training Ship Makes Initial Flight; 24 Seaplanes Leave Base for Winter Maneuvers; Navy's Nervy Pilots Guide Seaplanes on Hop from Deck; Laying High Power T.N.T. Mines to Try Out Their Efficiency as Part of Harbor Defense; Mines Exploded from Shore Station.

The pacific individual is usually cast, in longer reels, to look like a consumptive or a bomb-thrower.

Will Hays is now a lieutenant-colonel in the Adjutant-General's Department Reserve, and Jesse L. Lasky is a major in the Signal Corps Reserve. If there are enough official titles to go around, movie stars may yet receive a solace for the terrors of the "talkies."

The greatest need of the Big Navy Brothers is a huge merchant marine, and their latter-day propaganda has been focused on that end. There is a certain patness, therefore, in the fol-

lowing letter regarding a film, "Don't Give Up the Ship." This
letter was sent out to theater managers by a film board of trade:

In event you do not wish to use this subject on the dates designated kindly advise, giving us full information as to the reasons
why you do not wish to use it, as this has been requested by the
Naval Department through Mr. Will Hays, President of the
Motion Picture Producers and Distributors of America. And further, remember this is gratis, the posters are gratis, and again let
us draw to your attention the naval recruiting station in your city.
They will assist you with flags, weapons and other material that
can be used to decorate your lobby. Their own sheet boards will
be turned over to you for one sheet of "Don't Give Up the Ship"
with the name of the theatre on it. Kindly advise if the above
meets with your approval and, if not, let us know the reason. Yours
for a greater Navy and 100 per cent representation of the showing,
"Don't Give Up the Ship." [20]

And radio—what more could any ardent military-methodist
hanker for than is ready to his hand? Upon every holiday
when there is the least excuse military and naval spokesmen
have access to the public ear, and often when excuse is lacking.
The more powerful the station the more certain it is that preparedness is continually kept alive. The United States Army,
Navy and Marine Bands have contributed no small amount—
as their sponsors are well aware—to the creation of a satisfactory public opinion. To the formation of an Army Music
School notable musical instructors lent their aid, just as scientists and others have unquestioningly given theirs for different
purposes. In 1911 the New York Institute of Musical Art
placed ten free scholarships at the disposal of the War Department, to train army musicians for band leadership. In 1928
announcement was made that

Army bands and orchestras have reached such a state of musical
excellence that the War Department has recently closed its Washington school. . . . [21]

Military bands, supposedly for the soldier's morale, are fully
as much for the morale of the band-loving public.

One of the recent devices for holding the people in line is
Navy Day. Mobilization Day was short-lived, thanks to a hos-

tile church, labor, and peace-group leadership; but its older, brinier brother still performs its annual task of making popular opinion seaworthy. According to a navy release:

Navy Day was first sponsored in 1922 by the Navy League of the United States, a volunteer association of individuals, who seek to place information concerning the Navy before the public, and since that time the official approval and cooperation of practically all patriotic and veterans' organizations have been offered in support of the observance of the day.

October 27 was selected for the event because it was the birthday of Theodore Roosevelt, who had done so much to build up a large navy. It was Theodore Roosevelt the younger who, as Acting Secretary of the Navy wrote acknowledging the Navy League's suggestion, in 1922 (the same year which signalized the leasing of Teapot Dome and the Elk Hills Basin to Doheny and Sinclair):

Your idea is sound in every way. I think it particularly good because of certain physical conditions we have in the country. The people of the seaboard are reasonably familiar with the Navy. They see the great ships. They know the Navy men. In the interior of our country it is, however, a different story. The people of Kansas and Oklahoma do not get the opportunity for first-hand information that their fellow-countrymen of California and New York do. They do not realize that the Navy serves them equally with the people of the seaboard. I hope you will make an especial endeavor to familiarize the citizens of our great inland states with the everyday service their Navy does for them. The Navy will be glad to cooperate with you in any way it can. . . .[22]

Not to be outdone, the War Department announced early in 1929 that April Sixth would hereafter be Army Day, to be celebrated by parades and displays. The purpose of such a Day was "to foster a clearer, more intelligent and more sympathetic understanding of the land forces of the country."

There are Days and days. Through them all runs a constant use of military symbolism. The flag, symbolizing the romance and splendor of historic battles, somehow catches no gloomy reflection in its bright folds to show what warfare actually is. The Massachusetts Legislature in 1927 appropriated five thousand dollars for the restoration of the State's historic flags of war. If a flag code becomes Federal law as provided, say, in the so-called Brand bill, saluting the flag whenever it passes may be compulsory to all. Even if this proviso be dropped, a standardization will result calculated to achieve a national mind-set toward the religion of patriotism. What a flag code might do is illustrated by the experience of our 1928 Olympic Game team in Holland. In a parade before the Prince Consort all national flags were dipped as a mark of courtesy, except one— the Stars and Stripes. The reaction of the Dutch was immediate, and a coolness became apparent toward Americans. Who shall say it was not merited?

Only a callous, unimaginative dullard could fail to understand the glamour of war flags and relics to those who ran grave risks to bring them back victorious. But only those who are incapable of seeing plain facts can fail to appreciate the important social effect of war relics, especially on youthful minds.

Ten years after the World War a great Sunday-school supply house was selling buttons to stimulate attendance records, depicting a soldier with poised bayonet leaping into an enemy trench, and bearing the legend "Over the Top."

Cannon that stand on countless village greens speak with an accent in peace time less gutteral than in war; but the language is the same. Looking back, we find *The Advocate of Peace* in 1840 saying:

The building of battlefield monuments—and will Bunker Hill monument be regarded as an exception?—seems to arise from the same element of our nature which prompts the Indian to preserve the scalps of the enemies whom he has slain.

We have in this country an active Battle Monument Association; but there are hundreds of them traveling under other names. Every body of veterans, every town council, every civic improvement society almost, it appears, is bent on holding to the gaze of untold generations the things they want them *told*. Looking back on the bloody years and bitter decades that followed the Sumter episode, it seems a strange impulse that prompts the erection of a Sumter memorial flagstaff in our day. Equally odd in the sight of that angelic tourist described by Franklin to Priestly would seem the erection, at government expense, of a monument to the Battle of Long Island.

All over the country, however, the surveys of battlefields continue, the erection of granite obelisks goes on. Sometimes a war memorial is removed; but such instances are rare.

Late in 1928 the War Department predicted that under the new act approved May 26, providing for the loan or gift of World War relics to soldiers' monument associations, Grand Army of the Republic posts, State museums and municipal corporations, a shortage would speedily develop of captured field pieces and other trophies. More green lawns will bear these hideous blooms of hell, and more minds will be indoctrinated with the fiendish Great Gun Gospel.

The town of LeRoy, New York State, had the sense and courage in 1926 to bury in the soil of its parks two huge Revolutionary cannon; but such news is rarer than that of the man who bit a dog.

The shrine of the Unknown Soldier is a symbol doing its grievous share, perhaps, to create more Unknowns in Unknown wars to come. Lindbergh, the great Known to all, was captured by pursuit planes of the army's press bureau, and the whole world knew that "he was army trained." Even the old ship *Constitution*, rehabilitated for its trip along the coasts and through the inland waterways (and in part by funds raised through the use of franked envelopes by the navy), bears a mute testimony to the glory that was grease and the grandeur that was gore. Or, it may be, as stated in *The Mission and the Needs of the United States Navy*, published by the same:

Thus it will be possible for great numbers of grown people and children to see this relic of old times, to realize her history and battles, and feel the inspiration of her presence. To them she will represent sea power, the protection of merchant vessels and commerce, the establishment of freedom on the sea.

. . . The lessons of the early history of this country and the demonstration of the value of sea power by the *Constitution*, are lessons in good citizenship, of great spiritual value. And these lessons furnish an effective antidote to radical subversive doctrines in schools and among the people.

There are vast possibilities for the reservoiring of emotion behind such symbols, as the professional war-advertisers well know. But greatest of all as sales talks are the vast dramatic demonstrations of war machinery with none of war's effects.

All the artillery booming and machine gun fire in a sham battle between 18,000 citizen soldiers at Camp Henry Knox, Ky., will travel through the ether tomorrow night in an attempt to broadcast by radio from a battlefield, under direction of the United States Signal Corps. Citizen soldiers from three States will repulse an "enemy attack" and the progress of the warfare will be related over the radio by Col. Mark E. Hamer.[23]

And here is drama:

An attempt to "capture" this city will be made today by a theoretical army which has landed on the New Jersey coast during the last few days and has driven back the advance guard of the defending forces of the city and is now massing for an attack on Staten Island.[24]

And here:

While in Westchester the soldiers will enact seven realistic demonstrations showing how an enemy air attack would be repelled, bringing into play the latest type "archies" or anti-aircraft guns. . . . In the air raid demonstration, a huge searchlight with a beam of one million candlepower will be employed to "spot" imaginary enemy airmen. Approach of the theoretical aviators will be recorded by a highly intricate sound-detecting apparatus located on the ground near the guns. . . . For the first time a public demonstration of the army's new 50-calibre anti-aircraft machine gun will be given.[25]

Just stack this up in emotional appeal against the demonstration of a new peace proposal, proffered to the public by the people who have been described by the dramatist, Percy Mac-Kaye, as those who

read dry pamphlets in separate homes, or in offices to the clicking of typewriters, or at best . . . gather chaotically together in a rented hall, listening to drab-coated talkers from a platform, or waving drab handbills for rallying banners. Drab—that is their disease. Their dreams are more glorious than the dreams of war; their dreams are incarnadine, flushed with fighting angels; but they clothe them—and they stifle them—in drab."

Is this the fault of the peace movement? No; for that movement cannot afford to put on such displays.

Is this the fault of the peace movement? Yes; for it has too scant excitement to put on. There is drama in peace effort of a radical kind; but from that sort of effort the peace movement flees as from a plague.

It is enough to query who, in such a competition, is the certain winner, for the answer is but automatic. Thus equipped, reënforced by traditional emotion, sponsored by clever men who know how to extract from their gaudy toys the last ounce of unrealistic appeal, it is not strange that the mobilization of arms, industry, science and government is being matched and sustained by a vast mobilization of popular thought and feeling.

Left to themselves, the people want no war and no war truck or trappings. Left to themselves, however, they cannot be.

Is all of the foregoing merely a repetition of the old complaint against propaganda which in a previous chapter was classed as a skirmish in the fight for peace? Perhaps it is; but there is a difference, clearly, between a whipping up of popular opinion by newspapers which for sensationalism drive governments into war, and the deliberate official and semi-official use of every conceivable agency by what are nothing else than vested military interests. A military officialdom bent on efficiency to carry out the public will is also very different from a vested interest determined to use its power in order to create an overwhelming demand for more of the same vast power. That road when tried elsewhere has in the long run led to war.

How far we have traveled in this Via Dolorosa is suggested by a recent newspaper comment:

The most astounding part of it is that we Americans are becoming infected with the European spirit.

We are not only glad to scrap our beautiful dreams but we display a new and surprising interest in military subjects.

There never was a time, perhaps, when the news dealt more generously with war scares and war possibilities, when the magazines were so filled with war stories and war articles and when one could see so many movies depicting war romances.

Shall we attribute this to natural reaction or take it as a sign that·America has fallen in step with the Old World she professed to disagree with and is about to adopt a more aggressive policy? "

We may attribute it to the new power of mobilization. The masses are being used. They are being used to the limit of saturation by earnest madmen who learn nothing from the tragic blunders of humankind except the art of moving the world toward their ultimate repetition.

CHAPTER XVI
RIVAL TACTICS OF THE EARLY YEARS

The armies of peace, like the hosts of war, must have an advance guard, a forlorn hope, which may fall while leading the way to assault and victory. But in this, as in other cases, the post of danger is the post of honor. And who would not wish to share that honor? Who, after the glorious victory shall be won, will not wish to have been among the few who first unfurled the consecrated banner of peace?—EDWARD PAYSON, 1782-1827.

CHAPTER XVI

RIVAL TACTICS OF THE EARLY YEARS

Most of those in the peace movement have found it possible to support every war. Each war has been steadfastly opposed by a handful; at times some of the movement's leaders have been uncompromising. But an overwhelming majority in the rank and file have always subordinated their peace loyalties to the war cause and have been against all wars excepting the ones that have occurred.

For this inescapable fact the reason must be sought primarily in the peace-time tactics of the movement itself. What those tactics have been can be understood only by an examination of the sincere rivalry within the movement, of different ideals, personalities, and social principles.

"The long night of darkness, delusion, and war is far spent," Noah Worcester asserted in 1818; "the reign of light and love and peace is approaching." The almost millennial hope of Worcester is something hard to account for in view of his incisive intellect; but it makes his justification of defensive war the easier to understand.

David Low Dodge, on the other hand, was never guilty of a facile optimism. A radical on war, he looked forward with a more accurate vision, however reluctantly he faced the prospect.

David Low Dodge—Radical Pacifist

The "father of the peace movement" was a stout conservative in religion, in economics, in morality, in parental authority. In regard to war his was an untamed opposition.

The publication of his anti-war tracts was a startling challenge to accepted military orthodoxy. Unlike Ladd, who entered the peace movement as a middle-of-the-road peace advocate and gradually adopted a more drastic position, Dodge in his first pacific steps put both feet down firmly against all varieties of warfare. It was not a post-war period that witnessed the appearance of his writings, it was a time of gathering warlike bitterness. How few were the outside influences which impressed upon him the pacifist view, he later on attested. Like Francis of Assisi, he dated his conversion from an illness:

Until 1806, when I moved from Hartford to New York, I do not recollect that I ever found an individual but what advocated defense with carnal weapons. In New York I met with two persons, beside those who belonged to the Society of Friends, who advocated pacific sentiments. I continued my inquiries and investigations until 1808, when I was visited with the spotted fever, and was so low that two doctors told me I should probably live but a few hours. In this situation, my mind was calm and lucid. The question of war and self-defense came in review before my mind, and, in the light of the gospel, I had not a remaining doubt of the unlawfulness of all kinds of carnal warfare.

There is a biographical method which sees the cause of every deviation from standardized attitudes in some kind of abnormal mental state. Lest any such practitioner ascribe Dodge's pacifism to a depressed mental condition due to illness, I lose no time in saying that there had been earlier incidents which undoubtedly exerted an influence on his thinking.

For that matter, his mind remained alert. When his doctors advised against his plan to take warm baths, he overrode them and was benefited; whereupon they began to use this treatment successfully with other cases. It was during an unexpected relapse suffered at Litchfield, Connecticut, that his narrow escape occurred. It appears to be a wonder that he survived, for there was not a single "bathing tub" in the town; but he hastily devised a water-tight box which was built for him to order and immediately brought a gain in his condition!

He had been born of stock with military records; as a young man in Windham County, one of Connecticut's most war-revering strongholds, he had served as lieutenant in an artillery company for whose cannon his father had fashioned the wheels. He had, however, as a boy seen his two older half-brothers enticed into the Revolutionary army at the ages of fourteen and sixteen, respectively, by a man who had been promised a captaincy if he could obtain forty enlistments. Dodge writes touchingly of these fair-haired lads whose long sufferings followed by their death during the later years of the war all but drove his mother insane.

He describes with neither scorn nor self-righteousness the men who returned from the Revolutionary conflict demoralized and dispirited and "were generally addicted to low gambling, profanity, intemperance, and widely diffused a most unwholesome moral influence, which we might naturally expect as the fruits of war." He recalls the almost ludicrous sham fights with mock Indians staged in the military musters. And seared into his memory forever was the experience he once had while traveling and stopping at an inn, when in the night he narrowly escaped shooting the tavern keeper upon mistaking him for a burglar.

It was the fashion in those days to avoid trouble by signing pen names to controversial documents. William Ladd, partly from modesty and partly for prudential reasons, employed a score of pseudonyms. His more important series of essays were published as signed by "Philanthropos," and he often used such names as "Spectator," "Pacificator," "Justice," "Philo-Pacis," or "Philanthropist." Other writers on peace wrote as "Eirenikos," "A Poor Man's Son," etc.; Samuel Whelpley's public cognomen was "Philadelphus," and Noah Worcester, chiefly to satisfy the fears of his printer, consented to sign his stirring *Solemn Review of the Custom of War* with the innocuous "Philo Pacificus." A saber-rattling, pro-war pamphlet published in Dodge's bailiwick just prior to his own first tract, and called *War or No War—Introduced with a View of the Causes of Our National Decline* [sic] *and Present Embarrassments,* was signed "Lycurgus."

Dodge, also, launched his first bold tract under the authorship of "An Inquirer." The polemics which followed it, with blast and counter-blast, however, soon drew him forth from anonymity. In the open, with undiminished boldness, he hacked away at the sacred ikons of the patrioteers. His later writings, for example *The Kingdom of Peace under the Benign Reign of Messiah,* were perhaps a bit more carefully scrutinized, at his request, by various members of the New York Peace Society— such men as the Reverend Samuel Whelpley and his son the Reverend Melanchthon Whelpley, the Reverend Eleazer Lord, the Reverend H. G. Ufford, and the Reverend Doctors E. D. Griffin, E. W. Baldwin and M. L. Parvine.

Save when the duty of parental authority was involved or some public lapse outraged his moral sense, Dodge had a mellow disposition. He was intense with devotion to a multitude of humanitarian causes. His autobiography points an ideal he held up to himself:

. . . Intelligent piety is calm, contemplative, and seeks by prayer the guidance of the Holy Spirit in the way of duty. Such a course is not inconsistent with being zealous in a good cause or ardent in endeavors for the salvation of souls.[1]

Of that, Dodge himself was a living proof. He was no temporizer. Striding into the middle of a most ticklish subject, he even queried the wisdom of the Revolutionary Fathers:

In fact, the great barrier to our progress was the example of our fathers in the American Revolution. That they were generally true patriots, in the political sense of the term, and many hopefully pious, I would not call in question, while I consider them as ill directed by education as St. Paul was when on his way to Damascus.[2]

The resentment of war zealots and the alarm of conservative "peace men" can be understood when Dodge's clear-cut pacifism is studied through his own expression of it. His theoretical position on "defensive" war has been quoted in an earlier chapter. Here is his fearless application of it:

Offensive war, by all professing Christians, is considered a violation of the laws of Heaven; but offensive war is openly prosecuted by professing Christians under the specious name of self-defense. France invaded Spain, Germany, and Russia; England invaded Holland and Denmark; and the United States invaded Canada, under the pretense of defensive war.[3]

David Low Dodge was born on June 14, 1774, in what is now Brooklyn, Connecticut, and died on April 23, 1852, in New York City, after stating with quiet conviction in the morning, "I shall go home to-day." His was a mind of strange alliances, and yet no cause ever had a founder of greater loyalty, nor one with a more flaming passion to see and proclaim the whole truth, impatient of all equivocation. To the end his principles of non-violence possessed him utterly, and he could traffic with no part of any war at all.

Near-Pacifist: Noah Worcester

More than the New York Peace Society, the organization in the Bay State catered to the patronage of the eminent. Its leaders were often men of intellectual, political, and religious repute. College presidents, legal lights and political idols were all fish for Noah Worcester's net. Among those who met in Channing's study were President Kirkland of Harvard and the Governor and Lieutenant Governor of the Commonwealth. Inevitably, such a policy brought into the Society some who were attracted as much by the respectability of its sponsors as by the appeal of the cause.

Yet never were these really representative; still too unpopular was the very thought of anti-war activity. Worcester himself markedly combined a quill of vitriol with a hesitancy to accept a radical pacifist position, especially since the latter in his day was invariably an accompaniment of religious literalism which he as a liberal found hard to stomach.

Like many another person of sturdy speech, Worcester shrank from the open hostility of important people. He never desired classification as an ally of the radicals who refused to perform military drill, once going so far as to deny them access to the peace movement through the pages of his journal. He was a man of indubitable courage, but always something of a stage manager who prized the power of attraction over the populace wielded by star actors.

But if he ever remained a little cautious about adopting thoroughgoing anti-war positions, he knew no hesitancy when it came to attacking the citadels of war-upholding churchdom. He took a savage relish in pointing out the ludicrous alarums sent up over the uncivilized customs of backward peoples. When infanticide was a subject for horrified gestures in earnest pulpits he hastened to pillory the churches in this wise:

The more enlightened people called Christians, do not thus destroy their *female* infants. The very thought of doing this would fill them with horror. They have, however, another custom which is esteemed very honourable. They train up many of their *male* children in habits of vice that they may become heroic and dexterous *man-killers.*

With all of such biting sarcasm went a true humility which endeared him to all who knew him, including both those who deprecated his boldness and those who deplored his persistent approval of "defensive" wars.

When he printed letters in *The Friend of Peace* he scrupulously cut out any portions expressing tributes to his personal labors. He was a Congregationalist of strong liberal convictions, who had edited *The Christian Disciple* and had once published a *Solemn* (Worcester, in common with most disputants of the time, became "solemn" when acting as mouthpiece for the Deity) *Reason for Declining to Adopt the Baptist Theory and Practice in a Series of Letters to a Baptist Minister.* Nevertheless he came to see that if peace could be hoped for among nations, it was almost as possible to conceive of it between religious sects. Therefore while editing *The Friend of Peace* he brought out some pamphlets intended to aid interdenominational harmony. "Party spirit," he said, "is the principal obstacle to the progress of pacific sentiments"; and he felt that "Party Spirit among the different denominations of Christians, is but the War Spirit in a modified form. . . ."

Noah Worcester was born in Hollis, New Hampshire, on November 25, 1758. On December 2, 1828, having seen the American Peace Society's federative program accomplished, he laid down his "arms" and retired from active leadership. He lived for ten years more, as devoted as ever but with his hands off the movement. Upon his retirement he wrote to the Society he had founded:

More than thirty years ago, from what I had witnessed, I formed the opinion that old men are often unapprized of the decay of their mental powers, after the fact had become obvious to their friends—and that too frequently they wish to retain responsible situations, when others believe that they would evince greater wisdom in leaving those situations to be occupied by men of more vigor. Having formed this opinion, I then resolved to profit by it, should I be spared to old age.

I have now passed the boundary of "three score years and ten"; my former resolution has occurred with force to my mind, and I have felt it to be a solemn duty to reduce it to practice. I have therefore determined to discontinue my labours as Editor of the Friend of Peace. For several years I have wished to retire; but I saw no one disposed to take my place or to continue a similar work.

The elderly leader went on to rejoice at the appearance of *The Harbinger of Peace,* published by the American Peace. Society, and continued his valedictory:

The objects of the Society are still dear to my heart, but I have become too infirm any longer to sustain, without injury, the cares and responsibilities attached to the offices with which the Society has honored me for thirteen years. . . .

The Friend of Peace, from its commencement, has been printed at my own expense and my own risk—having never charged the Society with any copies except what have been distributed for it—just as I charged the copies purchased by other societies or individuals; always taking on myself the risk of selling the overplus copies. But without the patronage of the Society, and the contributions of friends, I could not, with safety, have continued the work one year. . . .

I entertain a cheering hope that my retiring from the responsible situations, which, perhaps, I have too long occupied will be so far from retarding the progress of the society, that it will occasion an addition to its members, its strength, its activity, and its success.[5]

In its write-up of Channing the *Encyclopedia Britannica* states that a sermon against war preached in 1816 resulted in the organization of the Massachusetts Peace Society. Unquestionably, Channing greatly influenced Worcester; but on this subject the truth was the other way around, the Society antedating the sermon. Channing's biographer, John White Chadwick, says of the great Unitarian, "The Peace Society of Massachusetts was instituted in his own parsonage, and of all his personal tributes, that to its secretary, the Reverend Noah Worcester, preëminently the peace advocate of his time, has the accent of profoundest admiration." Driving once with a friend at Newport, and discussing a non-resistant pamphlet written by Samuel J. May, Channing had clenched his featherweight, pale fist and cried, vehemently, "Brother Farley, sometimes we *must* fight!"

The Massachusetts Peace Society, which believed in one more kind of war than the radicals did, took an official position strikingly less bold. In its constitution it declared that

We wish to promote the cause of peace by methods which all Christians must approve—by exhibiting with all clearness and distinctness the pacific nature of the gospel and by turning the attention of the community to the nature, spirit, causes, and effects of war.

With a program like that, the Society was beaten before it started. How far it could go toward approving war with such a platform may be seen from the speech made to the Society in 1820 by the Honorable Josiah Quincy, legislator plenipotentiary of the adoring Federalists, who had indeed opposed the War of 1812. The Congressman who was later to be President of Harvard said, with "martial logic":

Even our militia system, although regarded by many zealous advocates of peace as stimulating war, is, in fact, the most powerful means of preventing its recurrence. In the present condition of the world [sic], a well-appointed militia is unavoidable, in every state, which would escape the necessity of "a state of soldiery professed." The right to defend its own territories against actual invasion is the last, which society can permit to be questioned.

Fifty years later Henry Ward Beecher was to proclaim the same sentiments and also in the name of peace. And in the name of peace they are proclaimed to-day.

Noble though he was, Noah Worcester must share some of the responsibility for this argument's perpetuity. His influence was great, and though he did not agree with such views as those of Quincy, the official attitude he had urged led directly to their spread.

Ladd paid Worcester a glowing tribute:

> No one, on this side of the Atlantic, has done so much for the cause of peace, as Dr. Worcester. His "Solemn Review of the Custom of War" had an irresistible effect on all who read it. No modern tract has had a greater circulation, both in Europe and America, or has been translated into a greater number of languages, perhaps excepting a few religious tracts.[6]

In terms of immediate influence, Worcester was indeed supreme. At this time Dodge had ceased the output of literature and of course his radical attitude automatically reduced the size of his following however high it was in intellectual clarity. The peace society in Warren County, Ohio, second in order of formation, grew to four branches with a hundred members or more, chiefly Quakers, but distributed the writings of Dodge, Worcester, Ladd and others without creating either new ideas or policies, or lending any appreciable vigor to the enterprise.

In a later chapter some reasons will be suggested as to why the radicals made it none too easy for careful thinkers to espouse their view; the moderates had good reason, sometimes, for their caution, entirely apart from the specific issues at stake. Yet the same essential forces were operative then that have served to guide men's minds these hundred years. Always the social rewards and satisfactions bend to those who can announce, "I am for peace, and yet . . ." Says Edwin D. Mead, with understanding:

> This famous essay of Worcester's represents the platform of the great body of American peace workers for a century, the position of men like Channing and Ladd and Jay and Sumner; but to a non-resistant and opponent even of self-defence like David Dodge, these seemed the exponents of a halfway covenant.[7]

In view of the rush to get on the war bandwagon that has so often characterized the peace movement as a whole, "halfway" seems almost too generous an adjective.

William Ladd: Pacifist-to-Be

Windham County, Connecticut, was not only the abode of
a flamboyant militarism; it was the home of a live peace
society, led for a time by Samuel J. May, whose peace work
seems all but unknown despite his fame as an abolitionist. The
Windham County Peace Society as a group stated in its constitution, "Although as a Society we do not denounce *defensive*
war, we are cordially united in opposition to all *offensive* or
aggressive wars." Their report for 1832 is lugubrious about
the support vouchsafed to peace work, but rejoices at the "mar-
vellous change wrought in the opinions and habits of our people
respecting the use of ardent spirits." The Hartford County
Peace Society also justified *defensive* war, and the same is
true of most others.

William Ladd held the same opinion, and had written *The
Christian Register* to allay the fears of a suspicious public:

> It is thought that the views of Peace Societies are in general
> extreme; that they condemn as unchristian, every species of self-
> defence, national or individual, and recommend a passive non-
> resistance, which would offer up a sacrifice of every right and com-
> fort to the aggressions which, it is premised, are ready to approach
> from all around if thus invited.
>
> To this belief, it is sufficient to reply, by a simple denial. What-
> ever may have been the authority upon which particular indi-
> viduals may have drawn from Scripture or elsewhere, to disclaim
> the right of self-defence,—few Peace Societies anywhere, and none
> in this country, have assumed this ground in their collective
> capacity. It is believed that the great majority of their members
> are in fact of a different opinion; and they meet and act on the
> common belief, that offensive war may be prevented, by measures,
> which will render the recurrence to self-defence, and the question
> respecting it, quite unnecessary.

Ladd had good reason, based on a disillusionment over the
failure of one idealistic venture earlier in his life, to be skeptical over "extreme" positions; and more basic still, his nature
was not that of one who could insensitively withstand the
assaults of critics. A bit of a glad-hander, a man who was
a good manager of affairs and knew it, he did not see any-

thing to be gained by an espousal of radical views. The time came when he did, and then he did not flinch; but he could rarely escape entirely from a tolerant sympathy with opposing ideas, and was not cast for the part of fiery champion.

William Ladd * was added to the unexcited population of Exeter, New Hampshire, on May 10, 1778. When he was seventeen his family moved to Portsmouth, where a lichened monument now stands in memory of his career. He was sent to Exeter Academy, and thence to Harvard, graduating, as was not uncommon then, at the age of nineteen. His father was a prosperous shipowner, and after leaving Harvard Ladd went to sea on one of the paternal vessels as a common seaman. Disappointing his parents' hopes that he should become a physician, he stuck to the sea and in a year and a half was a full-fledged captain.

When he married a London girl, Sophia Ann Augusta Stidolph, a more domestic career lured him to try his luck at Savannah as a merchant; he did not stay long there, but moved on to Florida. He raised cotton and owned slaves, a fact which burned into his conscience until at length he set out to strike at slavery by the fantastic—and issue-dodging—scheme of importing European labor. His plan fell flat and his pocketbook was in much the same sad case.

His father died in 1806, adequately rectifying this pecuniary condition, and William once more plowed the seas, until driven from them by the War of 1812. Thereupon he went to reside on a many-acred farm where his father had lived at Minot, Maine. In the old white homestead on the Minot hilltop most of Ladd's pacific projects were conceived. A contented agriculturist he would very likely have remained to the end of his days if he had not been contaminated by "the peace folly."

The infection accomplished by President Appleton and later developed to a fever by Noah Worcester plus Ladd's own fertile brain, never left him; from that time until his lips grew cold in death his veins never ceased to carry the warm blood of devotion. He could no more be cooled by discouragement, as he once said, than a volcano could be subdued by throwing snowballs into its crater.

His active peace work began in 1823, with the writing of the essays of "Philanthropos." He gave life to the Maine Peace Society and took the initiative in planning the amalgamation of some fifty peace groups which culminated in 1828 with his election as General Agent of the American Peace Society.

Before him now stretched thirteen years of life—years filled with opportunities but also titanic obstacles. During that time there was no war against a foreign foe; but there were frequent slaughters of the first Americans, there was almost a war with France, and sharp conflict over the northeastern boundary. It may have been true, as Madison had said, that "the most noble of all ambitions is that of promoting peace on earth and good-will to men"; but if so, it was news to the general public.

Nevertheless, one of the measures of a prophet's effectiveness is the number of lives set on fire by his words and deeds. And just as Worcester sired Ladd, so Ladd fathered a goodly company of the faithful. Among these were Andrew Preston Peabody, Thomas C. Upham, George C. Beckwith, William Watson (Hartford leader), Thomas S. Grimké, and Charles Sumner. Despite Josiah Quincy's sentiments on preparedness, his address had moved Sumner, who, at the age of nine, had heard it; and a lecture by Ladd shortly after Sumner had gone through Harvard, sharpened his conviction as one puts a point on a hitherto useless pencil. When Sumner stood forth in 1846, five years after Ladd's death, and, fearlessly looking down on rows of gay uniforms, shocked Boston by his sensational address on "The True Grandeur of Nations," Ladd spoke through him.

But Ladd, struggling against an overwhelming lethargy, was forced to say, in 1833:

We hesitate not to confess, that our pacific principles are not in our vicinity or elsewhere, either so greatly or so rapidly advanced, or so fully admitted, as we could wish; or as we had reason to expect, or as we may have led others to anticipate.⁹

The bulldozing of France by Old Hickory and the stubborn disregard by the French of their obligations owing the United States from spoliation and ship seizures ever since their war with Britain, had almost precipitated open combat; but Jackson was restrained by economic realities and a threat of unconquerable division politically. Ladd sought to take credit for this on behalf of the peace societies; but this claim rested on facts thinner than gossamer.

To be sure, new groups were springing up to propagate the peace idea; young men were responding fairly well in Lane Seminary, Amherst College, and Andover Theological Seminary.

Nearly three hundred ministers were preaching on peace—once a year!—and new ones were steadily pledging themselves to do so. What even this meant to some of them is indicated by a letter sent to Ladd from Vermont:

> The request to preach in December on this subject, was complied with, of course, readily. "But truly," said one of my deacons, an intelligent man, "you disappointed many of our good people last Sabbath." "Why?" "They expected that you would say *something*, at least, in favor of war!"[10]

It was bad enough to find it impossible to justify a printing of more than fifteen hundred copies of *The Harbinger of Peace,* later *The Calumet.* But even the subscribers did not pay for it, so many, said the man of Minot, "that our proceedings have been embarrassed." Hardly a month passed without the question of suspension being frankly faced, but always Ladd sighed, protested the unwisdom of such a policy in theory, and then put his hand still deeper into his jeans. "The work shall go on," he insisted, "whether our personal sacrifices be increased or diminished." The "last number" of *The Calumet* was published at least four times; but Grimké and others came to the rescue, Grimké once by dying—for after a genuinely final suspension had been decided, it was found necessary to get out an issue in his memory!

The handful were justified in complaining that the largest contributor, next to Ladd, was J. N. Mooyaart, a magistrate in far Ceylon. Any official of the modern peace movement will chuckle at the recognition of a familiar enemy that was faced just the same in 1836, when the Reverend William Ely, agent of the American Peace Society for Tolland County, Connecticut, reported:

The great number of objects demanding contributions, now before the public, will prove a great hindrance to the success of a peace agent.

'Twas ever thus! But Ladd's troubles were not all financial. An epidemic of cholera set back the work; his own illness, finally enfeebling him, in 1833, by a paralytic stroke the effects of which lasted acutely for many months, necessitated relinquishment of his editorial labors. Richard M. Chipman, who had won a peace prize at Dartmouth, and was studying in New York for the ministry, was selected as editor, but was adjudged too indiscreet; Professor George Bush, of the "New York City University," was editor for a time but made the journal even duller than usual. Finally Ladd was able to take up the work again, but so long an interregnum out of the thirteen years allotted him by fate constituted no slight setback. And always his health seemed below par. The paralysis plagued him again and again. His death, in 1841, occurred a few hours after his return from an arduous speaking trip, on which his iron will had refused to let him quit, moving him to deliver some of his talks in a kneeling position on the platform, leaning across a chair for support. Never, after 1833, could he be called a heartily well man.

Well or sick, he never forgot to keep up a neighborly interest in his home community and its people. He used his superior financial position to aid those in distress, and was able to help the poor without injuring the relations of friendship; there was nothing patronizing in his nature. Perhaps the strongest tribute paid to him after his death came from Reuben Merrow, who worked for Ladd as a farm hand for eleven years:

I loved him. I had reason to. He was good to me. I knew him by day and by night. I know much about men. Mr. Ladd came the nearest to being a perfect man of any man I ever knew.

Childless, Mr. and Mrs. Ladd spent upon the whole town the affection they might have shared with children of their own. On the town—and on each other. Their marriage had been a *bona fide* romance, and it never ceased to be one. Their youthful love to each other, carried through many years, was a source of general comment among their intimates. But the issues of the cause were insistent and could not be denied.

Along with other problems Ladd had gone through some travail of conscience. For a quartet of years his war position remained the same. But by 1832 it had been shaken. Now there was another Ladd, in a way, for he became a complete pacifist and paved the way for a swing to that view which carried one leader after another and finally the Peace Society itself. Partly the explanation of the change lies in the increased study of war their work had forced upon them; partly responsible, of course, were the inadequate answers they had been able to find to their own hearts' questionings. But for the direct incitement to a shift like that, one must journey to Charleston, South Carolina, where lived a pious brother of two crusading sisters, a crusader too, who was not the least courageous member of a courageous family.

Judge Grimké

Sarah Grimké lived until 1873; Angelina Grimké Weld until 1879. But Thomas Smith Grimké died in 1834 at the age of forty-eight. That is why the sisters are famous and the brother far less well known. All the stirring days of the anti-slavery conflict were unexperienced by Grimké; it would have been interesting to see whether this sterling pacifist could have repressed his peace views as the bulk of his fellows succeeded in doing.

Grimké was far from a pacifist in his early manhood. After graduating from Yale in 1807 his rise as a lawyer was rapid and consistent. From 1826 to 1830 he was a state senator in South Carolina; he became a respected judge; he was a member of the Cincinnati, that closed corporation of military aristocracy based on descent from officers in the Revolution.

In 1809 he delivered a Fourth of July oration at Charleston which was printed jointly by the Society of the Cincinnati and the American Revolution Society. It was an eloquent plea for national unity, showing something even then of an ideal which fruited later into his lonely vote against "nullification," the breaking of South Carolina's tie to the Union. It was also a glorification of the Revolutionary War. He said, in an apostrophe to his military ancestors:

. . . often in the calm shades of domestic life, shall we regret that we did not share in your dangers, because you "fought to protect, and conquered but to bless."

And this is the respected patriot who later on in life wrote to his state legislature notifying it that he should never aid war or the military system again, who was chiefly the cause of William Ladd's change to pacifism, and who of all Americans dared to utter the strongest declaration against the necessity of the Revolutionary War ever made, not even excepting the later one by Garrison!

Ladd and Grimké rose to their radical positions with the aid of each other, much as two gamesters keep raising their bids. In the first place, Ladd was impressed with Grimké's forceful piety—his plea that "the Bible should be the Text book of duty and usefulness in every scheme of Education, from the primary school to the University." The Southerner in 1830 made the Phi Beta Kappa address at Yale, along these very lines. Ladd, who counted Grimké "the most firm and substantial pillar in our temple of Peace," was stirred as early as 1827 by the latter's daring in challenging classical education despite his own status as a classical scholar. As the Minot pietist put it, "He fearlessly exposed the demoralizing effects of classical literature on the youthful mind, and counted all such high attainments 'but as filthy rags' when there was danger that they would injure the cause of virtue and piety."

Yet it was correspondence with Ladd which first wakened Grimké to a consideration of war from a new angle. While pondering this new and disturbing idea, Grimké was given by Dr. Hubbard of the Windham County Peace Society the best book available—possibly even now of its kind—on successful non-violent resistance. It was a study of Quakerism in the midst of the Irish Rebellion, written in 1825 by Thomas Hancock, M.D., of the English peace movement.[11] From that time on, Grimké was a peace enthusiast. He republished Hancock's detailed work, which he called "this precious seed," in a large edition, and contributed heavily to Ladd's endeavors. "If we were before him in the race," wrote Ladd, "and had got midway ere he entered it he soon outstripped us."

Prior to the circulation of Hancock's book, about the best example of a non-military oasis citable were the islands of Loo Choo, which furnished the theme of Stephen Thurston's satire, but whose inhabitants had had to be fed in 1832 by the United States Navy. Although the Reverend Cyrus Yale of New Hartford directed the gaze of the local peace society to this spot "which has remained for centuries without weapons of war and without hostile invasion," the public failed to be heartily impressed. Hancock's survey was an admirably documented report of dramatic and irrefragible accomplishments by non-violent methods.

Grimké, asked to speak in May of 1832 before the Connecticut Peace Society at New Haven—with the state legislature and general public invited—went to work with the zest of any other discoverer. His address was nothing less than a knockout, as it would be called in our pacific vernacular; for sheer audacity coupled with cogent pacifist apologetics, its equal is almost non-existent. Dehydrate it by removing the sanctimonious verbiage and the rhetorical flourishes *au fait* of the period, and the effort is extraordinarily powerful.

Recognizing, as only an ex-idolater could, the appeal of the Revolution as a perpetual argument against non-violent methods, Grimké stoutly asserted that

America, as the land of christian freemen, calmly, resolutely, self-devoted to martyrdom, returning good for evil, and blessing for cursing, unprovoked by indignities and unpolluted by hatred, anger or violence, must have conquered that monarch, with his ministry, his parliament and his people.

Our new radical was of course more than a bit Quixotic; for he showed no appreciation of the high degree of social control necessary to any such disciplined solidarity. Nevertheless, he was not vague and did not await requests for a bill of particulars. Said he:

I would have had them say to the British king and his ministry, to the parliament and people of England, "We are your children and your brethren: protection and justice, encouragement and assistance from you, are our birthright. We have a British title to be free, prosperous and happy. Yet have you dealt with us, as strangers and hirelings, and even as enemies. We have petitioned and expostulated and reasoned in vain. We have besought you, by the ties of a common ancestry, by the exalted privileges of a free constitution, and the holy fellowship of christians, to spare us the bitter cup of a brother's contumely, of a parent's anger. To mockery you have added revilings, to revilings injustice, to injustice threats, to threats violence and punishment. We have borne it all, as becomes those on whose soul is the vow to love our enemies; to bless them that curse, to do good to them that hate us. We have borne it, as becomes those whose trust is in God, not as the god of battles, but as the God of mercy and righteousness, of peace and love. Go on then in your career of injustice and contempt and injury. Double the measure of our humiliation and sufferings. Brand our entreaties with the name of cowardice; call our humility meanness; our respect for you, the language of servility; and trample on our love, as the folly of the dotard or the ravings of the enthusiast. Send among us the insolent tax gatherer and the more insolent soldier. Command the delegates of your power in the chair of state or in the courts of justice, in the army or the navy, to harass and persecute and oppress. Cast the father into prison, confiscate his property, banish the wife of his bosom, scatter the children of his affections. Let the perjury of magistrates, and the corruption or timidity of jurors, condemn the innocent to death, and stain the scaffold or the faggot, with the blood of christian martyrs, in the cause of christian freedom. All this, and more than this, we are ready to bear, with a love that cannot be quenched, with a constancy inflexible and undying, with a faith calm and humble, yet fixed and invincible. Yours is indeed the power to afflict and torment, be it our lot to suffer with fortitude and resignation; for ours is a nobler, better power, to bless and forgive. In vain may you hope to prevail. Yours are the instruments of weakness and fear, of tyranny and violence. We shall prevail; for ours are the weapons of righteousness, peace and love, the gift of God himself. As there is truth in his promises, you must yield, we shall conquer. Passion and prejudice, pride and disappointment may sustain you for a while; but our love and hope, and faith, are imperishable, inconquerable. Our purpose is irrevocably taken; we will be free: we will have the precious rights of British freemen; but, never shall violence and blood-shed be our arms. We must conquer, if we faint not. We know that passion and prejudice, anger and pride must yield, to firmness, reason, good sense, and candor. We know, that you yourselves, when the season of wrath and arrogance shall have passed away, will wipe the tears from our eyes, and wash out the blood-spots from our garments. We know, that, you yourselves will break the chains of the captive father, and recall the exiled mother, and gather their wandering children into your own bosoms. We know that the very tongue which has mocked our sufferings and uttered the sentence of imprisonment or death, will ask forgiveness in the accents of returning love. We know that the very hands, which stained the scaffold or kindled the fire, will build the monument of your own victims, and accord to the land they loved and died for, the precious privileges purchased by the love of Christian patriots, by the death of Christian martyrs.[12]

If the effect was to induce the public as a whole to think of Grimké as more to be pitied than scorned, certainly in some quarters his words ran like a train of gunpowder to a magazine. The explosion required five years to be set off; the whole policy of the American Peace Society was shifted to that of opposition to *all* war in 1837.

At once, however, Ladd was personally budged, and a host of others moved leftward with him. A renewed courage and momentum were given to the radical peace wing, and Ladd himself was stirred to remark that "one is astonished at his former opinions."

With all of Grimké's devout earnestness, his sister Sarah wrote to William Ladd that "he was the *happiest* person I ever saw. He seemed to *enjoy* life with a zest and unvary'd cheerfulness which was very remarkable." He is described as always a delightful companion.

History contains not a few records of personalities coupled in spirit and greatly moving each other, although never seen face to face. It was so with these two; but the peace movement reveals no case of similar attachment across cold space. "We never enjoyed the happiness of seeing him," said Ladd, "though for many years closely allied to him, as to a kindred spirit of much higher attainments."

But almost a century before Andrew Carnegie's advocacy of reformed orthography, Grimké was venturing to use such spelling as "nativ," "lovd," "honord," "developd," and "afection." And when it came to this particular innovation, William Ladd did as others of the bravest have always done. He paled before it, and confessed, "We have not yet examined this new mode of spelling, but whatever may be hereafter our convictions as to its utility, we fear we shall not have sufficient moral courage to follow the example."

Pacifism Triumphant

Even before Grimké's impetus, a few voices were raised on behalf of pacifism in the American Peace Society. A tract was put out by one "Pacificus" in New York in 1830 under the imprint of the Society's Executive Committee, entitled *Appeal to American Christians on the Practice of War*. This pamphlet lost no time on side issues:

Stand forth, then, an advocate for the principles of the early Christians, for the true spirit and teaching of Christianity, and the only doctrine which will ever despoil the monster war of his dominion over Christendom and the world. The toleration of defensive warfare would perpetuate his reign till the final conflagration. There can be, I am persuaded, no end to this plague of man and beast, except through a practical union of good and philanthropic men in the pacific principle, that wars, aggressive and defensive, are totally inconsistent with the spirit and principles of the Christian religion.

The Reverend R. V. Rogers, of St. Philips Church in Circleville, Ohio, wrote strongly against "defensive" war in 1833.

Thomas Cock, M.D., of New York, in 1835, called for "total abstinence" from war. The Reverend Dr. Nathan Strong surreptitiously confided to some influential friends in his Hartford study that privately he had become convinced of the wrongfulness of even the wars men called defensive. Reverend Jonathan Coggswell, at Hartford in the same year, addressed the Hartford County Peace Society and in the names of Jerome and Chrysostom called for a return to the peace stand of the church fathers. Meantime, Ladd's own change of view wielded a potent influence.

When William Ladd stirred up Professor Thomas C. Upham of Bowdoin, he let loose upon the peace problem an able thinker, a vigorous writer, an energetic and fearless prophet. Still in his early thirties, he was acknowledged as a brilliant student of philosophy and religion. He, too, was subject to the inadequate critical knowledge of his time, yet his vocabulary seems less colored with theological phantasms than that of some pacifists who were contemporaneous.

His *Manual of Peace,* published in 1836, covered the whole war against war as thus far conceived. He argued for world organization, urged removal of war's causes, but most of all he called for a more strenuous anti-war campaign by the peace societies themselves. More detailed than that of any other was his argument, more difficult to surmount. His book was sold out in a few months but its effect lingered. Looking back from the vantage point of almost a century's perspective, his insight seems astonishingly accurate:

Every one must admit that, in effecting a great moral object, everything depends upon the adoption of a correct moral principle. If the societies should be so unfortunate as to start upon an unsound principle as their basis, they may certainly count upon finding themselves practical nullities. We submit, then (in concurrence with the opinions of others whose views are entitled to much consideration), that it is necessary to adopt, as a fundamental article of these societies, the principle, that all wars whatever, both offensive and *defensive* are repugnant to the precepts and spirit of the gospel, and are sinful. . . .
It will be found on experience, if it has not already been, that

Peace societies, which admit the lawfulness of Defensive war, do not essentially disturb the quiet of warriors and politicians, with whatever prudence and zeal they may be conducted. These persons will even become polite and laudatory, and pronounce such societies very good.

This, as it happens, precisely describes the American Peace Society in its later days, the Lake Mohonk Conferences, the heavily endowed peace organizations, in fact, most peace groups—as the chapters yet to come will certainly disclose.

However, Upham's plea, for a time, was not devoid of results. Faced by this growing rebellion at the Society's equivocal position, and spurred also by the refusal of some groups to join the larger body, the A. P. S. officials began to consider a formal change.

In anticipation of it, the President of Bowdoin made strenuous objections. There were two William Allens to be counted in the peace movement—the thoroughgoing English Quaker, and this stern New England educator. President Allen wrote a number of articles for the magazines, upholding defensive war. One of these, during Ladd's disability, was run in *The Calumet* without comment. In the next issue Ladd, greatly concerned, made an elaborate explanation, and also defended the complete anti-war view:

Although I am myself opposed to all war in every form, as utterly inconsistent with the spirit of the Gospel, I am willing, that the sincere friends of Peace, who do not yet see their way clear to take that high ground, should have liberty to state their objections to it in candor—for how else can those objections be met? Truth should never fear a candid discussion, especially when it comes in the spirit of Peace. Nevertheless, I think that articles in favor of war in any shape, should not have been published, without, at least, a temporary answer, or something to show, that, although the Society might think itself in honor and in duty bound to publish them, it did not adopt the principles contained in them, as its own creed; but reserved to itself the right of withholding its judgment at least for the present.[11]

One can sympathize with President Allen without agreeing with him; for his arguments were able ones, and he probed unanswerably into the literal fundamentalism on which Ladd, at least, rested so much of his case. When he lost out, however, he withdrew none too gracefully from the Society altogether.

All the opposition was not intellectual. Economic considerations constituted a brake on pacifism. Protests came in from the field. One rather naïve and revelatory complaint came in from the Reverend Mr. Ely in the northern part of the Nutmeg State:

> In my opinion, serious injury has been done to the society by placing defensive and offensive wars upon the same ground. The opinion among the people of all classes, is nearly universal, that wars *strictly defensive may sometimes* be demanded. *So far as I know, no* objection is made to the course which the American Peace Society pursues.[14]

Having thus uttered a warning against the pacifist agitators, Mr. Ely went on to state that in asking for contributions he had found it advisable to solicit no donations that would interfere with other benevolences or "which would subject the donor to inconvenience." There's a sacrificial spirit for you! Also:

> I found it important to state, that no opposition was designed against the regularly instituted authorities of government. In repeated instances I solicited and received donations from members and officers of military companies at the same time publishing to them the principles of peace.

No warning like this could deter men who were clearly able to see how weak-kneed a movement would inevitably follow the employment of such tactics to build it up. The official change was made, and with William Ladd's approval.

Originally the Society's object had been

> . . . to diffuse light respecting the evils of war and the best means of effecting its abolition.

In 1837 a new constitution was adopted. It democratized the Society by transferring final power from a hand-picked board of directors to a voting rank and file with elective officers. The object clause was stiffened to read:

> This society, being founded on the principle that all war is contrary to the spirit of the gospel, shall have for its object to illustrate the inconsistency of war with Christianity, to show its baleful

influence on all the great interests of mankind, and to devise means for insuring universal and permanent peace.

Since William Ladd's will making the Society a legatee had directed that the object of the Society should never be changed and since he was still functioning, those who felt this object insufficiently explicit had a high barrier to leap. They made it, however, by working out a scheme of explanatory resolutions. Several of these were passed: one, designed to show that war was meant, and that individual use or non-use of force was not involved; another, to make it clear that no member was obliged to take a formal pledge. The most significant of these interpretations stated, of the object clause:

We consider it as designed to assert, that all national wars are inconsistent with Christianity, including those supposed or alleged to be defensive.

Just prior to his death three years before, Grimké had ventured a prophecy:

The principle for which I contend, has not as yet been adopted by the American Peace Society, but I do not entertain a doubt that many years will not elapse, before it will become an article of the constitution.[15]

Right he was! The pacifist principle of opposition to all war and the whole war system was now the normal, official organization view. What this meant to the peace movement, if not shown by the chapters thus far covered, assuredly will be by the story of the later years. The various emphases that had been tried by the peace societies were interestingly summed up by Ladd in *The Calumet* for May-June, 1834. This summary will be found as Appendix IV. It reveals that the ideology and tactics of 1834 are separated by an astonishingly slender margin from the ideology and tactics of to-day. Even this new basic objective, focused as it was so exclusively on an undependable church factor and associated with evanescent theological irrelevancies, was to be scarcely more effective a control than the others.

The pacifists were gravely glad, and settled down to build

more vigorously than ever, let the outward opposition be however strong. But it was not the attack from without they needed to reckon with. From the disgruntled and the shocked and the "compromised" conservatives came a counter-revolution. From a stormy area of political, economic and social movements far beyond their control also emerged a dozen compelling cross-currents that were destined to swamp the frail bark before its sails were fully spread.

Pacifism had triumphed; but it was to be a Pyrrhic victory.